Student Study Guide

EDUCATIONAL PSYCHOLOGY

Third Edition

Margaret M. Bierly
California State University at Chico

David C. Berliner
University of Arizona

N. L. Gage
Stanford University

HOUGHTON MIFFLIN COMPANY · BOSTON

Dallas · Geneva, Ill. · Hopewell, N. J.
Palo Alto · London

8565

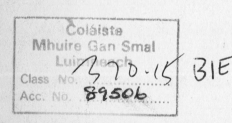
Printed in the U. S. A.

IBSN: 0-395-32764-4

DEFGHIJ-H-8987

CONTENTS

INTRODUCTION TO THE STUDY GUIDE

This study guide aims to help you master the subject matter of educational psychology as presented in the third edition of Educational Psychology by N. L. Gage and David C. Berliner. A thoughtful reading of the various chapters of the book, with particular reference to the key words in the text margins, and active use of this study guide should ensure your mastery of the subject matter. We intend that the level of competence you reach by studying in this way will meet your personal needs for achievement in your educational psychology course.

STUDYING EDUCATIONAL PSYCHOLOGY

There is no way in which this guide can substitute for reading the text. This guide supplements the text. It can help you understand and remember more of the facts, concepts, and principles presented in Educational Psychology. We want you to master these ideas for their immediate and long-term value. We expect your present learning to be maximized and your future teaching to reflect what you learned from this course. What you learn is, as usual, regulated by you. Motivation, more than any other factor, is what accounts for differences in achievement at the college level. Beyond your desire to learn, your study habits and attitudes will determine what you get out of Educational Psychology.

The text discussed studying (p. 526). You should read that section. The SQ3R method of study mentioned there is as useful a technique as any for studying Educational Psychology. That method requires:

Survey

Before you begin reading a particular chapter, go over the subheads listed in the contents at the beginning of each chapter. These headings are constructed to let you see rapidly the structure of the chapter. Read the summary for each chapter, too. It will give you additional help in grasping the content of the chapter.

Question

Turn each heading into a question to arouse your own curiosity. Thus, when you read the heading "Concepts and Principles in Educational Psychology," ask yourself, What are the concepts and principles in Educational Psychology? Why do I need to know them? How will they be useful to me? How does a concept differ from a principle? Etc.

Recite

Close your book and try repeating (out loud, if possible) the main points of what you have read and the questions you asked, with their answers. Repeat the questioning, reading, and reciting pattern as you go through a chapter.

Read

If your mind wanders, and you reach the bottom of a page without remembering what you read, you need more active patterns of reading. Try reading aloud (in a place where you won't disturb others, of course). Try answering your own questions while you read, or make up new ones. You might ask, what does this mean for me? Did this ever happen to me? Have I ever encountered an incident like this? Questions like these will keep you more active as a learner (see pp. 320-329 for more on active learning).

Review

This is the first step in effective studying where this study guide will prove to be most useful. This guide helps you review the material in each chapter of the text. A description of the review techniques that are used with each chapter follows.

REVIEWING EACH CHAPTER OF THE TEXT

This guide contains review exercises to give you practice at remembering important facts, definitions, concepts and principles. For each chapter, the study guide contains the following elements:

1. a statement of <u>Objectives</u>, which tells, at a general level, the goals the authors had in mind for you when the text was written

2. a <u>Reminder</u>, which reviews briefly what was taught in the chapter

3. <u>Definitions of Key Concepts</u>, exercises that provide you with a chance to evaluate whether or not you know the definitions of the key concepts in the chapter

4. <u>Application of Key Concepts</u>, exercises that help you to classify events as exemplars or nonexemplars of important concepts in educational psychology

5. a <u>Multiple-Choice Self-Test</u>, which gives you experience with items similar to those you might encounter on a test

The Objectives, Reminder, Definitions of Key Concepts, Applications of Key Concepts, and Mulitple-Choice Self-Tests are designed to help you review a chapter in the text. The correct definitions, correct choice of concepts in the application exercises, and correct answers to the multiple-choice questions are given in the back of the guide.

OTHER AIDS TO STUDENTS OF EDUCATIONAL PSYCHOLOGY

This study guide also contains suggested <u>Projects and Activities</u> for each chapter. These are for the student who wants to learn more about a particular concept, to observe a specific classroom phenomenon, or to work with one or more other students to make educational psychology "come alive" by seeing how it really relates to life in the classroom. Even if you do not carry out all these projects, you should read them and think about their consequences.

Each also contains <u>Suggestions for Term Papers,</u> a brief listing of topics appropriate to the subject matter of a particular chapter. Preparing such a term paper will require you to study in depth and acquire some expertise in a topic that is relevant to most educational psychology courses. Some of the topics call for library work, specifically, an exploration of the research literature, whereas others -- the "think pieces" -- require an analysis of important problems in educational psychology. Sometimes a topic will include several variations, for example, "Ways to provide multiple associations for important ideas in the teaching of third-grade reading/anatomy/Russian/etc." You should choose the alternative that has the greatest interest for you. Or suggest an alternative of your own.

A few chapters in this study guide have Technical Notes appended. These notes elaborate on points in the text that may be of special interest to a number of students and therefore deserve more attention. Thus, we have included technical notes on how to compute a correlation coefficient and how to interpret statistics and experimental designs. Another technical note contains some of the fine points on the heredity-environment or nature-nurture argument. Information on factor analysis is included, as is a theoretical model for determining motivation to succeed and to avoid failure. Later technical notes, addressing measurement and evaluation, tell you how to compute and interpret statistics such as the standard deviation and the standard error of measurement, and how to weigh and combine test data. In other words, the technical notes are intended to help you by providing data or formulas that illuminate a point in the text.

Finally, after all the chapters are presented, the Student Study Guide provides a brief introduction to <u>Information Sources</u>. These sources will be of help to you throughout the course, whether you are doing research for a term paper or merely looking for more information on an issue that interest you. Moreover, throughout your career these references should give you a way to find information on most of the areas of educational psychology.

CHAPTER 1 HOW EDUCATIONAL PSYCHOLOGY HELPS
WITH THE PROBLEMS OF TEACHING

OBJECTIVES

The student should be able to

o describe five major contributions of educational psychology to understanding teaching and solving the problems of teaching

o describe a model of the teaching-learning process that guides teacher problem solving before, during, and after instruction

o tell how educational psychologists study the major variables of student characteristics, the learning task, and teaching methods.

REMINDER

This chapter provided an overview of educational psychology, focusing on how educational psychology helps teachers with their instructional problems. These problems occur before (for example, development of objectives and thinking about student characteristics), during (for example, selection and use of one or more teaching methods), and after (for example, evaluation of students, learning and achievement of objectives) instruction. The five areas of teaching in which educational psychology can be of help are:

1. ways of stating educational objectives

2. understanding the characteristics of students that affect learning

3. considering the nature of the learning process

4. selecting various teaching methods

5. evaluating learning

The chapter concluded with a discussion of the major variables in the teaching-learning process studied by educational psychologists, and the interaction between theory and application.

DEFINITIONS OF KEY CONCEPTS

The following key concepts were discussed in this chapter. In your own words, write the definition of each concept in the space provided.

1. Educational objectives _____
_____
_____

2. Individual differences _____
_____
_____

3. Correlation _____
_____
_____

4. Teaching methods _____
_____
_____

5. Evaluation _____
_____
_____

6. "Grading on the curve" _____
_____
_____

APPLICATION OF KEY CONCEPTS

The terms listed below refer to important concepts that were discussed in this chapter. Carefully read each descriptive statement, and identify the concept or concepts each statement implies. Place the corresponding letter(s) of the concept(s) you select in the space provided.

Concepts

A. "grading on the curve"
B. teaching method
C. individual differences in students

D. educational objective
E. preinstructional problem
F. correlation

Descriptive Statements

1. The physiology teacher is asking those students who did not take a course in anatomy the previous semester to supplement their studying with a programmed workbook.

2. I told Bob that if he wanted to learn about parasites, he should read independently.

3. Beth received an average grade on her music test -- about half the class scored higher than she, and about half scored lower..

4. Ms. Wesson, a fifth-grade teacher, can't decide whether to give her students their test before or after spring vacation.

5. It seems that in almost all my classes the students who usually get the highest grades tend to sit toward the front of the room.

6. I think Frances should be able to tell us how to make wine after her trip to the winery.

MULTIPLE-CHOICE SELF-TEST

Select the response that best answers the question or completes the statement. Place the letter of the chosen answer in the space provided.

1. Designing procedures to find out how well students have achieved educational objectives refers to which component of the teaching-learning model?
   A. Student characteristics
   B. Learning processes
   C. Motivation
   D. Evaluation

2. Educational objectives are stated in terms of the
   A. capabilities of the teacher.
   B. behavior required from students.
   C. characteristics of the school environment, for example, whether urban or rural.
   D. method of teaching to be used.

3. Kinds of individual differences in students refer to which of the following?
   A. Use of different teaching procedures for different students
   B. Setting different objectives for different students
   C. Variability among students in age, intelligence, and previous achievement of certain kinds
   D. Different skills to be learned by different students

4. Many psychologists believe that the kind of learning process that occurs
   A. depends on the content of what is learned.
   B. is universal, and not related to the content of what is learned.
   C. is related to student motivation.

5. When can evaluation take place?
   A. Before instruction
   B. During instruction
   C. After instruction

D. During and after instruction

E. Before, during, and after instruction

6. Approximately what percentage of former teachers do the authors suggest most students rate as "really good" teachers?

   A. 5

   B. 10

   C. 25

   D. 50

   E. 75

PROJECTS AND ACTIVITIES

1. Try role playing instances of several of the important concepts introduced in this chapter with a few of the people in your class. Take turns role playing and observing to see who is the "best actor" and who is the "best guesser." Situations that demonstrate concepts might include a teacher employing the discussion method of teaching; a teacher practicing humanistic teaching, for example, by taking a very student-centered approach and showing concern for the feelings of students; a teacher explaining to parents their child's unique individual differences in comparison with other students; two teachers dealing with preinstructional problems of teaching, for example, discussing the pro's and con's of whether to reprimand John in front of the class or wait until after school to speak with him; a teacher giving a very unfavorable evaluation of a student.

   Try role playing several examples of each concept as you imagine they might actually occur in a classroom. If you need a "student" or "students" for your skit, ask some friends to help. You'll not only have fun and get to know some of the people in your class, you'll also gain a better understanding of some of the essential concepts around which this text on educational psychology is built.

   If you enjoy this activity, you might want to try it with some of the concepts presented in later chapters of the text.

2. Imagine that someone -- a friend or parent -- has just asked you, "What is it exactly that you study in an educational psychology class?" In fact, this may have already happened to you. How would you respond to this question? You may find it useful to write a brief outline to help you organize your thoughts.

SUGGESTIONS FOR TERM PAPERS

1. The usefulness of educational psychology for the classroom teacher

2. What educational psychologists do

CHAPTER 2   THE CONTENT AND METHOD OF EDUCATIONAL PSYCHOLOGY

OBJECTIVES

   The student should be able to

o analyze some of the obvious generalizations believed by nonresearchers about teaching and
  learning

o distinguish between possibility and probability in interpreting research findings

o compare and contrast concepts, principles, and methods

o state the differences between understanding, prediction, and control

o describe instances of logical, temporal, and causal relations

o contrast the experimental and correlational methods

o identify the independent and dependent variables in an experiment

o state why correlation does not mean causation

o compute a correlation coefficient (see Technical Note A at the end of this chapter)

o judge the adequacy of the methods used in an experiment (see Technical Note B at the end
  of this chapter)

REMINDER

   The second chapter pointed out that reliable knowledge is necessary for reaching
accurate educationally significant generalizations. Such knowledge is gained by understanding, predicting, and controlling phenomena. As you will recall, understanding depends on
logical relationships, prediction depends on time relationships, and control depends on causal
relationships. The two prevalent ways of studying these relationships are the correlational
and experimental methods. Correlation helps in prediction, whereas experimentation helps in
prediction and control by discovery of causal relationships. Both methods can be applied by
educators solving problems in their classrooms and schools.

DEFINITIONS OF KEY CONCEPTS

The following key concepts were discussed in this chapter. In your own words, write the definition of each concept in the space provided.

1. The empirical approach _____

_____

_____

2. Variables _____

_____

_____

3. Concepts in educational psychology _____

_____

_____

4. Principles _____

_____

_____

5. Laws _____

_____

_____

6. Understanding _____

_____

_____

7. Prediction _____

_____

_____

8. Control _____

_____

_____

9. A correlational relationship _____

_____

_____

10. A causal relationship _____

_____

_____

11. Manipulation of a variable _____

_____

_____

12. Independent variables _____

_____

_____

13. Dependent variables _____

_____

_____

14. Random assignment _____

_____

_____

15. Correlation coefficients _____

_____

_____

16. Experimentation _____

_____

_____

17. Statistics _____

_____

_____

APPLICATION OF KEY CONCEPTS

The terms listed below refer to important concepts that were discussed in this chapter. Carefully read each descriptive statement, and identify the concept or concepts each statement implies. Place the corresponding letter(s) of the concept(s) you select in the space provided.

Concepts

A. experimentation
B. correlation coefficient
C. independent variable
D. dependent variable
E. principle
F. control
G. concepts

H. causal relationships
I. understanding
J. manipulation of a variable
K. prediction
L. correlational relationship
M. random assignment
N. law

Descriptive Statements

_____ 1. Persons who score high on intelligence tests tend to score low on measures of authoritarianism.

_____ 2. The school nurse warned the high school students that people who are overweight, exercise little, and have a family history of pulmonary problems are prime candidates for a heart attack.

_____ 3. The more I tell Janie how well she's doing in class, the more her motivation to complete a task increases.

_____ 4. When the number of hours of French instruction in the audio mode and student achievement on a standardized French test were related, an $r = .78$ resulted.

_____ 5. The achievement scores of French students in Group 1 (10 hours of audio instruction), Group 2 (15 hours of audio instruction), and Group 3 (20 hours of audio instruction) were measured and compared at the end of the quarter.

_____ 6. The number of hours of audio instruction to French students in groups 1, 2, and 3 was 10 hours, 15 hours, and 20 hours, respectively.

_____ 7. To examine the effects of instructional time, the number of hours of audio instruction to French students in Groups 1, 2, and 3 was 10 hours, 15 hours, and 20 hours, respectively.

_____ 8. Twenty students from each of the ninth-grade French classes in the school district were randomly assigned to three groups. Each group received a different number of hours of audio instruction. Achievement scores on a standardized French test were measured and compared at the end of the quarter.

_____ 9. To see whether the new curriculum was effective, we created a new class that included 30 children from all over the district, and we chose them by pulling their names out of a hat.

_____10. Social class, motivation, attitude, and achievement are all examples.

_____11. Minority students didn't do as well in the spelling contest because they were not as familiar with standard English as some of the other students.

_____12. In mathematics we know that the following relationship uniformly exists: $(\underline{a} + \underline{b})\underline{c} = \underline{ac} + \underline{bc}$.

MULTIPLE CHOICE SELF-TEST

Select the response that best answers the question or completes the statement. Place the letter of the chosen answer in the space provided.

_____ 1. The "obviousness" of the concepts and principles of educational psychology is something that
A. must be accepted as an inevitable characteristic of the field.
B. is illusory because many apparently obvious conclusions turn out to be invalid.
C. occurs because of unfamiliarity with the discipline.
D. results from the non-researcher's tendency to overgeneralize.

_____ 2. Which of the following is an example of a concept in educational psychology?
A. Scholastic achievement is measured by the total score on the final examination.
B. Students learn more when they are reinforced more frequently.
C. Abler students require less time to study.
D. Verbal ability and mathematical ability are positively correlated.
E. Student achievement and student aptitude are positively correlated.

_____ 3. Which of the following states a principle?
A. Ability to solve problems is one component of intelligence.
B. Scholastic achievement can be measured by the grade-point average.
C. Intelligence can be either verbal or nonverbal.
D. Motor skill improves with practice.

_____ 4. To say that scientific principles, including the relationships between the variables of educational psychology, must be derived empirically is to say that they must be
A. carefully defined.
B. logically consistent.
C. consistent with observations in the real world.
D. partially based on moral considerations.

_____ 5. Which of the following is an empirical observation?
A. Sally's general intelligence
B. Number of times Sally volunteers to solve an algebra problem on the chalkboard
C. Sally's motivation for completing her algebra homework
D. Sally's math aptitude

_____ 6. Although unalterable variables cannot be changed to improve education, they are worthy of study because they help educators
A. understand certain situations.

B. control certain situations.
C. manipulate certain situations.
D. predict certain situations.

_____ 7. In order to demonstrate the probability of any phenomenon, which type of research approach is necessary?
A. Quantitative
B. Qualitative
C. Anthropological

_____ 8. The relationships between variables in educational psychology are
A. matters of definition or logic.
B. derived empirically.
C. qualitative.

_____ 9. The students in the class sometimes gawk at Shirley because she is the first fifth grade girl to show signs of physical development. This is an example of which type of variable?
A. Alterable
B. Unalterable
C. Maturational
D. Predictive

_____10. Control depends on which type of relationship between variables?
A. Logical
B. Temporal
C. Causal

_____11. The home economics teacher computed a correlation coefficient between the number of minutes students spent in the washroom during class time and their scores on the final exam. Since the correlation coefficient was −.45, he concluded that
A. students who spend a good deal of time in the washroom score higher on the final exam.
B. low scores on the final exam are associated with spending little time in the washroom.
C. there seems to be no relation between the amount of time students spend in the washroom and final exam scores.
D. students who spend a good deal of time in the washroom score lower on the final exam.

_____12. A teacher finds that if he increases the frequency of tests in his course, his students get much higher scores on the final examination than similar groups of students got on the same examination in previous years. Other teachers report the same phenomenon. If it were substantiated with adequate and valid research methods, this finding would illustrate the achievement, through scientific method, of
A. understanding.
B. prediction.
C. control.
D. balance.

_____13. In a study comparing the effects of black-and-white illustrations with those of color illustrations on reader interest, an investigator administered an interest

inventory after the treatment. She found that interest scores were higher for the group that saw color illustrations. What is the independent variable in this study?
A. Presence or absence of color in illustrations
B. Interest inventory score
C. Color illustrations
D. Black-and-white illustrations
E. There is no independent variable because the situation described is not an experiment

_____14. What is the dependent variable in the study described above?
A. Presence or absence of color in illustrations
B. Interest inventory score
C. Color illustrations
D. Black-and-white illustrations
E. There is no dependent variable because the situation described is not an experiment

_____15. A correlation coefficient between two variables tells us
A. how the first variable affects the second variable.
B. the strength, but not the direction, of the relationship between the variables.
C. the direction, but not the strength, of the relationship between the variables.
D. both the strength and the direction of the relationship between the variables.

_____16. A correlation coefficient of —.58 could be interpreted as indicating
A. a relationship in which increasing values of one variable are associated with increasing values of the second variable.
B. a relationship in which increasing values of one variable are associated with decreasing values of the second variable.
C. a lack of any relationship between two variables.

_____17. When choosing participants for an experiment, one of the best ways to ensure that causal effects are creating differences in measured or observed performance is by
A. assigning students alphabetically to the control and treatment conditions.
B. assigning "bright" students to one group and "dull" students to another.
C. assigning some students randomly to treatment groups and placing the remaining students in the control group.
D. allowing students to choose the group in which they'd like to participate.

PROJECTS AND ACTIVITIES

The text discusses some obvious principles in educational psychology, and shows that it is not always safe or wise to trust your intuition when it comes to thinking about teaching and learning. It is also important to note that some principles are obviously intuited and correct. But how do you know? You cannot always have access to just the right research study that can answer your question, and so you will want to know how to test your own assumptions empirically. But first, you must develop skill and accuracy in observing and recording behavior.

1. Try the following exercise to sharpen your skills of observation. As you are sitting through one of your lecture classes, observe, "um, um, um . . ."; "you know." The first day determine the two such phrases the professor seems to use most frequently. Then for the following two class periods, carefully record the number of times the professor uses the two phrases in a 30-minute interval.

2. When you feel comfortable observing and recording verbal phrases of hesitation, begin observing the nonverbal behaviors of hesitation the professor uses, for example, shuffling of notes at the lecture podium, silent pauses, head scratching, etc. Select two such target nonverbal behaviors used frequently by the professor and begin to carefully record these as well as the two target verbal behaviors you previously observed.

3. Now, ask a friend in your class to do the same: record the same two verbal phrases and the same two nonverbal behaviors of hesitation used by the professor. At the end of several classes compare your observation records for accuracy.

SUGGESTIONS FOR TERM PAPERS

1. The current concerns of educational research as reflected in recent educational research journals

2. Designing an experiment for an educational problem

3. A critical examination of some obvious statements taught to teacher trainees

4. How the teacher can be an experimenter in the classroom

5. Determining the correlation between heights of students and a test of classroom achievement/estimated parental income (high, medium, low) and a test of classroom achievement/students' standardized achievement test scores and a test of classroom achievement

6. Trying to understand the low-achieving child: Developing a theory

TECHNICAL NOTE A

HOW TO COMPUTE A CORRELATION COEFFICIENT

Information on correlation coefficients is presented in Chapter 2 of the text. You should have gained enough information to interpret correlational data, and you should also be able to compute these useful statistics for yourself. This technical note will help you.

The two most widely used coefficients of correlation are the Spearman rank-difference coefficient and the Pearson product-moment coefficient. The former is easier to compute when the number of pairs of measures is 30 or less. Also, the Spearman rank-difference coefficient shows well enough the nature of such coefficients, and so it is the one that we shall describe.

Table A-1
Three Sets of Paired Variables and the Corresponding
Rank-Difference Coefficients of Correlation

Set 1

Column 1	Column 2	Column 3	Column 4	Column 5	Column 6	Column 7
Student	Score Test (a)	Score Test (b)	Rank Test (a)	Rank Test (b)	Rank Difference	Difference Squared (D^2)
A	85	88	10	9	1	1
B	88	85	9	10	1	1
C	90	93	8	7	1	1
D	96	92	7	8	1	1
E	98	98	6	6	0	0
F	100	100	5	5	0	0
G	110	114	4	3	1	1
H	118	113	3	4	1	1
I	132	130	2	2	0	0
J	140	142	1	1	0	0
						$\Sigma D^2 = 6$

The formula, developed by statisticians, for determining the correlation coefficient is

$$rho = 1 - \frac{6\Sigma D^2}{N(N^2-1)}$$

$$= 1 - \frac{6(6)}{10(100-1)} = 1 - \frac{36}{990}$$

$$= 1 - .036$$

$$= .964$$

where rho = the rank difference coefficient of correlation
ΣD^2 = the sum of the squared differences-between-ranks
N = the number of pairs of measures

Table A-1 shows three sets of paired scores. Each set consists of measures of two variables for 10 students. Set 1 consists of the scores of the 10 students on (a) an individual test of IQ, the Stanford-Binet scale of intelligence, and (b) a group-administered test of scholastic ability, namely, the California Test of Mental Maturity. In correlating these two variables, we might be asking, How does the student's score on one test of mental ability correlate with the score on the other? Set 2 consists of the student's scores on (b) the

Set 2

Student	Score Test (b)	Score Test (c)	Rank Test (b)	Rank Test (c)	Rank Difference	Difference Squared (D^2)
A	88	18	9	10	1	1
B	85	21	10	8	2	4
C	93	19	7	9	2	4
D	92	25*	8	3.5	4.5	20.25
E	98	23*	6	5.5	.5	.25
F	100	22	5	7	2	4
G	114	27	3	2	1	1
H	113	23*	4	5.5	1.5	2.25
I	130	29	2	1	1	1
J	142	25*	1	3.5	2.5	6.25

$\Sigma D^2 = 44.00$

$$\text{rho} = 1 - \frac{6 \Sigma D^2}{N(N^2 - 1)}$$

$$= 1 - \frac{6(44)}{10(100-1)} = 1 - \frac{264}{990}$$

$$= 1 - .266$$

$$= .734$$

*Where there is a tie for the rank, the midpoint of all the ranks that could have occurred is used. Thus the two scores of 25 would occupy the third and fourth ranks, and are therefore both given the midpoint or 3.5. If there had been three scores of 25, they would encompass the third, fourth, and fifth ranks and would all have been assigned the rank of 4. The next rank to be assigned would be 6, the rank following all those that could have been used.

Set 3

Student	Score Test (c)	Score Test (d)	Rank Test (c)	Rank Test (d)	Rank Difference	Difference Squared (D^2)
A	18	165				
B	21	125				
C	19	143				
D	25	140				
E	23	155				
F	22	170				
G	27	150				
H	23	180				
I	29	165				
J	25	175				ΣD^2

$$\text{rho} = 1 - \frac{6\Sigma D^2}{N(N^2-1)}$$
$$=$$
$$=$$
$$=$$

Test a = Stanford-Binet IQ test
Test b = California Test of Mental Maturity IQ
Test c = Teacher-made test on colonial period in American history
Test d = Standardized test of achievement in American history

17

California Test of Mental Maturity and (c) a teacher-made test of understanding of the colonial period in American history, the subject of a recently studied unit. The correlation here would show the degree to which the student's achievement in this unit could have been predicted from a measure of general scholastic ability. Set 3 consists of the student's scores on (c) the achievement test on the colonial period and (d) a standardized test of achievement in American history. How well does performance on the teacher-made test on one unit correlate with the standardized test covering the whole field of American history?

The computation of the correlation, called rho, is straightforward. In Set 1, students are identified in Column 1, and the numerical values of the variables whose association we are examining are listed in Columns 2 and 3. We assign a rank order to the person's score on a and list that in Column 4. We list the ranks on b in Column 5. Thus Student B, with an IQ of 88 on the Stanford-Binet, ranks next to lowest, or ninth in the group of 10. In Column 6, we record the difference between ranks on the two tests. Finally, in Column 7, the last column, we compute the square of that difference between ranks. When Column 7 is summed, everything we need to put into the formula for determining the rank-difference correlation coefficient is available. We have computed the correlations in Sets 1 and 2, but have left Set 3 incomplete so that you can practice computing a correlation coefficient.

As Table A-1 shows, the three coefficients vary considerably. The correlation between variables a and b (rho$_{ab}$) is very high, .96; rho$_{bc}$ is high, .73; rho$_{cd}$ is low, .14.

Figure A-1a shows these paired scores plotted on a scattergram, a graphic way of showing a group's scores on two variables at one time. Note that, when the correlation is high, as in Figure A-1a, the paired scores tend to fall very close to an imaginary diagonal line running from the lower left-hand corner to the upper right-hand corner. This scatttergram shows that high scores on the one test are closely associated with high scores on the other test, and that low scores on one test are closely associated with low scores on the other test. If the correlation described were negative, say, —.96, the diagonal line would run from the upper left to the lower right-hand corner. In this case, being high on one test would be associated with being low on the other test. The closeness of the association would nevertheless be as great as it is when the relationship is positive. When the correlation is lower, the tally marks do not fall as close to such a diagonal line. Indeed, for rho$_{cd}$, shown in Figure A-1c, the correlation is almost zero, and the tally marks do not fall at all close to such a line.

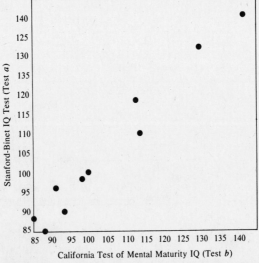

Figure A-1a
Scattergram of data in Set 1: IQ s of 10 pupils on two intelligence tests.

Figure A-1b

Scattergram of data in Set 2: IQs and scores on teacher-made history test.

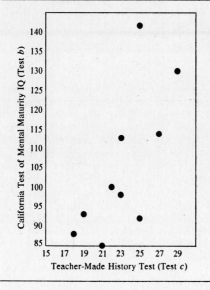

Figure A-1c

Scattergram of data in Set 3: Scores on teacher-made and standardized history tests.

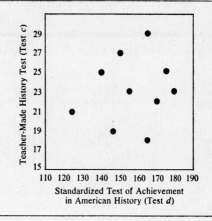

TECHNICAL NOTE B

SOME METHODOLOGY FOR INTERPRETING EXPERIMENTAL RESEARCH

The text briefly introduced you to experimental research in Chapter 2. Because so much of what educational psychologists do is experimental in nature, and because many journals in the field publish only articles reporting experiments, you need a working knowledge of what a "good" experiment is. You also need to be able to interpret the results of experiments. This technical note will help you to judge the quality of experiments, and it will give you at least some practice in interpreting the results of such experiments.

Experiments are used to determine causal relationships. Variations on the research methods used in designing experiments are presented over and over in research journals and reports. In this brief introduction you will learn some important considerations to be taken into account when studies are designed to determine causality. However, the best way to learn how the experimental method is used in educational psychology is to read some articles that use the experimental method. The list of references in the text cites many such articles. When you are finished with this technical note, pick a few journal articles on topics that interest you and read them. You will quickly get a feeling for how experimental researchers go about their business.

RANDOM ASSIGNMENT AND CAUSALITY

The inference as to causality is justified if the different values of the independent variables were applied to groups of subjects (such as students, classes, schools) that differed only randomly in variables other than the manipulated variable.

Suppose that in our explanation experiment (see text p. 23) one of four groups of students was extremely bright. Then an inference that causally relates types of explanation to differences in understanding is mistaken. The same mistake might be made if one group of students were poor, or one group were females, or three groups were from parochial schools, whereas the fourth was not. The many student characteristics that exist, if not randomly distributed, would hinder our making inferences that we would trust. It is therefore crucial that persons who receive the different treatments or values of the independent variable be made equivalent with respect to all the other variables possible, except for the variable we are trying to manipulate. And the best way to ensure such equivalence is to assign subjects to treatments at random. In this way, the irrelevant variables in an experiment will probably be equally represented in all experimental groups. Roughly equal proportions of subjects who are high and low in intelligence, rich and poor financially, parochial and nonparochial school students, or black or white or brown will be present in all treatments. Such random assignment marks the true experiment.

If such randomization is impossible or not feasible, less convincing but still valuable studies aimed at determining causal relationships can be made. Such compromises, called quasi-experiments (Campbell & Stanley, 1966), can often suggest whether a causal relationship exists.

DESIGN AND CAUSALITY

Thus randomness in assignment of subjects is a major consideration. But another factor, the design of the experiment, also plays an important role in determining the validity of the inferences that can be made from an experiment.

Suppose you randomly picked 30 students to study a unit of French taught by your own special method. You wished to determine whether there was a difference betweeen the average pretest and posttest scores in French pronunciation. We might schematize the design of this particular experiment as follows:

$$\underline{O}_1 \ X \ \underline{O}_2$$

where $\underline{O}$ is an observation of the subjects, say, a test (tests are systematic observations), which is given as a pretest ($\underline{O}_1$) and also as a posttest ($\underline{O}_2$), and $\underline{X}$ is a treatment, your method of teaching this particular French unit. This kind of one-group experiment would be inadequate because the difference between pretest and posttest scores might be attributable to factors other than the treatment. A number of these other factors have been identified by Campbell and Stanley (1966), who named them as follows:

(a) "History," that is, events other than the treatment that occurred between the pretest and the posttest. For example, if the treatment is a unit of instruction in French, the difference between the pretest and the posttest might result from coincidental lessons in French on the local television station, at the neighborhood movie theater, or in a weekly magazine. Thus the personal history of the subjects in the study could affect the results. Then the experimenter might never know that the treatment was not responsible for any changes that occurred.

(b) "Maturation," for example, mere growth in mental maturity in the interval between the pretest and posttest. Thus, suppose the treatment is instruction in basketball. We cannot attribute improvement to the instruction unless we are sure that the students would not have improved just as much merely as a result of their growing older, taller, and stronger.

(c) "Practice," or the improvement on the posttest due to the practice gained from taking the pretest. Improvement on a French reading test may result merely from the practice effect of taking a series of such tests. Students learn to pace themselves and spot the kinds of points likely to be dealt with in the test questions. These factors will produce improvement between pretest and posttest for reasons other than experimental treatment. Taking one test provides a kind of "practice" that improves scores on subsequent tests.

(d) "Instrumentation," or change in the measuring instruments used in the pretest and posttest. Such change is easy to comprehend when these "instruments" are human raters. Suppose the ratings on a pretest of French pronunciation are made by severe judges, but the ratings on the posttest are made by lenient judges. (The same judges might become more lenient as time went on.) Then we shall obviously find an improvement from pretest to posttest. But such improvement should not, of course, be credited to the experimental treatment.*

Each of these sources of invalidity can threaten the internal validity of an experiment. Internal validity is the degree to which the difference between the pretest and posttest (or the difference between two groups on a posttest) may justifiably be attributed to the treatment. Internal validity bears upon the question: Did, in fact, the experimental treatment make a difference in this specific experimental instance? It is distinguished from external validity, that is, generalizability. Problems of generalizing from an experiment seem to fall into two broad classes:

> (1) Those dealing with generalizations to populations of persons (What population of subjects can be expected to behave the same way as did the sample experimental subjects?), and (2) those dealing with the "environment" of the experiment (Under what conditions, i.e., settings, treatments, experimenters, dependent variables, etc., can the same results be expected?). These two broad classes correspond to two types of external validity: population validity and ecological validity (Brach & Glass, 1968, p. 438).

To use experimental evidence as a guide to practice, you must ask two questions of any internally valid experimental findings:

1.   Does the reported experiment allow me to infer that the same kind of results will occur with my subjects (students, teachers, administrators, etc.)? In this case, you are asking whether your population of subjects is similar enough to the population used in the experiment to assure that the finding might be generalizable to your own people.

2.   Does the reported experiment allow me to infer that the same kind of results will occur under the conditions present in my situation (type of physical setting, time of day, length of treatment, equipment available, etc.)? In this case, you are asking whether the environmental setting in your situation will affect the outcome reported in the experiment, or whether that outcome is dependent upon particular factors present when the experiment was conducted.

How can the problems of the external validity and internal validity of experiments be overcome? We noted the vulnerability to criticism of the "one-group pretest-posttest design" schematized above. Now suppose that, in addition to the single group portrayed above, we have another group, a "control group." This group receives the pretest and the posttest at the same time as the experimental group. But it does not receive the experimental treatment. The control group is probably made equivalent to the experimental group in all respects by randomization (R); that is, the students are assigned to the experimental or the control group at random. Now we have the following pretest-posttest control-group design:

> Experimental Group $\underline{R}$ O_1 X O_2
> Control Group $\underline{R}$ O_3 X $\overline{O_4}$

Then the comparison of effects is made between O_2 and O_4. The question we would ask is, Do the posttest scores of the two groups differ? Or a comparison can also be made between O_1 and O_2 and between O_3 and O_4. The question we would ask here is whether the former difference ($O_2 - O_1$) is greater than the latter difference ($O_4 - O_3$).

* Campbell and Stanley (1966) discuss four additional sources of invalidity in attributing causality to a treatment: "regression," "selection," "mortality," and "interaction of selection and maturation." The interested reader will find their discussion enlightening and understandable even without knowledge of statistical methods.

The reader who wishes to understand experimental design, of which only the simplest notions are presented here, will gain much from trying to describe the ways in which this design does or does not ward off the various threats to internal and external validity described above -- namely, "history," "maturation," "practice," and "instrumentation." The discussion and schematization of experimental and quasi-experimental designs provided by Campbell and Stanley (1966) present a researcher with many alternatives to consider when an experiment is to be undertaken.

STATISTICS AND CAUSALITY

Our causal inferences about the outcomes of experiments are justified by the random assignment of the subjects to treatments and the kind of design used in the experiment. Even when the criteria for conducting valid experimentation are well met, we are faced with a problem of inferring whether real differences or chance differences between groups are occurring. Let us use a practical example. Suppose you wanted to train teachers to ask questions that were "higher order," that is, questions that required students to give an answer based on processes more complex than simple memory. You might demonstrate how to ask this kind of question by showing one group of teachers a set of transcripts displaying higher-order questions. You might present to another group of teachers a videotaped version of the same transcript. The experimental question you are asking is, Does the transcript treatment (X_t) work better (or worse) than the videotape treatment (X_v) in changing the frequency of occurrence of higher-order questions? Your experimental design is:

$$\underline{R}\ \underline{O_1}\ \underline{X_t}\ \underline{O_2}$$
$$\underline{R}\ \underline{O_3}\ \underline{X_v}\ \underline{O_4}$$

Teachers are randomly assigned ($\underline{R}$) to the two conditions, X_t and X_v. Each treatment group receives a pretest in which the number of higher-order questions asked in a 10-minute period of teaching is counted. Both groups receive a posttest, which is a repeat of the pretest.

Now, suppose that the subjects in Treatment X_t produced, on the average, 19 higher-order questions when the O_2 observation was made. Further, suppose that the subjects in Treatment X_v produced, on the average, 14 higher-order questions when the O_4 observation was made. May we infer that the transcripted method of training in higher-order questioning is superior to the videotaped method of training this behavior? It certainly appears so, since 19 is greater than 14. But is the difference between the two treatments subject to chance variation? Probably it is, since if we checked at another time we might find that the mean or average score for treatment X_t was 16 and the mean score for treatment X_v was 15. Do the two treatment groups still show a difference greater than chance fluctuations could probably account for? Scores are always expected to fluctuate a little. Differences in the results for different treatments are always likely to occur. Therefore, how big a difference is needed to let us infer that a real difference and not a chance difference is present? In fact, if we taught two randomly selected groups of subjects the same thing in the same way, would we not also be likely to find slight differences in final performance? That is, would it not be a remarkable coincidence if the final performances were exactly the same?

We make the decision about whether a difference can or cannot be attributed to chance fluctuations through the use of statistical methods. These methods are used to describe and make inferences from data. On the one hand, when we mentioned the mean number of higher-order questions, we used a descriptive statistic: the mean. When we report the range of scores, or percentages, we are using other descriptive statistics. On the other hand, inferential statistics are methods that allow us to infer characteristics of a population on the basis of a sample drawn from the population. Statistical measures based on samples, because they never completely encompass all the cases possible, are always subject to fluctuation. Our sample of teachers will show this kind of fluctuation in our measurement of higher-order questions. Inferential statistics provide us with a way of estimating what the characteristics of the entire population might be. In that way, we can have some guide as to the amount of fluctuation that might be possible within the smaller sample.

We might, through our statistics, find that the population mean for Treatment X_t is 19, but we can expect that 68 percent of the time a sample mean will fall between 16 and 22 points. Likewise, we might, through our statistics, find that the population mean for Treatment X_v is 14, but we can expect that 68 percent of the time a sample mean will fall between 11 and 17 points. These statistically estimated distributions of sample means are plotted in Figure B-1. Notice the shaded area of overlap between the two estimated distributions of sample means, given population means of 19 and 14, respectively. If there were no overlap in the distributions, we could clearly infer that Treatment X_t is superior to Treatment X_v. Because, in our samples, the number of higher-order questions asked after Treatments X_t and X_v might sometimes be very close to each other, we need statistics to decide whether the difference that we actually obtained in our experiment is "real" or merely one of those chance fluctuations that occur.

Figure B-1
Estimated distribution of sample means for two treatments: Videotaped (X_v) and transcripted (X_t)

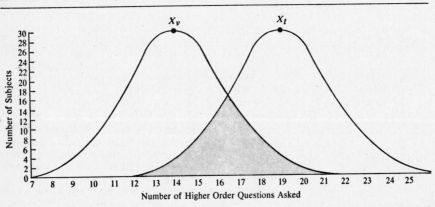

Our decision about whether differences between groups are real or chance is usually based on the estimated probability of obtaining by chance a difference as large as the difference obtained in our experiment. If the statistical procedure we use provides us with an estimate that the probability of obtaining by chance a difference between means as large as 5 points (19 — 14) on our measure of higher-order questions is .05, we usually accept the difference as nonchance. We call that difference significant. The probability that the obtained difference in mean scores would occur by chance 5 times out of 100 different draws of two samples from the same population is a small one. Since the probability of this difference by chance is small, and since we obtained it on our first and only draw of two samples, it is likely that a real difference exists between treatment populations. To infer that significant differences exist, research workers prefer probabilities of less than .05 or .01 (usually written $p < .05$ or $p < .01$). Such small probabilities of occurrence give the experimenter and readers the assurance that if they infer that a treatment produces some effect, they will not be wrong too often. But they will still, sometimes, make a wrong inference.

Even a probability that a difference as large as the one obtained could occur by chance less than once in 1,000 samples ($p < .001$) still leaves open the possibility that the difference really did occur by chance. But the possibility is now a remote one. The possibility of an error is conceivable because in the experiment you might have drawn the one sample per 1,000 that yielded, by chance alone, the difference you obtained. Clearly, because we use probabilities that are never perfect, we can never achieve complete certainty. But we can approach certainty so closely that we have great confidence that our results are not due to chance.

We can achieve greater confidence by replication, or repetition, of experiments. That is, we can trust several studies of the same or similar treatments, produce the same or similar effects much more than we can trust a single study in which statistical measures were used to make inferences about whether the effects were real or chance.

To round out the reader's appreciation of the value of inferential statistics in educational experimentation, we offer some illustrative studies, using several different statistical tools:

1. Berliner (1969) compared the effectiveness of transcripted and videotaped examples of higher-order questions in training teachers. An analysis of variance (a statistical technique) produced an F ratio of 1.23, $p < .05$.

The statistic called the F ratio used with two or more samples was obtained when the means of the two samples of teachers (the transcripted and videotaped groups) were compared. An F ratio is associated with particular probabilities. In this case it is estimated that the F ratio of 1.23 has a probability p of occurring by chance more than ($>$) 5 out of 100 times ($p > .05$) in the population from which the sample of teachers was drawn. Since this is not a very rare event, we may conclude that the difference between the two groups may be simply a chance difference. A nonchance difference between the two methods of teacher training cannot be said to exist. In such a case, we say the difference was not significant. Either videotaped or transcripted instruction is probably appropriate, if no other criterion of the effectiveness of the instruction (for example, trainee attitudes) is used.

2. Ausubel and Tenzer (1970) compared learning from prose material in dogmatic students who either read a special introduction to counter their dogmatism or read no introduction to the material. A t test (a statistical test used with two samples) of the difference between these two groups in average amount learned was significant ($t = 2.22$, $p < .05$).

The t distribution also yields a probabilistic figure. A t of 2.22. is estimated to occur by chance less than 5 times in 100 ($p < .05$). Thus the size of the difference between the groups -- the one that had the special introduction and the one that did not -- is considered large enough to be nonchance, or statistically significant. Other things being equal, we would conclude that, in the population from which this sample was drawn, dogmatic people learn better when instructions to counter the dogmatism are provided. We can put 95 percent confidence in that statement because we expect to be wrong, that is, to have such a difference occur by chance, less than ($<$) 5 out of 100 times ($p < .05$).

3. Schwebel and Cherlin (1972) did a study of physical and social distance in teacher-pupil relationships, using the statistic called chi square (written X^2) to test their data. In the

25

study, students were moved to new seats in their classrooms. The movement was either forward, backward, or lateral within the same row. The purpose was to determine whether a change in the location of the student within a classroom was functionally related to the teacher's ratings of how well the teacher liked the student. The relationship of direction of seat movement to teacher's ratings of likability showed a chi-square value of 6.14, $p< .05$.

Table B-1
Effect of Seat Change on Likability of Students

Seat Change	Direction of Change in Ratings			
	More Likable	No Change	Less Likable	Total
Moved forward	23	28	12	63
Moved backward	13	35	22	70

$$\chi^2 = 6.14, p<.05$$

Source: Andrew I. Schwebel and Dennis L. Cherlin, "Physical and Social Distancing in Teacher-Pupil Relationships," *Journal of Educational Psychology*, 63:548. Copyright 1972 by the American Psychological Association. Reprinted by permission.

As shown in Table B-1, of the 63 students moved forward, the teachers rated 23 as more likable and 12 as less likable. Of the 70 students moved backward, the teachers rated 13 as more likable and 22 as less likable. Teachers' ratings for the other students in the sample did not change. The χ^2 equaled 6.14, $p< .05$, indicating that the change in seating resulted in a change in the teacher's liking of students. Changes of this magnitude in the rating of a student's likability could have occurred by chance less than 5 times in 100 studies of this kind. It appears that the closer a student sits to a teacher, the more the teacher tends to like the student.

The many kinds of statistical tests available are designed to put a probabilistic estimate on the "nonchanceness" of the differences that we find in our data. You need not know the nature of the F ratio, t test, or chi-square test, but you should understand the probabilistic statements that are associated with the statistical tests. We ask whether the differences we find are significant or merely chance events. The methods of inferential statistics, by providing probability estimates of the likelihood of the occurrence of events, are tools that give us confidence in a statement that two or more variables are related.

REFERENCES

AUSUBEL, D.P., and TENZER, A.G. (1970) Components of and neutralizing factors in the effects of close-mindedness on the learning of controversial material. American Educational Research Journal, 7:267-273.

BERLINER, D. C. (1969) Microteaching and the technical skills approach to teacher training. Stanford, Calif.: Stanford Center for Research and Development in Teaching. Technical Report No. 8.

BRACHT, G. H., and GLASS, G. V. (1968) The external validity of experiments. American Educational Research Journal, 5:437-474.

CAMPBELL, D. T., and STANLEY, J. C. (1966) Experimental and quasi-experimental designs for research. Chicago: Rand McNally.

SCHWEBEL, A. I., and CHERLIN, D. L. (1972) Physical and social distancing in teacher-pupil relationships. Journal of Educational Psychology, 63:543-550.

CHAPTER 3   THE FORMULATION OF OBJECTIVES AND THEIR JUSTIFICATION

OBJECTIVES

The student should be able to

o state why the formulation of objectives is useful in teaching and in evaluation of students' learning

o write an objective that describes precisely what student behavior is required, specifies the conditions for performance of the task, and states the minimal level of acceptable performance

o construct a behavior-content matrix in some curriculum area

o discuss five criticisms of behavioral objectives, and respond to each from a pro-objective point of view

o distinguish between expressive and behavioral objectives

REMINDER

This chapter taught you why and how to write educational objectives. You will recall that the essential components of a good objective are specifying evidence of achievement, stating conditions of performance, and stating acceptable levels of performance. You also learned how to construct a behavior-content matrix, a framework for formulating useful objectives. Arguments against the use of objectives were also examined. These arguments included the notions that only trivial objectives can be behaviorally stated, that only a few subject areas lend themselves to behavioral objectives, and that objectives are mechanistic and inhibit spontaneity. A reply to each criticism was provided. A review of research on the effectiveness of objectives concluded the chapter.

DEFINITIONS OF KEY CONCEPTS

The following key concepts were discussed in this chapter. In your own words, write the definition of each concept in the space provided.

1. Objectives _____

_____

_____

2. Terminal behaviors in educational objectives _____

_____

_____

3. Conditions of performance in educational objectives _____

_____

_____

4. Levels of performance in educational objectives_____

_____

_____

5. A behavior-content matrix _____

_____

_____

6. Expressive objectives _____

_____

_____

APPLICATION OF KEY CONCEPTS

The terms listed below refer to important concepts that were discussed in this chapter. Carefully read each descriptive statement, and identify the concept or concepts each statement implies. Place the corresponding letter(s) of the concept(s) you select in the space provided.

Concepts

A. terminal behavior
B. conditions of performance
C. level of performance

D. behavior-content matrix
E. expressive objective

Descriptive Statements

_____1. Those students trying for an A grade must correctly perform five of the chemistry experiments; those trying for a B grade must correctly perform three of the chemistry experiments.

_____ 2. At the end of the project, Robert proudly showed the teacher his collection of five different types of marine crustaceans.

_____ 3. He told his students to write the essay in class, without using the text or lecture notes.

_____ 4. I'm being more systematic this year in my planning and evaluation of the tennis unit. I've drawn a chart for myself listing the key areas to cover, combined with rows outlining how students will show their mastery.

_____ 5. I told Jennifer that during lunch times she could use any of the materials on the dissection table she wished.

MULTIPLE-CHOICE SELF-TEST

Select the response that best answers the question or completes the statement. Place the letter of the chosen answer in the space provided.

_____ 1. What is a major pitfall for teachers who do not formulate objectives?
   A. Presentation of content too difficult for students to comprehend
   B. Concern with only the content of instruction
   C. Focus on outcome rather than process
   D. Time constraints preventing the covering of essential content

_____ 2. Mr. Jones is teaching an art appreciation class. He states as an objective "The students will attain an appreciation of historically significant works of art." This objective can be criticized on the grounds that

   A. "historically significant" is too vague and ambiguous.
   B. it does not specify student behaviors observably enough.
   C. it has insufficient educational importance.
   D. A and B

_____ 3. A "good" educational objective" aids in student evaluation because
   A. it is written to meet criteria that the author deems important.
   B. it specifically states what the student is expected to do to show achievement of the objective.
   C. it is written to conform to the curriculum in use.
   D. it specifically tells when testing will take place.

_____ 4. In order to be useful, a list of objectives for a unit of instruction
   A. must specify every student behavior that is required.
   B. need only state conditions of performance.
   C. must be made available to students at the beginning of the school year.
   D. should provide an uncluttered set of guidelines for planned instructional activities.

_____ 5. Which of the following statements contains both components of what should be included in a cell of a behavior-content matrix?
   A. "Define and give an example . . ."

B. "Without using notes, compute from memory . . ."
C. "Tomorrow be prepared to discuss and write one instance of . . ."
D. "Write your first reactions to Longfellow's poem . . ."

_____ 6. Of the following behavioral terms, which would you consider to be highest in "observability"?
A. To understand
B. To appreciate
C. To learn
D. To arrange

_____ 7. Some critics of the use of behavioral objectives believe that the really important goals of learning cannot be put into behavioral terms. Which of the following best refutes that belief?
A. Learning minute behaviors is necessary to reach the larger, more all-encompassing goals.
B. Evaluation of students will be more valid if objectives of limited scope are used.
C. It has been found that vague statements of educational goals can be translated into observable behaviors, thereby allowing the teacher to determine whether such goals have been reached.
D. Educational goals can be broken down into their most minute components.

_____ 8. The statement that although behavioral objectives are appropriate for some subject-matter areas, they are difficult or impossible to formulate for certain other subject areas is
A. false, because regardless of whether the curriculum emphasizes process or product, the teacher has criteria in mind for determining whether the goals are reached, but may be reluctant to describe them in terms others can see.
B. false, because only teachers who are unsure about the goals of their course will be unwilling to formulate behavioral objectives.
C. true, because a curriculum that emphasizes a process to be participated in does not have criteria for evaluating student achievement, since there is no product to be evaluated.
D. true, because it is impossible to state behavioral objectives for classes such as art, music, or creative writing, where the student's interpretation is just as valid as the teacher's.

_____ 9. One refutation of the argument that behavioral objectives are antihumanistic is that
A. it is more humane to make clear the criteria of success than to keep them from students.
B. as long as teachers treat students intelligently, behavioral objectives cannot be antihumanistic.
C. the teacher can be imaginative and flexible in evaluating whether or not behavioral objectives have been achieved.

_____ 10. The planning of behavioral objectives should be such that
A. every classroom will be anticipated by the teacher.
B. all educational goals, both short-term and long-term, are prespecified.
C. they always keep class activities from wandering in irrelevant directions.
D. unanticipated outcomes and developments are not necessarily hindered.

_____11. An expressive objective is one that
A. specifies the terminal behaviors of students.
B. specifies the conditions under which the objective is to be met.
C. describes an educational encounter.
D. specifies aesthetic educational goals.
E. specifies what it is that students are to learn from an educational encounter.

_____12. Which of the following is an example of an expressive objective?
A. "Given three hours to experiment, students will learn how to . . ."
B. "Students should be able to write five reasons . . ."
C. "Students will be able to construct . . ."
D. "Students will go on a field trip . . ."

_____13. What does current research as a whole indicate is the general relationship between use of objectives and student learning?
A. Learning is enhanced.
B. Learning is depressed.
C. Certain types of learning are enhanced, whereas others are depressed.
D. There is no basis for drawing a conclusion.

PROJECTS AND ACTIVITIES

1. Select a chapter from a textbook from which you are studying this term and construct a behavior-content matrix covering the material. Practice this with different chapters if you feel the need. This will also help you in your study and preparation for the tests you must take. Next, from a text library, pick a text you may have to teach with, for example, a third-grade reader or a high school civics book. Develop a behavior-content matrix covering all the material in the text. Try to formulate at least two educational objectives for each cell of the matrix. If you were teaching the material, with which cells of the matrix do you think you would be most concerned? Imagine how you would evaluate whether students achieved the objectives designated for each cell.

2. Here are some examples of "word magic." Try translating each into a useful educational objective.
A. The student will appreciate art forms of the Renaissance period.
B. The student will understand the function of the cardiovascular system in endurance tasks.
C. The student will learn to be more polite in social situations.
When you compare your new list of objectives with those of other students who tried this activity, you will note the diversity in the modifications that were made, an excellent example of why the original objectives were "word magic."

3. Actually collect data on student opinion regarding courses guided by educational objectives. If you are a student teacher, you might try the following: Develop a short student questionnaire to tap opinion about teachers' use of educational objectives. For one week instruct your students, using carefully planned behavioral objectives. At the end of the week, administer the questionnaire to the students. The second week, instruct students without using behavioral objectives. Again, at the end of the week, administer the same questionnaire. Compare students' responses for the two weeks. This exercise will help you in developing and using educational objectives.

SUGGESTIONS FOR TERM PAPERS

1. A translation of the statement of goals for the _____ School District into useful objectives

2. Determining terminal behaviors in biology/second-grade math/seventh-grade social studies/chemistry/etc.

3. Development of a behavior-content matrix for anatomy/auto shop/music/etc.

4. Determining the conditions and level of performance for behavioral objectives

5. Problems in the use of educational objectives

6. How to help teachers of English literature/creative writing/primary reading/etc. develop sensible behavioral objectives

7. The students' point of view about courses that are guided by behavioral objectives

8. How to use behavioral objectives with a humanistic approach to teaching

CHAPTER 4   DIFFERENT KINDS OF OBJECTIVES AND THEIR ORGANIZATION

OBJECTIVES

The student should be able to

o describe the three domains of the taxonomy of educational objectives

o order the levels of ability within the cognitive domain from simple to complex

o write objectives at different levels of the cognitive domain

o critique the notion of a hierarchy of skills within the cognitive domain

o construct a structure for learning some particular skill or piece of information

o discuss the concepts of economy, power, and mode of knowledge and their application to teaching/learning

REMINDER

Chapter 4 addressed the teacher's problem of optimally organizing and structuring educational objectives.   One major classification scheme divides objectives into three domains: cognitive, affective, and psychomotor.   Although the behaviors associated with objectives for each domain are not independent, it is useful to focus on one domain at a time. Another way to organize objectives is to examine the different types of learning that take place. You will remember the hierarchy of seven types of learning -- ranging from simple signal learning to rule learning -- based on the premise that the learning of some behavior may be a prerequisite for the learning of another behavior. A structure for learning number operations illustrated how such a taxonomy of learning tasks may aid the teacher.   The chapter concluded with a discussion of how an analysis of the structure of the tasks to be learned is useful to the teacher and the student.

DEFINITIONS OF KEY CONCEPTS

The following key concepts were discussed in this chapter. In your own words, write the definition of each concept in the space provided.

1. Taxonomy of educational objectives _____

_____

_____

2. Cognitive objectives _____

_____

_____

3. Affective objectives _____

_____

_____

4. Psychomotor objectives _____

_____

_____

5. Knowledge _____

_____

_____

6. Comprehension _____

_____

_____

7. Application _____

_____

_____

8. Analysis _____

_____

_____

9. Synthesis _____

_____

_____

10. Evaluation _____

_____

_____

11. Learning hierarchy _____

_____

_____

12. Signal learning _____

_____

_____

13. Stimulus-response learning _____

_____

_____

14. Chaining _____

_____

_____

15. Verbal association learning _____

_____

_____

16. Discrimination learning _____

_____

_____

17. Concept learning _____

_____

_____

18. Rule learning _____

_____

_____

19. Structure of content _____

_____

_____

20. Mode of knowledge _____

_____

_____

21. Economy of knowledge _____

_____

_____

22. Power of knowledge _____

_____

_____

APPLICATION OF KEY CONCEPTS

The terms listed below refer to important concepts that were discussed in this chapter. Carefully read each descriptive statement, and identify the concept or concepts each statement implies. Place the corresponding letter(s) of the concept(s) you select in the space provided.

Concepts

A. economy of knowledge
B. learning hierarchy
C. psychomotor objective
D. mode of knowledge

E. cognitive objectives
F. affective objectives
G. power of knowledge
H. structure

Descriptive Statements

_____ 1. The seventh-grade teacher wants her students to be able to compare and evaluate capitalism and socialism.

_____ 2. Marian has to understand the use of indirect objects in English grammar before she can learn the use ot the dative case in Latin.

_____ 3. After Willard learned the formulas for how light refracts in water, he was able to increase the number and sharpen the quality of his underwater pictures.

_____ 4. Mr. Plant has found that his students do best when he teaches horticulture of forest lands by starting with concerns about ground soil, then weather patterns, then root systems of plants and trees, then life cycles of plants and trees, and ending with ecological forest systems.

_____5. The art teacher conveyed the concept of texture by having students actually feel five different objects of varying texture, examine a painting in which the use of texture was particularly striking, and read a chapter on the importance of texture in artistic expression.

_____6. The home economics teacher has students organize their present thinking about what they will be doing in five years by asking them to formulate three goals they have for themselves.

_____7. Freud categorized personality into id, ego, and superego processes.

_____8. On the first day of typing class, Ms. Simmons taught her students three different finger exercises, which they are to practice daily.

MULTIPLE-CHOICE SELF-TEST

Select the response that best answers the question or completes the statement. Place the letter of the chosen answer in the space provided.

_____ 1. Taxonomies of learning tasks are especially useful and relevant for those who believe that
A. certain behaviors must be learned before others.
B. behaviors that are learned are independent of one another.
C. all behaviors are learned simultaneously but at different cognitive levels.
D. teaching is an art.

_____ 2. A particular usefulness of the taxonomy in the cognitive domain has been to
A. enable teachers to increase their specification of objectives in the "knowledge" area of the cognitive domain.
B. provide specific evaluation procedures to measure student performance.
C. help teachers specify objectives throughout the entire range of areas in the cognitive domain.
D. help teachers include more attitudinal concerns in the curriculum.

_____ 3. Three of the following categories of objectives belong in the cognitive domain. Which category does not?
A. Comprehension
B. Discrimination
C. Evaluation
D. Application

_____ 4. Since taking a course in nutrition, Nancy no longer drinks carbonated cola after school, but now has grapefruit juice. At what level of the cognitive domain is Nancy operating?
A. Knowledge
B. Application
C. Synthesis
D. Evaluation

_____ 5. The previous question is an example of a test item that taps the _____ level of the cognitive domain.
A. knowledge
B. application
C. synthesis
D. evaluation

_____ 6. A student can tell you why he thinks Pittsburgh was built where it was. What behavior category does this illustrate?
A. Knowledge
B. Comprehension
C. Analysis
D. Evaluation

_____ 7. A recent survey of test items from world history textbooks revealed that most items tap
A. higher-level cognitive processes, such as analysis.
B. lower-level cognitive processes, such as comprehension.
C. about equal amounts of lower-level and higher-level processes.

_____ 8. In a task sequence that demands both horizontal and vertical learning,
A. the lower-order learning must take place after the higher-order learning.
B. the hierarchy of learning must be empirically derived.
C. vertical learning is a prerequisite to horizontal learning.
D. horizontal learning should take place before vertical learning.

_____ 9. Which of the following kinds of learning are ordered from simplest to most complex according to Gagne's taxonomy of learning tasks?
A. Discrimination, concept, rule
B. Signal, concept, discrimination
C. Rule, signal, chaining
D. Discrimination, concept, verbal association

_____10. Which of the following is primarily an example of discrimination learning?
A. Matching names of United States presidents with their pictures
B. Learning to dress oneself
C. Translating from Spanish to English
D. A child saying "boat" at the sight of a sailboat

_____11. Learning that "cerveza" is the Spanish equivalent for "beer" is an example of which type of learning?
A. Stimulus-response
B. Chaining
C. Verbal association
D. Discrimination
E. Rule learning

_____12. The power of a structure of knowledge is best indicated by which of the following properties?
A. Its applicability to a wide variety of apparently unrelated phenomena
B. The way in which the knowledge is represented or communicated
C. The sharpness of the steps in the hierarchy of the structure
D. Its ability to incorporate many facts into a single formula
E. The number of different steps or levels in the hierarchy of the structure

_____13. What is the value of the taxonomy of educational objectives?
A. It helps teachers focus on academic, knowledge-based areas of instruction.
B. It provides an impetus for teachers to consider a wider range and variety of objectives.
C. It stimulates more emphasis on lower-level objectives that are realistically attainable by students.
D. It creates equal teacher emphasis on all three domains of objectives.

PROJECTS AND ACTIVITIES

1. Select three tests to which you have access. These may be tests from previous courses or, if you are a teacher trainee, tests used by a supervisory teacher. Carefully analyze the content of the test material in terms of the taxonomy of cognitive objectives. Do the tests reflect all six categories of cognitive objectives, or mostly knowledge and comprehension? If the latter is true, how would you modify the test items to tap application, analysis, synthesis, and evaluation?

2. Locate a text used at the level you are most likely to be teaching. Also obtain any accompanying workbooks, test booklets, and teacher's manuals. If you are a student teacher, you can easily borrow materials. If not, check the curriculum or textbook section of your college/university library. Randomly sample the test items contained in these materials, then classify items into the six skill levels -- knowledge, comprehension, application, analysis, synthesis, evaluation -- of the cognitive domain. Tally your results and compute the relative frequency of occurrence of items at each of the skill levels. What do your findings imply regarding student learning?

SUGGESTIONS FOR TERM PAPERS

1. An analysis of the content of some current tests in terms of the taxonomy of cognitive objectives

2. A survey of teacher attitudes regarding higher-level cognitive processes: Intention and reality

3. A philosophical critique of the hierarchical notion of learning

4. Developing a learning hierarchy for an objective in third-grade reading/junior high music/microbiology/etc.

5. How to present material in different modes when teaching art history/U.S. government/botany/etc.

CHAPTER 5   THE DEFINITION, MEASUREMENT, AND ORGANIZATION OF INTELLIGENCE

OBJECTIVES

The student should be able to

o define <u>intelligence,</u> <u>norms,</u> <u>percentile rank</u>, and <u>test reliability</u>

o distinguish between general and specific mental abilities

o describe factor analytic approaches used to study intelligence (see Technical Note C at the end of this chapter)

o describe the normal curve distribution associated with IQ scores

o compare and contrast intelligence and achievement tests

o define <u>self-fulfilling prophecy</u> and give an example

o discuss the appropriate use of intelligence tests

REMINDER

In this chapter you read about how intelligence is defined -- the ability to deal with abstractions and solve problems; how intelligence is measured and related to the performance of others through the use of norms; and how intelligence is organized -- the degree to which ability consists of one dimension or a subset of dimensions. Chapter 5 also discussed the differences between intelligence and achievement tests, and the timely issue of the appropriate use of intelligence tests in schools, namely, as part of the process of diagnosing needs for special education.

DEFINITIONS OF KEY CONCEPTS

The following key concepts were discussed in this chapter. In your own words, write the definition of each concept in the space provided.

1. Intelligence _____

_____

_____

2. Binet intelligence tests _____

_____

_____

3. Raw Test scores _____

_____

_____

4. Test norms _____

_____

_____

5. Standardized test scores _____

_____

_____

6. Standard deviation _____

_____

_____

7. Percentile rank _____

_____

_____

8. A normal distribution _____

_____

_____

9. Reliability _____

_____

_____

10. Achievement tests _____

_____

_____

11. Crystallized intelligence _____

_____

_____

12. Fluid intelligence _____

_____

_____

13. The self-fulfilling prophecy _____

_____

_____

APPLICATION OF KEY CONCEPTS

The terms listed below refer to important concepts that were discussed in this chapter. Carefully read each descriptive statement, and identify the concept or concepts each statement implies. Place the corresponding letter(s) of the concept(s) you select in the space provided.

Concepts

A. raw test scores
B. test norms
C. standard deviation
D. standardized test scores
E. achievement test
F. normal distribution
G. reliability
H. percentile rank
I. crystallized intelligence
J. fluid intelligence
K. self-fulfilling prophecy

Descriptive Statements

_____ 1. Nine-year-old Billy's performance on the test more closely matched the average for the sixth graders than that for the fourth graders.

_____ 2. All his teachers agree that Josh is very bright; he always gets A's in his math, English, and science courses.

_____ 3. To make the assignment of grades easier, I have a system of converting exam scores so that the class mean on a particular test is always 50 and the standard deviation is 10.

_____ 4. My last test must have been quite different from the tests I usually give. In the past, students' scores seemed to cluster pretty closely around the average score, whereas on this test nearly a quarter of the students scored really high and nearly a third scored very, very low, with only a few scores falling somewhere in between.

_____5. Darlene is quite adaptable. She accurately solved the maze problems in no time, and I don't think she's ever worked on that type of problem.

_____6. The school nurse plotted the frequency distribution of the weight of all the second-grade boys in the district.

_____7. In this test you are to read each short passage, then answer the factual questions following the passage.

_____8. Bobby was put in the Bluebirds Group (medium-low group) six months ago; since that time his reading scores haven't improved at all.

_____9. The principal congratulated me for the way in which my eighth-grade class's high math scores compared with those of the other eighth-graders in the school on the same test.

_____10. Her total number of correct answers to all the questions on the exam was 157.

_____11. Hank was pleased that he scored better than three-quarters of the students in his class on the test.

_____12. The students filled out the Questionnaire on General Study Habits during homeroom on Wednesday and again on the following Monday; on the average, their responses were just about the same.

MULTIPLE-CHOICE SELF-TEST

Select the response that best answers the question or completes the statement. Place the letter of the chosen answer in the space provided.

_____1. Why was a standardized test needed to differentiate intellectual ability of school children if teachers' judgments were to be used as the criterion for test validity?
   A. Extraneous factors not related to intelligence, such as appearance, influenced teachers' judgments.
   B. Teachers were able to correctly classify brighter students, but not students representative of the full range of intellectual ability.
   C. Teachers were able to correctly classify less bright students, but not students representative of the full range of intellectual ability.

_____2. Intelligence encompasses
   A. general mental ability only.
   B. general mental ability plus nonintellectual components, such as ability to withstand stress and emotion.
   C. general mental ability plus specific abilities, such as artistic and musical ability.
   D. all important kinds of abilities, skills, and capabilities.

_____3. We observe 12-year-old Paul performing very well on a block-sorting task, a vocabulary comprehension task, and a numerical reasoning task. On the basis of these measures, we would be most safe in describing Paul as being high in
   A. numerical abilities.
   B. special abilities.

C. general mental ability.
D. social and verbal abilities.

_____ 4. John received a percentile rank of 70 on a foreign language aptitude test. This score is interpreted to mean that
A. 30 percent of the people who might ever take this test would score lower than John.
B. 30 percent of the people who have taken this test scored higher than John.
C. 70 percent of the people who might ever take this test would score lower than John.
D. 70 percent of the people who have taken this test scored higher than John.

_____ 5. The normal curve is a graphic representation on a score scale of a group of scores that has
A. many cases near the midpoint and many at the high and low ends.
B. many cases near the midpoint and few at the high and low ends.
C. few cases near the midpoint and many at the high and low ends.
D. few cases near the midpoint and few at the high and low ends.

_____ 6. Mr. Blake received the IQ scores for pupils in his class recently and noted that most of them were quite a bit different from what they had been a year before in the seventh grade. Should he be surprised?
A. Yes, because IQ scores are generally quite constant after about age 10 to 12.
B. No, because IQ scores are quite variable at this stage in children's development (ages 13-15).
C. No, because there is a typical decline in IQ scores associated with the onset of puberty.
D. Yes, because there is typically an increase in IQ scores when students enter high school and begin to be concerned with their future careers.

_____ 7. The Highbar Test of Mental Gymnastics, a brand new intelligence test, was given to a sample of students on March 1, 1983. The same test was readministered on April 10, 1983, and the students' scores on the two test administrations were correlated. The correlation coefficient is best labeled as a coefficient of
A. regression.
B. determination.
C. validity.
D. reliability.

_____ 8. Dennis, a junior high school student, was just given an intelligence test that has a reliability coefficient of .87. Next year Dennis's score on the intelligence test will very likely
A. increase, because he will have more experience.
B. decrease, because he will be bored taking the same test again.
C. be about the same.
D. be unpredictable.

_____ 9. Which of the following statements accurately describes the relationship between an individual's intelligence score and age? The correlation between intelligence at a given age and intelligence at maturity
A. increases.
B. decreases.
C. remains about the same.

_____10. To make it possible to compare one person's test performance with those of other persons in some defined group, test developers usually make available test
   A. standards.
   B. validity data.
   C. reliability data.
   D. norms.

_____11. On an intelligence test that makes possible the computation of an intelligence quotient (IQ), an IQ of 100 has a percentile rank of about
   A. 50.
   B. 68.
   C. 95.
   D. 100.

_____12. If the magnitude of a variable is determined by a large number of equal, independently operating factors, the resulting frequency distribution will tend to be
   A. biomodal.
   B. negatively skewed, that is, with a tail to the left.
   C. positively skewed, that is, with a tail to the right.
   D. normal.

_____13. Which of the following does not belong in the psychologist's conception of intelligence?
   A. Ability to deal with abstractions
   B. Ability to solve problems
   C. Ability to behave morally
   D. Ability to adapt to a new situation

_____14. Currently, measures of intelligence are most frequently used by educators for
   A. selection of teaching methods to fit ability patterns of students.
   B. placement of students in educational programs, because the tests help predict success in various programs.
   C. both selection of teaching method and placement.

_____15. Tests of cognitive ability that differ in content and type of reasoning processes required correlate
   A. positively.
   B. negatively.
   C. randomly.
   D. not at all.

_____16. The function of a test's norms is to
   A. define standards of acceptable performance.
   B. convert raw scores to percentage scores.
   C. make possible comparisons with the performance of other persons.
   D. indicate the nature of a normal performance.

_____17. The problem of the organization of intelligence is one that relates to questions like:
   A. Is there only one general mental ability, or are there a number of special abilities?

    B. Are differences in heredity or environment more important in producing differences in intelligence?

    C. Can intelligence tests be freed of cultural bias?

    D. Is intelligence pretty much determined before age 10?

_____18. Intelligence tests have been found to have the most validity for the prediction of
    A. school grades.
    B. occupational success.
    C. earning power.
    D. motivation.

_____19. Which of the following is an instance of the use of norms in the interpretation of test scores?
    A. A raw score of 68
    B. A percentile rank of 68
    C. A reliability coefficient of .68
    D. A validity coefficient of .68

_____20. Which type of tests correlates most highly with job success?
    A. General intelligence tests
    B. Special abilities tests
    C. Verbal ability tests
    D. Spatial ability tests

_____21. Which of the following types of tests is most useful for predicting achievement in school subjects?
    A. General intelligence tests
    B. Tests of special mental abilities
    C. General and special ability tests are of about equal predictive value

_____22. The best conclusion to draw about the relationship between IQ score and job success is that
    A. there is no relationship.
    B. a high IQ score in high school is the most important factor contributing to later income level.
    C. the high correlation between the two indicates that the skills required for job performance are the same as those measured by IQ tests.
    D. IQ score is a better than chance predictor of job success.

_____23. How do intelligence tests differ from achievement tests in terms of measuring content of what is taught in schools?
    A. Qualitatively
    B. Quantitatively
    C. Both qualitatively and quantitatively
    D. Neither qualitatively nor quantitatively

PROJECTS AND ACTIVITIES

1. Go to a kindergarten classroom and randomly select one child to observe. Observe the child for one hour as he or she engages in work and play activities. Record the problems (academic, social, etc.) encountered by the child and carefully note how he or she tries to solve them. Is what you're seeing intelligence in action? What do you think is the relationship between what you've noted and tests of intelligence?

2.   Take an adult individual intelligence test. You can arrange for this by either volunteering to be a subject for graduate students in an advanced course in psychological testing; going to your college's testing office; or, if you're a student teacher in a school district, asking one of the district's school psychologists to administer the test. Ask for your score and an interpretation of that score. What were your feelings as you were taking the test? How did you feel as you were told about your performance according to the test norms? At the end of your interview, you might also ask if you could observe a child being tested with one of the individualized intelligence tests. Do you think the tests "capture" the child's intelligence?

3.   Interview a special education teacher in your district regarding the use of tests in diagnosis and placement of special learners. Be sure to ask about the role of intelligence tests, achievement tests, and any special ability tests. What other systematic information is collected before a placement decision is made for a given student? How is this information, including test results, weighted in decision making, that is, do standardized test scores "count" more or less heavily than teacher observation and recommendation? Finally, ask about how information gathering varies by exceptionality. As a result of your findings, would you conclude that intelligence tests are "alive and well" or on the decline?

SUGGESTIONS FOR TERM PAPERS

1.   Appropriate use of intelligence testing

2.   The history of intelligence testing in the United States

3.   How we might go about measuring social intelligence

4.   Is intelligence many separate abilities or one general ability

5.   Why schools are eliminating intelligence testing

6.   Intelligence testing and special education

TECHNICAL NOTE C

FACTOR ANALYSIS AND THE ORGANIZATION OF INTELLIGENCE

There is a raging battle, with a long history, about whether intelligence has one dimension or many. The text touched only briefly on this issue. Now we take the time to explore it in more depth.

Factor analysis is the main tool for investigating the organization of intelligence. It is a mathematical technique for determining the number of underlying dimensions, or factors, necessary to account for the intercorrelations among the scores obtained by a number of persons on a set of tests. Nine of the 21 tests used in one factor analysis are described in Figure C-1. These tests illustrate the kinds of things measured by intelligence tests. The set of tests, or test "battery," is administered to several hundred persons. A score is obtained for each person on each test. Then the scores on Test 1 are correlated with those on Test 2 to obtain r_{12} (where r is the symbol for the correlation coefficient). Similarly, r_{13}, $r_{14}, \ldots, r_{23}, r_{24}, r_{25}, \ldots, r_{(n-1)n}$ are computed. That is, all possible pairs of tests in the battery are correlated. These r's are then arranged in a "correlation matrix," which lists the various tests along both the columns and the rows, as illustrated in Table C-1, which is an excerpt from the full 21-test matrix. Each cell of the table contains the coefficient of correlation between the tests corresponding to the cell's column and row.

Table C-1
Correlation Coefficients for the
Selected Test Battery

Test	7	8	9	13	14	15	16	17	18
7. Sentences		.83	.77	.11	.03	.11	.30	.31	.35
8. Vocabulary			.78	.12	.06	.13	.32	.35	.57
9. Completion				.27	.21	.24	.30	.27	.39
13. Flags					.64	.63	.25	.18	.37
14. Figures						.71	.14	.09	.25
15. Cards							.19	.10	.29
16. Addition								.65	.53
17. Multiplication									.54
18. Three-higher									

Source: Data from Thurstone and Thurstone (1941, p. 90).

A method of factor analysis is then applied to this correlation matrix. The factor analysis shows how the tests in a battery fall along a few dimensions, where each dimension or factor is made up of a cluster of similar tests. Each factor is made as different as possible from another cluster or factor. The factor analysis yields a number of hypothetical factors or clusters. The correlation of a test with a factor, called its factor loading, tells us about the magnitude of the relationship between a test and the factor. Table C-2 shows the correlations of the nine tests with three factors that the factor-analysis technique identified through statistical manipulations. The factor measures whatever appears to be measured in common by the tests that have high loadings on it. Correlations, as you remember, can go from -1.00 to +1.00 and indicate no relationship when near .00. As shown in Table C-2, Tests 7, 8, and 9 have high correlations with the first factor. These are the Sentences, Vocabulary, and Sentence Completion tests. The nonverbal tests in the battery had low correlations, close to zero, with this factor. Hence, the factor was interpreted to be a "verbal comprehension" factor. Tests 16, 17, and 18, dealing with numbers, had high loadings on the second factor; low correlations on this factor were found for tests dealing with other kinds of material. Hence, that factor was called "number ability." A "spatial" factor also emerged from this battery of tests. By giving many tests of ability and factoring them, we can determine the different kinds of things that get measured. The important question is whether the things we actually measure when we attempt to measure intelligence are capable of being factored into subcategories, or really represent a more unitary kind of variable.

Table C-2
Excerpt from a Rotated Factor Matrix

	Verbal Compre- hension	Number Ability	Spatial Ability
7. Sentences	.66	.01	.08
8. Vocabulary	.66	.02	−.04
9. Completion	.67	.00	.15
13. Flags	−.01	.05	.68
14. Figures	−.02	−.06	.76
15. Cards	.03	−.03	.72
16. Addition	.01	.64	.05
17. Multiplication	−.03	.67	−.05
18. Three-higher	.06	.38	.20

Source: Data from Thurstone and Thurstone (1941, p. 91).

GENERAL-FACTOR AND GROUP-FACTOR MODELS

Research on the organization of intelligence dates from about 1905, when a British psychologist, Charles Spearman, applied mathematical reasoning to tables of intercorrelations among mental ability tests. He arrived at the theory that a general factor, which he called g, could account for the positive intercorrelations found among the many tests that were given. British psychologists have tended to support this conclusion. But American psychologists have often followed L. L. Thurstone, whose factor analyses during the 1930s and 1940s led him to infer various group factors.

To Thurstone, mental-ability tests seemed to have high loadings on some but not all the factors. He held that these group factors were relatively independent of one another. Some of the group factors proposed by Thurstone and Thurstone (1941) are shown in Table C-2, namely, verbal comprehension, number ability, and spatial ability. The other group factors proposed by the Thurstones are perceptual speed, word fluency, associative memory, and general reasoning ability. These factors were, to the Thurstones, the "primary mental abilities" that made up the complex variable we call intelligence.

Although L. L. Thurstone first concluded that no general factor of mental ability existed, his subsequent work revealed that his primary mental abilities were themselves positively correlated. Note that only positive correlations between the tests appear in Table C-1. This fact suggests that some comon general ability appears in all the test scores. Thus

Figure C-1
Nine tests used
in a factor analysis.

SENTENCES (7)

This test is a sentence-completion test.

An adult female of the human species is called
a/an _____.*

A heavenly body that revolves around the sun is
a/an _____.*

VOCABULARY (8)

This test is a synonyms test.

Huge: loud, heavy, enormous, filled, bright*

Brilliant: vast, brittle, shifty, honest, gleaming*

COMPLETION (9)

The following sentence has a word missing at the place indicated by the parentheses. You are to think of the word that best completes the meaning of the sentence. The number in parentheses is the number of letters in the missing word.

A (4) is a contest of speed . . . .
B=   F=   M=   P=   R━

The test contained sixty definitions.

FLAGS (13)

Here are two pictures of a flag. These two pictures of the flag are the same. You can slide one picture around to fit exactly on the other picture.

S is marked to show that the pictures are the *same*.

The next two pictures of the flag are different. You cannot slide the pictures around to make them fit exactly.

D is marked to show that the pictures are *different*.

The test contained forty-eight items.

FIGURES (14)

Some of the figures in the row are like the first figure. Some are made backward. The figures like the first figure are marked.

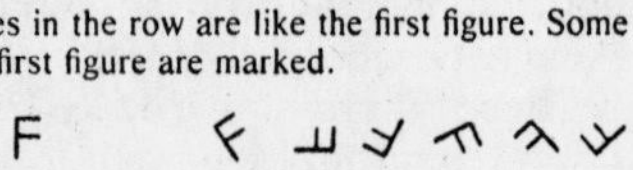

F   ⅃ ⅄ ⊼ ⋏ ⋎
━ = ━ = ━

The test proper contained sixty rows of seven figures.

*Items not from original battery.

CARDS (15)

Below is another row of cards. Mark all the cards which are like the first card in the row, when you slide them around on the page.

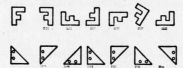

The test contained twenty rows of seven figures.

ADDITION (16)

Below are two columns of numbers which have been added. Add the numbers for yourself to see if the sums are correct.

16	42
38	61
45	83
99	176
R ▬	R =
W =	W ▬

The first sum is right, so the R below it is marked. The second sum is wrong, so the W is marked.

The test contained fifty-six columns of six two-place numbers.

MULTIPLICATION (17)

Below are two multiplication problems which have been worked out. Multiply the numbers for yourself to see if the products are correct.

64	39
7	4
448	166
R ▬	R =
W =	W ▬

The first answer is right, so the R below it is marked. The second answer is wrong, so the W is marked.

The test contained seventy problems.

THREE-HIGHER (18)

Here is another row of numbers. Mark every number that is exactly 3 more than the number just before it.

4 11 14 10 9 12 16 8 10 3 15 18 9
= = = = = = = = = = = = =

You should have marked 14, 12, and 18.

The test contained thirty rows of numbers.

Source: Thurstone, L. L., and Thurstone, Thelma G. Factorial studies of intelligence. *Psychometric Monographs*, 1941, No. 2. Reprinted with permission of the University of Chicago Press. © 1941 by The University of Chicago.

many factor analysts now agree on a general factor of intelligence -- one that underlies performance on all tests of mental ability. Beyond the general factor, most factor analysts also find some group factors. But the exact nature of the group factors varies from one investigator and his or her tests to the next. The debate goes on and can be expected to continue for some time. Meanwhile, using the best available evidence, theoreticians continue to put forth ideas about the nature of intelligence.

RECENT MODELS

Two recent attempts to describe the organization of intelligence are based on the accumulated findings of factor-analytic studies. These models go considerably beyond the research findings, but they illustrate current thinking.

Guilford's Structure-of-Intellect (SI) model is illustrated in Figure C-2. It has three basic dimensions: operations, referring to the kinds of mental activities or processes necessary in using information; products, referring to the form of the information being processed; and content, or the way in which the information is discriminable by the person (see Guilford, 1967). These dimensions will become clearer as we examine the subdivisions shown in the figure. That is, mental operations can take the form of evaluation (E) of some object or event, for example, judging the correctness, suitability, or adequacy of something; convergent production (N), dealing with operations that have correct or logical outcomes, as when factual information is processed; divergent production (D), dealing with creative or unique responses to stimuli; memory (M), processing of material in the form in which it was first encountered; or cognition (C), recognizing or comprehending an object or event. The operations dimension, then, is concerned with the kinds of mental processes a person engages in.

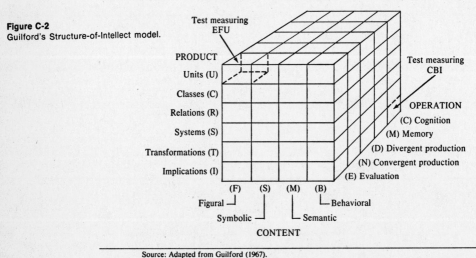

Figure C-2
Guilford's Structure-of-Intellect model.

Source: Adapted from Guilford (1967).

The processes need not be verbal, however. That is why the content dimension has to be specified. Content can be figural (F) (visual/spatial); symbolic (S) (letters, numbers, codes); semantic (M) (connotative responses to words and other things); or behavioral (B) (nonverbal information about people's needs, acts, attitudes, moods, etc.). In other words, the coding and processing of information, that is, the content, may be in the form of ☐☐☐☐☐ or $1 + 2 = 3$; in meanings associated with things like wonder, amazement, fear, stupefaction, and awe; or in an act such as tying a shoelace, drinking some milk, or perceiving a person's gloom. When the content being operated on takes the form of social interactive phenomena, such as perceiving the mood or intentions of another (B), we are dealing with "social intelligence," an area that is not well established in the psychological literature, but is commonly discussed by nonprofessionals.

The product of the operations with certain kinds of contents can be discrete events or units (U); classes (C) of things, as when grouping takes place; relations (R), as when units or classes of things are connected in some meaningful way; systems (S), structured aggregates of information; transformations (T), or changes of material from one form to another; and implications (I), which call for extrapolations and generalizations.

Thus we see that each factor in this model consists of a unique combination of operation, content, and product. For example, CSU is the factor standing for Cognition of Semantic Units. The test of such a factor would be a verbal comprehension test, such as finding the correct synonym for a word. DSU stands for the Divergent Production of Semantic Units. A test of word fluency, such as writing words that start with the letter R, would measure DSU. EFU, the Evaluation of Figural Units, would be measured by the kinds of tests shown in Figure C-3. CBI, the Cognition of Behavioral Implications, would

Figure C-3
Items in a short matching set of items for the factor of evaluation of figural units.

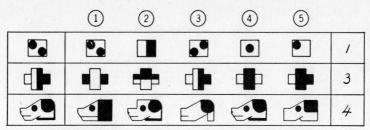

Which figure in each row is exactly the same as the one at the left? The answers are marked.

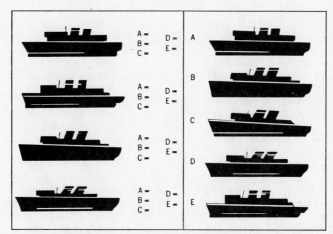

Identical pairs are to be matched exactly, where there are small but supraliminal differences among the objects.

Source: Guilford (1967, p. 187). From Part IV of the Guilford-Zimmerman Aptitude Survey, Courtesy of the Sheridan Psychological Services, Inc.

be measured by the kinds of tests shown in Figure C-4. The cells in Guildford's model of intellect in which these tests are located are identified in Figure C-2. With five types of operation, four types of content, and six types of product, it is possible to identify 120 (or 5 x 4 x 6) factors. Guilford (1967) has done so, describing possible or available tests for each one, and also the research evidence for that factor. Thus far, the structure-of-intellect model has served mainly to show in detail one kind of implication of the factor-analytic approach. Its main practical value until now has been to distinguish between divergent and convergent production operations as an approach to the study of creativity. In any case, the SI model shows fully the implications of regarding intelligence as a multifaceted ability rather than a single general factor.

Figure C-4
An item from
Cartoon Predictions.

Starting with the scene above, state which of the three alternative scenes below is most likely to come next, all visible cues being considered and human nature being what it is.

Source: Guilford (1967, p. 107). Courtesy of the Sheridan Psychological Services, Inc.

Critics have charged that the SI model excessively fractionates intelligence, lacks research support, and is of dubious practical value. Thus, Humphreys (1962, p. 475) was disturbed by "the proliferation of factors. . . . For example, Guilford now recognizes more factors than Thurstone had tests." McNemar (1964, p. 872) held that "the structure of intellect that requires 120 factors may very well lead the British, and some of the rest of us, to regard our fractionization and fragmentation of ability into more and more factors of less and less importance, as indicative of scatter-brainedness."

Vernon's hierarchical group-factor theory is shown in Figure C-5. Vernon (1965) incorporates in his model a general factor (g) and two major group factors: a verbal-educational factor (v:ed) and a spatial-practical-mechanical factor (k:m). The v:ed factor further includes minor creative, fluency, scholastic, and number subfactors. The k:m factor further includes perceptual, physical, spatial, and mechanical subfactors. Cross-links may appear. Thus, clerical ability may consist of verbal ability (v) and perceptual speed (p). Mathematical and scientific ability may depend on both number ability (n) and spatial ability (k).

Figure C-5
Diagram of the main general and group factors underlying tests relevant to educational and vocational
achievement.

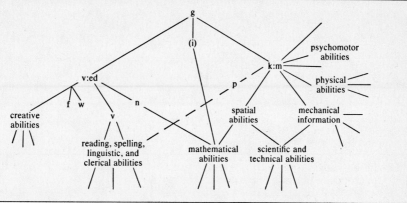

Source: Vernon, P. E. *Structure of Human Abilities*, 2d ed. (New York: Barnes & Noble, 1965), p. 725.

Most psychologists are currently inclined to accept some kind of hierarchical model of intelligence. The notion of a substantial general factor in intelligence, along with less substantial group factors, is widely accepted, because (1) mental-ability tests that differ greatly, such as tests representing verbal and mathematical factors, are nonetheless positively and substantially correlated (correlations between verbal and mathematical tests average about .45), and (2) practical uses of intelligence tests depend more on the general factor than on group or special ability factors.

REFERENCES

Guilford, J. P. (1967) The nature of intelligence. New York: McGraw-Hill.

Humphreys, L. G. (1962) The organization of human abilities. American Psychologist, 17:475-483.

McNemar, Quinn (1964) Lost: Our intelligence. Why? American Psychologist, 19:871-882.

Thurstone, L. L., and Thurstone, Thelma G. (1941) Factoral studies of intelligence. Psychometric Monographs, No. 2. Chicago: University of Chicago Press.

Vernon, P. E. (1965) Ability factors and environmental influences. American Psychologist, 20:723-733.

CHAPTER 6   HEREDITY, ENVIRONMENT, AND GROUP DIFFERENCES IN INTELLIGENCE

OBJECTIVES

The student should be able to:

o state the hereditarian and environmentalist positions with regard to influences on individual differences in intelligence test scores

o cite evidence regarding the differences in IQ between different social classes, and between those residing in rural and urban areas

o state three causes for group differences in IQ scores

o provide relevant data regarding the improvability of the IQ scores of children from different social classes and ethnic backgrounds

o compare and contrast the ways in which home variables affect children's intellectual achievement

o state both sides of the argument regarding the influence of black English on thinking and learning

o list outcomes from early education intervention programs

REMINDER

This chapter discussed how differences in intelligence are influenced by differences in heredity and environment. Individual differences in intelligence are largely determined by genetic makeup. However, the important questions are: What determines group (ethnic, cultural, geographic, social class) differences in intelligence, and are group averages in intelligence improvable? These questions about group differences are educationally important because group differences indicate the possibility of social inequality and injustice. Also, answers to these questions may provide a guide toward better accomplishment of equality of educational opportunity. You learned about environmental variables in the home and school that appear to affect children's intellectual achievement. Home environmental variables, such as parents' press for achievement and language development, along with parental provision of general learning opportunities, are more highly correlated with the intellectual performance of children than are social class and IQs of parents. This chapter examined school environmental variables, including the controversial language-training approach, and concluded with a summarization of the lasting effectiveness of early education intervention programs.

DEFINITIONS OF KEY CONCEPTS

The following key concepts were discussed in this chapter. In your own words, write the definition of each concept in the space provided.

1. Selective placement _____

_____

_____

2. Longitudinal studies _____

_____

_____

3. Social class _____

_____

_____

4. "The poverty circle" _____

_____

_____

5. Selective migration _____

_____

_____

6. Environmental influences _____

_____

_____

7. Test bias _____

_____

_____

8. Culturally fair intelligence tests _____

_____

_____

9. Early intervention _____

_____

_____

10. Cultural deprivation _____

_____

_____

11. The linguistic-deficit approach _____

_____

_____

12. Mediated learning _____

_____

_____

APPLICATION OF KEY CONCEPTS

The terms listed below refer to important concepts that were discussed in this chapter. Carefully read each descriptive statement, and identify the concept or concepts each statement implies. Place the corresponding letter(s) of the concept(s) you select in the space provided.

Concepts

A. linguistic-deficit approach   F. cultural deprivation
B. test bias   G. culture-fair intelligence test
C. selective migration   H. longitudinal study
D. early intervention   I. "the poverty circle"
E. selective placement   J. mediated learning

Descriptive Statements

_____ 1. Husén, a Swedish psychologist, obtained an r of .72 between the intelligence test scores of over 600 males who were measured in the third grade and again when they were inducted into the military.

_____ 2. "That was a really dumb test -- I didn't even know what the lady was talking about when she was telling me what to do."

_____ 3. In this preschool, the emphasis is placed on speech drills to teach the children a more standard form of English, because the director feels that only if children speak standard English will they be able to perform to their fullest cognitive capacity.

_____ 4. Jane has received a scholarship to attend the university, which is located at the state's capital city, more than 300 miles from her small hometown.

_____ 5. "Now, I want you to look at the pictures (common objects found in every household) in this row and put an X on the one that doesn't go with the others."

_____ 6. Marsha's biological father owned a realty company franchise in New England; her adoptive parents, who also live in New England, earn a moderate income as elementary school teachers.

_____ 7. Jeff's father left him and his mother when Jeff was an infant. His mother went to school only up to the seventh grade, and has had a very difficult time financially. She is rarely at home. At 15, Jeff is anxious to drop out of school and find any kind of job.

_____ 8. The goals of this preschool program are to provide children with resources -- I mean teachers, aides, and parents, in addition to books, games, and other materials -- so that when they are ready for elementary school they'll have a better chance to do well.

_____ 9. "That's not quite the correct answer to this test question. Let's look at it together and identify the steps needed to solve the problem. Why don't you describe the first step. . . . "

MULTIPLE-CHOICE SELF-TEST

Select the response that best answers the question or completes the statement. Place the letter of the chosen answer in the space provided.

_____ 1. Hereditarians tend to account for differences in IQ of various regional groups, such as northern and southern or rural and urban groups, in terms of the process of
A. selective heredity.
B. cultural transmission.
C. cultural migration.
D. hereditary transmission.
E. selective migration.

_____ 2. Which of the following is not one of the indices frequently used as a measure of social class?
A. Father's occupation
B. Family income
C. Place of residence
D. Citizenship in the United States
E. Parents' educational level

_____ 3. Which group of children could you expect to score the highest on an IQ test?
A. Urban, middle-class children
B. Rural, middle-class children
C. Urban, lower-class children
D. Rural, lower-class children

_____ 4. Which of the following is least often considered to explain the IQ differences between social classes, occupational groups, and urban and rural communities?
A. Teacher expectations
B. Test bias
C. Selective migration
D. Environmental influence

_____ 5. To determine the correlates of researchers' interpretations of their findings, Sherwood and Nataupsky surveyed 83 investigators of racial differences in IQ. They found that the more hereditarian interpretations of these racial differences tended to be made by those who
A. were born later in their families rather than first.
B. had grandparents born in the United States.
C. had lower grades in college.
D. grew up in urban communities.

_____ 6. A group of 100 tenth-grade children have their IQs measured by the same test on two different occasions, about a week apart. The correlation between their IQs on the first occasion and their IQs on the second occasion will be about the same as that between the IQs of
A. identical twins reared apart.
B. identical twins reared together.
C. fraternal twins reared apart.
D. fraternal twins reared together.

_____ 7. In general, within each of the various degrees of relationships between persons (unrelated, siblings, fraternal twins, identical twins), being reared apart rather than together tends to have what kind of effect on the correlation between IQs?
A. It raises the correlation.
B. It has no effect on the correlation.
C. It lowers the correlation.
D. It raises the correlation for some relationships between persons and lowers it for others.

_____ 8. In studies of correlations between the IQs of children and the educational levels of their real and foster parents, it has been found that the IQs of the children correlate
A. more highly with the educational levels of their foster parents than with those of their real parents.
B. more highly with the educational levels of their real parents than with those of their foster parents.
C. about the same with the educational levels of their foster parents as with those of their real parents.

_____ 9. Newman, Freeman, and Holzinger reported the correlation between educational differences in environment and differences in school attainment of identical twins reared apart. They obtained a correlation of about
A. .90.
B. .60.
C. .40.
D. .20.
E. .00.

_____ 10. The implications of the findings of the study cited above are that

A. differences in educational advantage produce IQ differences.
B. differences in educational advantage do not produce IQ differences.
C. the study was flawed because the correlation was not 1.00.
D. the differences in the environments of most identical twins reared apart were very great.

_____11. Consider the correlation between educational advantage and IQ difference of identical twins reared apart. It indicates convincingly that differences in educational advantage are nonexistent when genetic differences
A. are related substantially to differences in IQ and school attainment.
B. are related only slightly to differences in IQ and school attainment.
C. do not correlate with differences in IQ and school attainment.

_____12. It is possible to list types of person-pairings in rank order from least different to most different in heredity and environment. Which of the following pairs would be the most different?
A. Fraternal twins of different sex raised together
B. Ordinary siblings raised together
C. Unrelated persons raised together
D. Ordinary siblings raised apart

_____13. Whether individual differences between students are caused primarily by differences in hereditary or environmental factors should
A. not be an issue for the teacher.
B. be a major issue for each teacher.
C. be the first consideration of every teacher.
D. be a concern of school administration

_____14. Research indicates that, within the limits of environmental variation that occurred in northern Europe and the United States in various studies of kinship correlations, genetic differences determine about 75 to 80 percent and environmental differences about 20 to 25 percent of the individual differences in intelligence. We can conclude that
A. race differences in intelligence are largely genetically caused.
B. social class differences in intelligence are largely genetically caused.
C. 75 to 80 percent of the time it would be accurate to account for race differences in intelligence as genetically caused.
D. there is no clear evidence that race differences in intelligence are genetically caused.

_____15. Research examining the effects of adoption on IQ score indicates that
A. children's IQs are stable and will not change.
B. only white, adopted children's IQs will change if they are placed in a white, middle-class environment.
C. the home environment can affect IQ.
D. all adopted children showed above-average achievement when tested five years after adoption.

_____16. It is likely that most psychologists believe that low-income and minority-group members have lower IQ scores because they
A. have not had the kinds of childhood experiences needed to enhance one's performance on an IQ test.
B. have inherited inadequate value systems from their parents.

C. lack industry and achievement motive.

D. have poorly developed brain structures as a result of inadequate diet.

_____17. In a study investigating linguistic communication between mothers and their children, Hess and Shipman found that the children's ability to learn was most affected by their mother's

A. teaching behaviors.

B. display of love and affection.

C. academic achievement.

D. mean length of sentences used in speaking to their children.

_____18. According to Bereiter and Engelmann, programs designed to improve the academic success of children from low-income homes ought to concentrate on

A. enrichment programs.

B. creative skills.

C. social skills.

D. language development and usage.

_____19. Linguists, such as Labov and Ogbu, disagree with the linguistic-deficit approach. They suggest that black English

A. is only an interference to learning in standard English.

B. is complex enough for sophisticated communication, but not for learning to read.

C. is different from standard English, but not inadequate for communication on learning.

D. interferes only with reading in standard English.

_____20. The linguistic-deficit approach of Bereiter and Engelmann suggests that the achievement of poorer and ethnic minority children is lower than that of middle-class white children because

A. "disadvantaged" children require general environmental enrichment.

B. the language used by "disadvantaged" children is inadequate in its complexity for fostering communication and learning.

C. the language used by "disadvantaged" children is cognitively adequate, but superficially inferior for use in school settings.

D. the language of "disadvantaged" children sounds inferior, thereby resulting in a self-fulfilling prophecy.

_____21. An approach for improving intelligence during adolescence has been developed by Feurstein. He views cognitive growth as the result of incidental learning from exposure to the environment and

A. passive testing of intelligence.

B. mediated learning in the form of exercises in perceptual and cognitive skills.

C. practice in modeling parents' attitudes and perceptions.

D. physiological maturation that enables learners to control and regulate their thinking processes.

_____22. A comprehensive follow-up study examining the lasting effectiveness of early education programs indicates that in comparison with control children, the program children excelled on

A. math tests.

B. reading tests.

C. IQ tests.

D. math and reading tests.

E. math, reading, and IQ tests.

_____ 23. What is the best conclusion to reach regarding the overall effectiveness of early intervention programs for lower-class black children?
   A. Parents were satisfied with results, but actual competence did not improve.
   B. Maternal satisfaction with the child's school performance increased, as did actual student achievement.
   C. School achievement increased in the early grades following intervention, but "washed out" in the later grades.
   D. Since the children's attitudes regarding achievement did not change substantially, increased school performance was superficial.

PROJECTS AND ACTIVITIES

1. Go to your college counseling center or testing office and tell the counselors that you are a student in educational psychology. Ask to see examples of items from an individual intelligence test, a group intelligence test, a culture-fair intelligence test, and a standardized achievement test -- all for the same age level. Go through the tests, noting how they differ and how they are the same. Think of how you would respond to the items if you were a member of a minority, foreign-born, or bilingual group. Also look for instances of sex bias in the items. Do you think all the tests are measuring the same thing?

2. Take some common test-item formats that you have come across in IQ tests (for example, "A is to B as X is to _____), and develop some items of your own -- items that would be suitable for administering to a group of students to whom you have access, or a group of your peers. Create the items so that they are of three levels of difficulty, that is, very easy, moderately difficult, and very difficult, for the group to whom you plan to administer your test. Also include items that are obviously biased against minority and female students. After you've given your test to the students or your friends, ask them what they thought about the test. How did they feel when handling easy or hard material? How did they react to the biased items?

3. If you have an opportunity to observe children in school and also on the playground, try the following. Pick three students who, from your observations of their classroom behavior, you think are the least able students in the class. Then carefully observe them on the playground with their friends. Compare their ability to communicate in the two settings. Would your ratings of these students have been different if you had first observed them on the playground? Compare your observations in these two settings and think how often school judgments of IQ do not address the issue of social or functional intelligence.

4. Prepare a short questionnaire for students that will give you information about the kinds of pressure to achieve they are under at home. Ask such questions as, What do your parents or guardians want you to be? How often do your parents or guardians question you about your schoolwork? Do you talk about school at the dinner table? etc. After obtaining permission from the appropriate persons, such as teachers, principals, and parents, administer the questionnaire. Observe how the students vary in their report of the academic influences present in their homes. If you know the students well, predict their answers. And, if the classroom teacher has time, check the students' responses with the teacher's opinions to see what information or lack of information he or she possesses.

SUGGESTIONS FOR TERM PAPERS

1. The history of culture-fair testing

2. Intelligence measurement throughout the world

3. Test bias in supposedly culture-fair tests

4. The relative persuasiveness of the hereditarian and environmentalist positions

5. A teacher's guide to interpreting individual students' IQ scores

6. Social Darwinism: The schools and achievement

7. Nonstandard English: Linguistically different or linguistically deficient?

8. The case for early childhood learning

9. The research basis for day care centers

10. The verdict on early intervention programs for education of the disadvantaged

TECHNICAL NOTE D

HEREDITY AND ENVIRONMENT AS DETERMINANTS OF INTELLIGENCE

One of the burning issues in educational psychology is the controversy over whether heredity or environment is the dominant force in the determination of intelligence. The text presented some aspects of this issue. Now we look more carefully at the data and methodology used as the basis for discussions of the nature-nurture controversy.

THE CONTINUING CONTROVERSY ABOUT THE DATA AND METHODS

The nature-nurture controversy lay relatively dormant in the several decades before 1969. It had been the subject of a major yearbook (Stoddard, 1940), and writings had continued to appear on both sides (for example, Burt, 1958; Hunt, 1961). But the controversy flared anew with the appearance of a major review of the evidence by Jensen (1969a; 1969b; 1972, pp. 69-203). Of the many replies, rebuttals, and counterrebuttals that have appeared since then, only some of the more salient can be considered here. You should know enough about their content and flavor to have a basis for your own convictions or doubts about the many issues and subissues that have arisen around the major controversy. We shall not deal here with the question of the determiners of racial and other group differences; this question is considered in Chapter 6. Thus, we deal here only with the questions raised about the general conclusion that approximately 80 percent of the variance in the IQs of individual northern European and American whites is attributable to differences in genetic factors and, therefore, that attainment in schools, jobs, and life as a whole may be to a similar degree determined by genetic factors.

THE IMPORTANCE OF IQ

First, questions are raised about the social and economic importance of IQ. McClelland (1973) has questioned the causal nature of the correlations between IQ and occupational success, where such correlations exist, and the degree to which such correlations exist at all. Similarly, Jencks and his colleagues (1972) have questioned the importance of scholastic attainment, as indicated by school grades and scores on educational achievement tests, in determining economic and social status in American society. Granted, some people end up richer than others, but not necessarily because they have more adequate cognitive skills. Although it is true that children who read well, get the right answers to arithmetic problems, and articulate their thoughts clearly are more likely than others to get ahead, there are many other equally important factors involved. Almost as much economic inequality exists among those who score high on standardized tests as exists in the general population. Equalizing everyone's reading scores would not appreciably reduce the number of economic "failures" (Jencks et al., 1972, p. 8).

In short, IQ does predict school success, but school success does not greatly determine occupational or economic attainment. So the importance of IQ to such attainment is questionable.

THE DATA ON IDENTICAL TWINS RAISED APART

Second, questions are raised about the data on identical twins reared apart. As we saw in Chapter 6, the correlations between the IQs of such twins are central to the estimation of IQ heritability. Since the correlation coefficients in the four existing studies of such twins have ranged from .62 to .86 (Jensen, 1969a, 1972), the estimates of IQ heritability have run similarly high.

Yet the largest of these four studies, the one by Burt (1966), which dealt with 53 sets of twins, has been found to have serious shortcomings (Kamin, 1974). The correlations for various categories of kinship mysteriously stayed the same, although the number of pairs of twins increased by 20 over an 11-year period. The names and definitions of environmental variables, such as "economic conditions" and "cultural conditions," changed over the years in reference to the same data. The techniques Burt used in measuring intelligence were described in later reports by referring to earlier ones, which, when examined, turned out (in Kamin's view) to be ambiguous, referring to "personal interviews" and unspecified "camou-flaged tests." Furthermore, Burt seems to have used tests that were inadequately standardized for age and sex. Because of inadequate standardization, IQs can vary as a function of the age or sex of the persons tested. This means that the correlation between the twins' IQs will rise with the numbers of twin pairs of different sexes and ages. In short, as Jensen (1974) indicated, after reviewing all of Burt's data, they are characterized by "the reporting of kinship correlations at times with and at times without noting the sample size, the rather inconsistent reporting of sample sizes, the probably higher than ordinary rate of misprints in Burt's published tables (several of them acknowledged by himself), and the quite casual description of the tests and the exact procedures and methods of data analysis. . . . " Further analysis of Burt's articles reveals the possibility that the data may have actually been faked (Wade, 1976; Dorfman, 1978).

When identical twins are reared apart, the apartness should refer to psychological and educational differences in environments, not merely to physical apartness in different homes. Yet it appears that many of these pairs of twins were raised in the same villages, neighborhoods, streets, and schools, and, in some cases, in related branches of the same family, living next door to one another. Presumably, the apartness was therefore not very great in some instances. As Bloom (1964) showed for the 19 separated identical twins in the study by Newman, Freeman, and Holzinger (1937), the correlation between the IQs of the 11 pairs raised in the most similar environments was .91, whereas that for the 8 pairs raised in the least similar environments was only .24. Hence this extremely important coefficient turns out to depend for its value on the similarity of the environments of the two persons in each twin pair. And many such persons grew up, as we have seen, in apparently highly similar environments. Therefore, the average coefficient of about .80 between the IQs of identical twins reared apart cannot be regarded as reflecting only genetic factors. Environmental similarities must also be given credit in some substantial degree for the magnitude of that correlation.

The test data are also weakened by the fact that the identical twins were often tested by the same examiner, whose expectations may have unconsciously made the twins' IQs more similar. In one study (Shields, 1962), according to Kamin, the 35 pairs of identical twins tested by the same examiner differed in raw score by 8.5 points, whereas the 5 pairs tested by two different psychologists differed by 22.4 points (equivalent to an IQ difference of 17 points).

Kamin's conclusion thus disputes Jensen's estimate that the heritability of IQ equals .82. Rather, Kamin (1974, p. 67) states that "to the degree that the case for a genetic influence on IQ scores rests on the celebrated studies of separated twins, we can justifiably conclude that there is no reason to reject the hypothesis that IQ is simply not heritable."

However, a recent examination of Kamin's criticisms finds them, in turn, not altogether justified. Sifting the data with apparently equal or even greater care, Loehlin, Lindzey, and Spuhler (1975) have found Kamin's critique to suffer from logical and statistical difficulties. The thorough reader must now study carefully this latest review of the issue. Its conclusion, among others, is that "the data do place some real constraints on the plausible values of this [heritability] index, and that for at least the last 30 years these values have not included either zero or one" (Loehlin, Lindzey, & Spuhler, 1975, p. 299).

THE DATA ON FOSTER CHILDREN

As the text noted, the hereditarian position also seems to be supported by the higher correlations between the IQs and educational levels of natural parents and those of their own separated children than between the educational levels of foster parents and the IQs of their adopted children (Skodak & Skeels, 1949). Yet, here again there are reasons to question the findings. The foster mothers were much more homogeneous in educational level than were the natural mothers. (More than half of the foster mothers had attended college, whereas less than 10 percent of the natural mothers had done so.) Hence, it was more difficult for the foster mother's educational level to correlate with the foster child's IQ, because high homogeneity in any variable lowers its correlation with other variables.

But how can the environmentalist explain the correlation of .32 between the educational level of the natural mothers and the IQs of their own children whom they had not raised? Here the phenomenon of selective placement enters in. As shown in Table D-1, the children of better educated natural mothers were placed with foster parents of higher educational level. Similarly, the 12 "college" foster families, in which both foster parents had gone to college, received foster children whose true mothers had a higher educational level, as compared with the 22 sets of "grade school" foster parents, in which neither parent had completed high school.

Table D-1
Selective Placement in the Skeels-Skodak
Sets of Real and Foster Parents

For 8 natural mothers who had completed more than 12 grades of school, the foster mother's educational level averaged	13.9 years
For 12 natural mothers who had completed less than 8 grades of school, the foster mother's educational level averaged	11.8 years
For 12 college-level foster homes, the real mother's educational level averaged	11.3 years
For 22 grade-school level foster homes, the real mother's educational level averaged	9.1 years

Source: Adapted from Kamin (1974).

But the foster parents' educational level is merely a symptom of selective placement. In Kamin's view, the education of the foster parents correlated only moderately with the "goodness" of the foster home in the highly agricultural state of Iowa in the 1930s. Skodak and Skeels indicated in their report that many of the foster homes with the greatest cultural and environmental amenities belonged to successful farmers who had relatively little formal education (Kamin, 1974, p. 129). Hence, it is reasonable to find no correlation between the educational level of the foster parents and the IQs of their foster children.

Here again, however, the point has been argued by Loehlin, Lindzey, and Spuhler (1975, pp. 297-298). They pointed out that selective placement will explain the correlation of IQs of biological parents and their children only if the adoptive mother's educational level does affect the child's IQ -- an effect that Kamin had earlier denied. Thus they again conclude that "Kamin's interpretation seems much less plausible than a view that allows a place for substantial genetic factors . . . " (p. 298).

IN CONCLUSION

So goes the debate between the hereditarians and the environmentalists. What looks like conclusive data to one camp becomes extremely questionable data when viewed by the other. The debate, now many decades old, shows no signs of abating. The teacher and the educational policy maker may expect to witness further debate in the decades ahead.

REFERENCES

Burt, C. L. (1958) The inheritance of mental ability. American Psychologist, 13:1-15.

Burt, C. L. (1966) The genetic determination of differences in intelligence: A study of monozygotic twins reared together and apart. British Journal of Psychology, 57:137-153.

Bloom, B. S. (1964) Stability and change in human characteristics. New York: Wiley.

Dorfman, D. D. (1978) The Cyril Burt question: New findings, Science, 201, No. 4362.

Hunt, J. McV. (1961) Intelligence and experience. New York: Ronald Press.

Jencks, Christopher, et al. (1972) Inequality: A reassessment of family and schooling in America. New York: Basic Books.

Jensen, A. R. (1969a) How much can we boost IQ and scholastic achievement? Harvard Educational Review, 39(1): 1-123.

Jensen, A. R. (1969b) Reducing the heredity-environment uncertainty: A reply. Harvard Educational Review, 39:449-483.

Jensen, A. R. (1972) Genetics and education. New York: Harper and Row.

Jensen, A. R. (1974) Kinship correlations reported by Sir Cyril Burt, Behavior Genetics, 4:1-28.

Kamin, L. J. (1974) The science and politics of IQ. New York: Halsted Press.

Loehlin, J. C., Lindzey, Gardner, and Spuhler, J. N. (1975) Race differences in intelligence. San Francisco: W. H. Freeman.

McClelland, D. C. (1973) Testing for competence rather than for "intelligence." American Psychologist, 28:1-14.

Newman, H. H., Freeman, F. N., and Holzinger, K. J. (1937) Twins: A study of heredity and environment. Chicago: University of Chicago Press.

Shields, James (1962) Monozygotic twins brought up apart and brought up together. New York: Oxford University Press.

Skodak, Marie, and Skeels, H. M. (1949) A final follow-up study of one hundred adopted children. Journal of Genetic Psychology, 75:85-125.

Stoddard, G. D. (Chm.) (1940) Intelligence: Its nature and nurture. Part I. Comparative and critical exposition. Part II. Original studies and experiments. Yearbook of the National Society for the Study of Education, 39, Parts I and II. Chicago: University of Chicago Press.

Wade, N. (1976) IQ and heredity. Suspicion of fraud beclouds classic experiment. Science, 194, No. 4268.

CHAPTER 7 THE DEVELOPMENT OF COGNITIVE FUNCTIONS AND LANGUAGE

OBJECTIVES

The student should be able to

o list the stages of development in Piaget's theory

o describe and illustrate the cognitive capabilities of learners at each stage of development noted by Piaget

o describe two different conservation experiments and their results

o define assimilation and accommodation

o list characteristics of learners in the enactive, iconic, and symbolic stages of development described by Bruner

o state the rationalist view of language acquisition

o compare and contrast linguistic competence and linguistic performance

o increase students' metalinguistic awareness

o state how learners' sociolinguistic competence affects classroom behavior

REMINDER

In this chapter you learned how cognitive functioning at one age differs from that at another age. The major concepts used by Jean Piaget in his descriptions of the processes and stages of mental development were introduced. You'll recall Piaget's categorization of cognitive development into four stages: sensorimotor, preoperational, concrete operational, and formal operational. The chapter also explained Jerome Bruner's theory of cognitive growth, which categorizes mental development into three stages: enactive, iconic, and symbolic. The implications for teaching of these two views of cognitive development were discussed. You also read a description of language development and how this knowledge is important for teaching. A discussion of issues related to nonstandard English, bilingualism, metalinguistic awareness, and sociolinguistic competence concluded the chapter.

DEFINITIONS OF KEY CONCEPTS

The following key concepts were discussed in this chapter. In your own words, write the definition of each concept in the space provided.

1. Sensorimotor stage _____

_____

_____

2. Object permanence _____

_____

_____

3. Preoperational phase _____

_____

_____

4. Intuitive phase _____

_____

_____

5. Conservation _____

_____

_____

6. Concrete operational stage _____

_____

_____

7. Composition _____

_____

_____

8. Associativity _____

_____

_____

9. Reversibility _____

_____

_____

10. Former operational stage _____

_____

_____

11. Hypothetico-deductive thinking _____

_____

_____

12. Propositional thinking _____

_____

_____

13. Assimilation _____

_____

_____

14. Accommodation _____

_____

_____

15. Cognitive schema _____

_____

_____

16. Disequilibrium _____

_____

_____

17. Enactive stage _____

_____

_____

18. Iconic stage _____

_____

_____

19. Symbolic stage _____

_____

_____

20. Intellectual empathy _____

_____

_____

21. Inductive approach _____

_____

_____

22. A language acquisition device _____

_____

_____

23. A rationalist view of language acquisition _____

_____

_____

24. Holophrastic speech _____

_____

_____

25. Linguistic competence _____

_____

_____

26. Linguistic performance _____

_____

_____

27. Inflections _____

_____

_____

28. Metalinguistic awareness _____

_____

_____

29. Sociolinguistic competence _____

_____

_____

APPLICATION OF KEY CONCEPTS

The terms listed below refer to important concepts that were discussed in this chapter. Carefully read each descriptive statement, and identify the concept or concepts each statement implies. Place the corresponding letter(s) of the concept(s) you select in the space provided.

Concepts

A. associativity
B. sensorimotor stage
C. conservation
D. assimilation
E. iconic stage
F. metalinguistic awareness
G. inductive approach
H. preoperational stage
I. symbolic stage
J. linguistic performance
K. rationalist view
L. enactive stage

M. hypothetico-deductive thinking
N. concrete operational stage
O. inflection
P. linguistic competence
Q. propositional thinking
R. composition
S. formal operational stage
T. accommodation
U. intellectual empathy
V. holophrastic speech
W. sociolinguistic competence
X. object permanence

Descriptive Statements

_____ 1. To the very young child, the ball is something to hold in his hands.

_____ 2. I presented this problem to Rhonda: If Sueann is shorter tan Rose, and Sueann is taller than Roberta, who is the tallest? She thought for a moment and said, "Rose."

_____ 3. I asked Teddy which one of three dolls -- a Barbie doll, a Raggedy Ann doll, and a cowboy doll--didn't belong with the other two. He pointed to the cowboy doll.

_____ 4. My fourth graders are learning that you add "-ed" to most verbs to show that the action happened in the past.

_____ 5. T:Here's a dab of red paint and a dab of blue paint. Now, if I mixed these two paints together, do you think I would get this purple color, this pink color, or this turquoise color?
S:You would get the purple color.

_____ 6. Tom was quite upset when I gave him his milk in a regular glass instead of his own glass (which is narrower). He kept saying that it was not enough. I guess he thought that because the milk came only halfway up the regular glass and not all the way to the top as it does in his own glass, he wasn't getting as much as usual.

_____ 7. When my little brother says "more" and then looks at the refrigerator, I know he's really trying to communicate "I want some more milk."

_____ 8. This recipe calls for one and one-half cups of flour, but our measuring cup holds only one cup. That's right, it doesn't make any difference whether we put in the half cup first and then a whole cup or a whole cup first and then the half cup.

_____ 9. When I put the ruler in the glass of water, with one half in the water and the other half sticking out of the water, it appeared as if the ruler were bent in the middle. Some of the children were amazed and wondered how I had made the ruler bend!

_____10. I demonstrated the "ruler in a glass of water" phenomenon. Some of the children said they knew the ruler coudn't bend by itself, so why did it look like it had?

_____11. Even though I can't recite the grammatical rule for how to form the nonidentity pronominal referent, I must really know it since I can correctly use sentences that contain that form. I read that that's because people can figure out all the rules of the language they are exposed to without even knowing it.

_____12. In item 11 above, the statement, "Even though I can't recite the grammatical rule for how to form the nonidentity pronominal referent" is an example of this concept.

_____13. In item 11 above, the statement, "I must really know it since I can correctly use sentences that contain that form" is an example of this concept.

_____14. Whenever one of the preschoolers makes a mistake that I think is really obvious, I make a point of asking all about it so that I can better understand what things look like to a preschooler.

_____15. Instead of explaining and demonstrating to the third graders how light passing through a prism is broken into colors, I'm giving them a few cues, all the equipment they need, and a chance to discover it for themselves.

_____16. Annie will now look for the car keys when I hide them under the blanket. Last month when we played that "game" she would start playing with something else as if the keys had just disappeared!

_____17. Raymond is having difficulties in my class. When I ask him a question, he timidly looks down. I get the feeling that he doesn't know he's supposed to answer when I ask a question.

_____18. Alex said we know that the earth rotates as it revolves around the sun because it's light for part of the day and dark for part of the day, and on the other side of the earth it's just the opposite at the same time.

_____19. Today Pete went all around the house pointing to everything that was red and saying "red."

_____20. In our journalism unit, the teacher talked about how the use of alliteration often makes a headline more effective. That's when you begin all the words in a phrase with the same sound. It's fun!

_____21. I was amazed that Nancy could describe every detail of the living room in her grandmother's house; she hasn't been there in over a year.

_____22. Did you see how fast Sam crawled across the living room? He couldn't do that last week.

_____23. I was studying when it hit me that zero is simply a set with nothing in it.

MULTIPLE-CHOICE SELF-TEST

Select the response that best answers the question or completes the statement. Place the letter of the chosen answer in the space provided.

_____1. Which of the following is most justifiably considered an implication of Piaget's work?
A. The educator can predict a child's thought processes by examining his or her own.
B. The use of words and symbols promotes the most effective form of learning in the early years.
C. Children learn especially well from working with concrete objects, material, and phenomena.
D. Learning can be speeded up by introducing new concepts to a child before he or she would normally acquire them on his or her own.

_____2. The concept of accommodation is best described as
A. changing the cognitive structure to fit what is perceived.
B. changing what is perceivd to fit the cognitive structure.
C. an intellectual ability used to gain equilibrium.
D. the process involved in determining logical relations.

_____3. The concept of assimilation is best described as
A. an intellectual ability used to gain equilibrium.
B. changing what is perceived to fit the cognitive structure.
C. changing the cognitive structure to fit what is perceived.
D. the process involved in determining abstract relations.

_____4. Piaget's work does not imply which of the following for teachers?
A. New experience interacts with cognitive structure to arouse interest and develop understanding.
B. Through special teaching, a child can move quickly through the developmental sequence.

C. Children are not merely young adults in their thought processes.
D. Children learn well from working with concrete objects.

Classify the skills described in the following six items (Items 5-10) according to one of Piaget's four main stages of intellectual development. Choose the stage that the skill best characterizes and answer with the appropriate letter.
A. Sensorimotor stage (0-2 years)
B. Preoperational stage
   preoperational (2-4 years)
   intuitive (4-7 years)
C. Concrete operational stage (7-11 years)
D. Formal operational stage (11-15 years)

_____ 5. Tracy understands that oranges and other types of fruit are not exactly alike, but that they can all be grouped together and labeled "fruit." She also understands that she can subtract all nonoranges from the group that she has labeled "fruit" and obtain oranges.

_____ 6. John didn't recognize his little sister after their mother had dressed her in a lacy bonnet and dress for the first time.

_____ 7. Dana can work out logical possibilities when trying to solve a problem without needing to determine which ones actually occur in the real world.

_____ 8. Michelle is sure that the actual number of blocks changes depending on whether they are stacked one on top of the other or are lined up in a row.

_____ 9. Tony no longer looked for the squirrel after it became hidden from sight on the other side of the tree.

_____ 10. Brad can tell you that if you add two to three you get five. He also understands that if he reverses the order of the addends, that is, adds three to two, he still gets five.

_____ 11. According to Piaget, a teacher will gather more information about the cognitive level of a student by examining the student's
A. correct test responses.
B. incorrect test responses.
C. performance on a conservation task.
D. performance on a classification task.

_____ 12. One of the several teaching implications of Piaget's theory of cognitive development suggests that sequencing of instruction should have "proximal experience precede distal experience." Which of the following is an example of this principle?
A. Students should first learn about the properties of minerals in general, and then learn about a few minerals that are found in their geographical area.
B. Students should first learn about a few minerals that are found in their geographical area, and then learn about the properties of minerals in general.
C. Teachers should ask students who are proximal about their preference for the order of material to be presented in a given unit of instruction.
D. The most abstract information should be presented first, followed by first-hand experience.

_____13. Which of the following theoretical positions does not suggest that people possess common preconceptions about the formal nature of language, which then allow them to implicitly determine the rules of their speech community?
A. Rationalist
B. Nativist
C. Innate
D. Operant

_____14. Mr. Ware has a student in his class who consistently drops the g sound from words ending in -ing. For example, the student says readin', swimmin', and writin'. Based solely on this speech form, Mr. Ware should assume that the cognitive level of this student
A. is higher than that of standard English speakers.
B. is lower than that of standard English speakers.
C. cannot be estimated given only the above information.

_____15. Which of the following linguistic variables is affected by one's environment and, therefore, is of particular interest to teachers?
A. Linguistic competence
B. Linguistic performance
C. Language acquisition device
D. Language acquisition system

_____16. The child's grammatical knowledge is most influenced by
A. direct training procedures.
B. use of reinforcement and punishment.
C. exposure to speech of one's language.
D. modeling and feedback.

_____17. Proponents of cognitive psychology suggest that production of logical thought depends largely on
A. mental structures formulated through experience.
B. genetic components that are innate.
C. the information processing demands of the task.
D. systematic learning of problem-solving procedures.

_____18. Since Nick is a bilingual student, you would expect that
A. his competence in both languages will be poorer than if he were monolingual.
B. his IQ score will be lower than average.
C. his attitude toward members of both cultures will be more positive than if he were monolingual.
D. his linguistic competence will necessarily reflect his intellectual competence.

_____19. What can teachers accurately assume about their students' sociolinguistic competence?
A. Every child has the necessary competence.
B. Some children have the necessary competence and some do not.
C. All students lack the necessary competence when they begin school.

PROJECTS AND ACTIVITIES

1. Following the descriptions and diagrams in Figure 7-2 of the text (p.137), perform a few of the conservation experiments you've read about, using either clay or beakers of

water. Choose children of various ages, ranging from about five through eight. As the children make errors in answering your questions, ask them to talk out loud about what they're doing, and ask them why they've made those choices. Notice the differences in responses between the children of various ages.

2. Question two children about their dreams. One child should be under five years of age and the other over nine years of age. Get them to talk about the things that they remember being in their most recent dreams. Probe them for descriptions of the events. Is the younger child's world more visual than verbal or symbolic? How do the descriptions of the two children differ?

3. Observe the language used by a standard English speaker in both an academic and a social setting. Then observe the language used by a nonstandard English speaker of about the same age in both kinds of settings. What are the obvious differences? Think of these differences as reflecting different surface structures. What are the similarities between the language of the two students? Are both students able to express a variety of grammatical concepts, such as negation, question-asking, pluralization, pronoun substitution, and imperatives? How are these linguistic similarities related to cognitive development and cognitive ability? Of what importance is the setting, that is, academic or social, in contributing to the student's selection of a particular surface structure?

4. Interview parents of bilingual students. You might want to gather some descriptive information regarding specifics, language development, for example, did the child learn both languages simultaneously, or was exposure to one language earlier and/or more pervasive? Be sure you also ask parents about their views on language education in public schools. For example, do these parents want their child to be in a bilingual academic program? Do they want the cultural orientation of both languages explicitly taught in school? Compare the responses of parents of bilingual students with the responses of parents of monolingual students. Are there any patterns that emerge? Why or why not?

SUGGESTIONS FOR TERM PAPERS

1. The Montessori method and the theories of Bruner and Piaget

2. Implications of Piaget's theory for curriculum development

3. Bruner's ideas and the teaching of science/mathematics/social studies/etc.

4. The absurdity of trying to teach more and more complex conceptions and operations to younger and younger children

5. In defense of using nonstandard English in the schools

6. The need for bidialectal teachers

7. Designing a program to teach standard English to first/third/ninth/etc. grade students

8. The relation between language and cognition during the preschool/elementary/high school years

9. Five ways to increase students' metalinguistic awareness

10. Pros and cons of bilingual education for all students

CHAPTER 8   THE DEVELOPMENT OF PERSONALITY

OBJECTIVES

The student should be able to

o name the stages of personality development described by Erik Erikson

o describe the distinguishing characteristics of the crises that occur at each stage of personality development in Erikson's theory

o name the stages of development in moral reasoning

o describe the kinds of responses to a moral dilemma made by persons at different stages of moral development

o discuss both sides of the argument about whether traits are stable or unstable characteristics of individuals in different situations

o list ways to foster creativity in the classroom

o state how the classroom environment should be structured differently for high-anxiety and low-anxiety students

o explain the relationship between self-concept and achievement

REMINDER

Chapter 8 introduced you to Erik Erikson's global theory of personality development, which is based on the notion that an individual faces several crises during different stages of psychosocial development. The resolution of these crises helps determine whether one's personality becomes more integrated or more diffuse. You also learned about a less global theory of personality--the development of moral reasoning. You will recall that Kohlberg described three levels of moral thought, with two stages of development characteristic of each level. The chapter continued with a discussion of personality traits, specifically focusing on the traits of honesty, creativity, self-concept, and anxiety. You'll remember that traits are thought to be a pervasive aspect of one's behavior, yet consistency in behavior occurs only to the extent that the environment across situations is the same. Teachers need to be most careful about expectations for student behavior, since personality traits are not as stable as many people believe.

DEFINITIONS OF KEY CONCEPTS

The following key concepts were discussed in this chapter. In your own words, write the definition of each concept in the space provided.

1. Personality _____

_____

_____

2. Crises in psychosocial development _____

_____

_____

3. Crisis of trust vs. mistrust _____

_____

_____

4. Crisis of autonomy vs. shame _____

_____

_____

5. Crisis of initiative vs. guilt _____

_____

_____

6. Crisis of accomplishment vs. inferiority _____

_____

_____

7. Crisis of identity vs. confusion _____

_____

_____

8. Crisis of intimacy vs. isolation _____

_____

_____

9. Crisis of generativity vs. stagnation _____

_____

_____

10. Crisis of integrity vs. despair _____

_____

_____

11. Moral development _____

_____

_____

12. Preconventional level of moral development _____

_____

_____

13. Conventional level of moral development _____

_____

_____

14. Postconventional level of moral development _____

_____

_____

15. Morality _____

_____

_____

16. Convention _____

_____

_____

17. Traits _____

_____

_____

18. Creativity _____

_____

_____

19. "Governing skill" in problem solving _____

_____

_____

20. Self-concept _____

_____

_____

21. Anxiety _____

_____

_____

APPLICATION OF KEY CONCEPTS

The terms listed below refer to important concepts that were discussed in this chapter. Carefully read each descriptive statement, and identify the concept or concepts each statement implies. Place the corresponding letter(s) of the concept(s) you select in the space provided.

Concepts

A. crisis of initiative vs. guilt
B. conventional level of moral development
C. crisis of identify vs. confusion
D. trait
E. preconventional level of moral development
F. crisis of trust vs. mistrust
G. crisis of generativity vs. stagnation
H. crisis of autonomy vs. shame
I. crisis of intimacy vs. isolation

J. crisis of integrity vs. despair
K. crisis of accomplishment vs. inferiority
L. postconventional level of moral development
M. aggression
N. anxiety
O. self-concept
P. creativity
Q. personality

Descriptive Statements

_____ 1. Deborah, who is eight or nine years old, was quite pleased when I told her she had done her balance beam routine perfectly.

_____ 2. Caretakers of institutionalized infants do not have much time to give a lot of attention to each particular child.

_____ 3. I went to my teacher to tell her I was sorry and felt really bad about breaking the vase on her desk.

_____ 4. I enjoy reading Russell's short stories; they're always so original and entertaining.

_____ 5. It's fun to listen to old Mr. Felixbrad's stories about all his adventures. He seems to have really enjoyed his life.

_____ 6. She grabbed the puzzle away from me and wouldn't give it back!

_____ 7. He seems to be unsure about how to make really close friends.

_____ 8. My parents just don't understand at all!

_____ 9. Let's see, how can I describe Raymond to you? He's even-tempered, very popular, a good student, seems very mature for his age; he's just a really nice boy--I'm sure you'll enjoy having him in your class.

_____ 10. Arthur's mother is always following him around and watching that he doesn't get into anything.

_____ 11. Maybe you should ask Harry to lead the discussion. I probably wouldn't be very good at it.

_____ 12. Julie is always very shy and quiet with people she doesn't know well.

_____ 13. I get really nervous in the biology lab when I'm around the reptiles, especially the snakes.

_____ 14. I've raised my kids and now I'd like to just relax. Why should I take a job?

_____ 15. I knew I'd get caught, so I didn't cheat on the test.

_____ 16. I don't think you can ever make capital punishment acceptable to me; it seems so antihuman.

_____ 17. I don't jaywalk because if everyone did, there would be some mess!

MULTIPLE-CHOICE SELF-TEST

Select the response that best answers the question or completes the statement. Place the letter of the chosen answer in the space provided.

_____ 1. Erik Erikson's theory of personality deals with which of the following areas of human development?
A. Psychophysical
B. Psychosocial
C. Moral-ethical
D. Emotional

_____ 2. Use of psychological traits to describe the consistency of a person's behavior is difficult because
A. the behavior of a person with supposedly stable traits has not been studied in enough different environments.

B. the situations that a person is in are constant.
C. stimuli that are similar don't elicit similar responses by the same person.
D. a person's behavior can never be constant, so traits are not worth studying.

_____ 3. Many researchers who have studied the relationship between creativity and verbal intelligence believe that the correlation between the two is
A. highly positive--about .80.
B. slightly positive--about .20.
C. around zero.
D. slightly negative--about -.20.
E. highly negative--about -.80.

_____ 4. A ninth grader who says that it's wrong for students to smoke marijuana because it's against the law, and besides if they get caught they'll be expelled from school, is revealing what level of moral reasoning?
A. Preconventional
B. Conventional
C. Postconventional

_____ 5. When an attempt is made to modify moral development by training, you can expect
A. at best, a change by some students to a level just above the one they had possessed.
B. no change at all, since the stages are relatively fixed.
C. change by many, but not all, students to the top two levels of development.
D. change in behavior toward others.

_____ 6. Kohlberg's view suggests that moral reasoning is most closely related to
A. affective development.
B. social learning.
C. parental standards.
D. cognitive development.

_____ 7. The stereotype that girls behave more honestly than boys is
A. true at the elementary level, but not the high school level.
B. true at the high school level, but not the elementary level.
C. true at both the elementary and high school levels.
D. false at both the elementary and high school levels.

_____ 8. Student honesty has been found to be
A. a pervasive trait that is consistently revealed across all situations.
B. unchangeable in a variety of different tasks.
C. changeable in different situations.
D. changeable in similar situations.

_____ 9. The best conclusion to draw about the fostering of creativity in the classroom is that
A. since creativity is mostly heritable, it cannot really be taught.
B. teachers who are not themselves creative are limited in terms of providing experiences for highly creative students.
C. teachers can provide environments to increase student creativity.
D. unless the student has a high IQ, the impact of the environment on creativity will be negligible.

_____10. What aspect of personality is the general disposition to feel threatened by a broad range of nonharmful situations?
A. Anxiety as a trait
B. Anxiety as a state
C. Anxiety as a trait and a state
D. Anxiety as measured by a personality test

_____11. High-anxiety students perform best on tasks that are
A. challenging.
B. timed.
C. structured.
D. "open."

Classify the statements below (Items 12-19) according to one of Erikson's eight crises in personality development. Choose the crisis that best characterizes the statement and answer with the appropriate letter.
A. Autonomy vs. shame and doubt
B. Initiative vs. guilt
C. Trust vs. mistrust
D. Accomplishment vs. inferiority
E. Identity vs. confusion
F. Generativity vs. stagnation
G. Intimacy vs. isolation
H. Integrity vs. despair

_____12. There is a need to be able to do and make some things almost perfectly; however, feelings of worth must not be based solely on work.

_____13. As conscience develops, the person begins to exhibit independence.

_____14. There is a strengthening of creativity and productivity and a nurturance of ideas, things, and people in one's environment.

_____15. There is a sense of acceptance of this one and only chance at life on earth and of the important people in it.

_____16. One shares oneself by giving some piece of one's identity over to another.

_____17. One seeks to clarify who one is and what one's role in society will be.

_____18. A sense of security is established through the relationships of love, attention, and touch.

_____19. One develops a sense of self-control without loss of self-esteem.

PROJECTS AND ACTIVITIES

1. Write a small scenario depicting a moral dilemma (for example, cheating on tests, stealing food). Question students on whether the act was justifiable or not; probe for their reasons. Keep switching the circumstances under which the moral dilemma takes place (for example, if one is hungry, is it justifiable to steal food?) to see whether the circumstance affects children's responses. Raise moral issues at a much higher level in the Kohlberg classification scheme than the levels indicated by the students in their

responses, and see whether the children understand you. Pose the same moral dilemma with your peers. See whether their responses are much higher than those of the students you might teach. What are the implications for viewing behavior as a moral issue or as convention?

2. Observe some students at school and try to identify "creative" students. Ask yourself how you made your identification. Question the students, asking them how they would solve some major problems--corruption in government, pollution, etc. Do their responses surprise you or confirm your tentative identification of creative students? How would you foster creativity in your classrooms and how would you identify the truly creative student?

SUGGESTIONS FOR TERM PAPERS

1. Adolescence and the crisis of identity

2. Teaching for 20 years: The crisis of generativity vs. stagnation

3. Teaching morality: Can it be done?

4. Teaching morality: Should it be done?

5. Differences between creativity and intelligence

6. Fostering a positive self-concept in students

7. Relieving tension in the highly anxious student

8. Usefulness of personality tests

CHAPTER 9 THE DEVELOPMENT OF SEX DIFFERENCES

OBJECTIVES

The student should be able to

o list the findings on sex differences in cognitive and personality dimensions

o define the term undergyny

o describe how the schools train the sexes differently for socially acceptable roles

o name five ways in which the student's school district engages in sex discrimination of one kind or another

o describe in writing three ways in which schools can modify their curriculum offerings so as to include more students of the opposite sex in certain classes traditionally oriented toward either boys or girls

o state the relationship between the personality traits of passivity and boldness and intellectual performance for both sexes

REMINDER

This chapter summarized the research literature dealing with sex differences in cognitive abilities (verbal, numerical, spatial, and problem-solving) and personality characteristics (aggression, conformity and dependence, emotional adjustment, and achievement orientation). You read how different socializing processes for the two sexes account for most of the differences found. Also included in Chapter 9 was a discussion of androgynous individuals, that is, people whose sex-role adaptability enables them to behave effectively without concern about the sex-role stereotypes attached to such behavior. The remainder of the chapter discussed the effects of sex-role stereotyping in the schools, the home, and the mass media--and suggested several ways in which teachers might eliminate stereotyping from their behavior.

DEFINITIONS OF KEY CONCEPTS

The following key concepts were discussed in this chapter. In your own words, write the definition of each concept in the space provided.

1. Sex bias in intelligence tests _____
_____
_____

2. Cross-sex parental linkage _____
_____
_____

3. Spatial ability _____
_____
_____

4. Field dependence _____
_____
_____

5. "Category width" in conceptual learning tasks _____
_____
_____

6. Androgyny _____
_____
_____

7. Sex-role stereotypes _____
_____
_____

8. Title IX of the Education Amendments _____
_____
_____

APPLICATION OF KEY CONCEPTS

The terms listed below refer to important concepts that were discussed in this chapter.

Carefully read each descriptive statement, and identify the concept or concepts each statement implies. Place the corresponding letter(s) of the concept(s) you select in the space provided.

Concepts

A. field dependence
B. spatial ability
C. sex-role stereotype
D. sex bias in intelligence tests

E. "category width" in conceptual learning
F. cross-sex parental linkage
G. androgyny
H. Title IX of the Education Amendments

Descriptive Statements

_____ 1. Ann has decided to be a math major. Did you know that her father is a professor in the statistics department here? That's where she gets her ability.

_____ 2. Now, Cecil, you know that boys don't cry. So I want you to go right back outside and ask Don if you can share the ball with him.

_____ 3. If I turn this cube, which you'll notice has a different color on each side, 180° to the right, and then 90° downward, what will be the color of the side facing you?

_____ 4. I overheard her tell him that the current practice that limits membership in the high school computer science club to boys is illegal.

_____ 5. I got some really interesting questions from my fourth graders when I gave them this problem: "If Neal's mother gives him $3.75 to go to the store on an errand, and he buys bread for $.59, a quart of milk for $.49, and a carton of cottage cheese for $.55, how much money would he receive in change?" One of the girls asked why Neal didn't buy something for himself and another student asked whether he bought chocolate milk.

_____ 6. The Baileys are planning to raise their newborn in an environment that is as free as possible from sex-role stereotypes; the baby should be quite adaptable as a result.

_____ 7. I showed Marvin the two pictures and then asked him to describe what he had seen. He described the things that were alike about the pictures.

_____ 8. Pick the one word that doesn't belong with the others: GINGHAM   MADRAS   SEERSUCKER   CHECK

MULTIPLE-CHOICE SELF-TEST

Select the response that best answers the question or completes the statement. Place the letter of the chosen answer in the space provided.

_____ 1. There is some evidence that spatial abilities are
   A. genetically sex-linked, with the parental characteristic being transmitted to a child of the same sex.
   B. genetically sex-linked, with the parental characteristic being transmitted to a child of the opposite sex.

C. environmentally determined, and related to the mother's attitude toward mathematics.
D. environmentally determined, and related to the father's job.

_____ 2. Intellectual achievement is higher in girls who are
A. more conforming.
B. less impulsive.
C. more assertive.
D. less anxious.

_____ 3. Sex differences in achievement and personality variables are primarily determined by
A. genetic factors.
B. environmental factors.
C. hormonal factors.
D. biological-cultural factors.

_____ 4. The correlations between IQ and expected level of success on a given task were
A. moderate and positive for both boys and girls.
B. moderate and negative for both boys and girls.
C. moderate and positive for boys and moderate and negative for girls.
D. moderate and negative for boys and moderate and positive for girls.

_____ 5. In item 4 above, one would conclude that brighter boys are more likely to predict
A. lower level of success for themselves.
B. higher level of success for themselves.

_____ 6. In item 4 above, one would conclude that brighter girls are more likely to predict
A. lower level of success for themselves.
B. higher level of success for themselves.

_____ 7. Approximately what percentage of people studied by Bem could be classified as androgynous?
A. 10
B. 30
C. 60
D. 80

_____ 8. Research has indicated that high levels of mental health, self-esteem, and adjustment are found in men and women who score high on measures of
A. androgyny.
B. feminine characteristics.
C. masculine characteristics.

_____ 9. Both male and female teachers reinforce boys for play behavior that is rated as

A. masculine.
B. feminine.
C. androgynous.

_____ 10. Recent content analyses of school textbooks in both the United States and England indicate that sex-role stereotypes are
A. prevalent for boy characters but not girls.
B. prevalent for girl characters but not boys.

C. prevalent for both boy and girl characters.
D. not at all prevalent for either sex.

In general, if you had no other information, and were offered a $100 prize for every correct identification, which team -- Team 1, made up of Jane, Marian, and Margaret, or Team 2, made up of Robert, Willard, and David -- would you select to win the contests specified in Items 11-15?

_____11. Tests of verbal intelligence (when team members are second graders)
A. Team 1 will score higher.
B. Team 2 will score higher.
C. The teams will score about the same.

_____12. Tests of spatial ability
A. Team 1 will score higher.
B. Team 2 will score higher.
C. The teams will score about the same.

_____13. Tests of reading ability (when team members are in their teens)
A. Team 1 will score higher.
B. Team 2 will score higher.
C. The teams will score about the same.

_____14. Tests of mathematics achievement
A. Team 1 will score higher.
B. Team 2 will score higher.
C. The teams will score about the same.

_____15. Tests of religious values (when team members are young adults)
A. Team 1 will score higher.
B. Team 2 will score higher.
C. The teams will score about the same.

Use the following information to answer items 16-18. The School Board lost the captions to the table for expenditures in social studies, science, and athletics for males and females. The table, without identification, looks like this:

Curriculum Area	Column 1	Column 2
X	$150,000	$100,000
Y	100,000	100,000
Z	275,000	85,000

_____16. You might predict that Curriculum Area Z was
A. social studies.
B. science.

_____   C.   athletics.

_____ 17.   You might predict that Curriculum Area X was
             A.   social studies.
             B.   science.
             C.   athletics.

_____ 18.   You might predict that Column 2 was labeled
             A.   girls.
             B.   boys.

PROJECTS AND ACTIVITIES

1.   Go to the library and randomly select five children's books. First look at the pictures in the books. How do they portray men and women? How do they portray boys and girls? Then read excerpts from these stories. Who are the people in charge -- the boys or the girls? Who cries? Who is helpless? Who leads? Who makes decisions? How might what you observe affect the socialization processes of boys and girls?

2.   Take the list of masculine and feminine descriptors in Table 9-1 (p. 208 of the text) and make up a questionnaire asking students such questions as: Who in the class is very aggressive? likes math and science? is rough? is very emotional? is very passive? is illogical? and so forth. Did the questions consistently evoke a girl's name or a boy's name? In other words, were the descriptors associated differently with boys and girls in the class?

CHAPTER 10 INDIVIDUAL DIFFERENCES AND THE NEED FOR SPECIAL EDUCATION

OBJECTIVES

The student should be able to

o explain the impact of Public Law 94-142 on the education of all students

o list the essential components of an IEP

o summarize the research results on mainstreaming

o list four ways in which the classroom teacher can help educable mentally retarded children learn

o name five common observable signs of a student's behavior that might be indicative of a visual disorder

o contrast a specific learning disability with a behavior disorder

o describe aptitude-treatment interaction and give at least two hypothetical examples of interactions that could occur in teaching

REMINDER

This chapter introduced you to some of the unique abilities and needs of exceptional learners, who are increasingly attending school in regular classrooms. You learned that the general concerns of teachers of exceptional students are normalization, attitudes, assessment, and instruction. A categorical guide was provided that outlined some of the unique characteristics of students who are unusually high or low in intellectual ability and those with behavior problems, learning disabilities, and problems in speech, vision, and hearing. You also read about some ways in which teachers can optimally facilitate the learning of the many students in the least restrictive environment of the regular classroom. Finally, this chapter introduced you to a new approach -- the aptitude-treatment interaction (ATI) approach. ATI investigates how students with differing characteristics, or aptitudes, are affected by differing teaching methods, styles, or treatments.

DEFINITIONS OF KEY CONCEPTS

The following key concepts were discussed in this chapter. In your own words, write the definition of each concept in the space provided.

1. Exceptional students _____
_____
_____

2. P.L. 94-142 _____
_____
_____

3. The least restrictive environment _____
_____
_____

4. Mainstreaming _____
_____
_____

5. An individualized education program _____
_____
_____

6. Specific learning disablilities _____
_____
_____

7. Behavior disorders _____
_____
_____

8. Mental retardation _____
_____
_____

9. Severely or profoundly mentally retarded students _____
_____
_____

10. Trainable mentally retarded students _____

_____

_____

11. Educable mentally retarded students _____

_____

_____

12. Speech disorders _____

_____

_____

13. Language disorders _____

_____

_____

14. Hearing impairment _____

_____

_____

15. Visual impairment _____

_____

_____

16. Physical and health impairment _____

_____

_____

17. Giftedness and talent _____

_____

_____

18. Acceleration _____

_____

_____

19. Enrichment _____

_____

_____

20. An aptitude-treatment interaction _____

_____

_____

APPLICATION OF KEY CONCEPTS

The terms listed below refer to important concepts that were discussed in this chapter. Carefully read each descriptive statement, and identify the concept or concepts each statement implies. Place the corresponding letter(s) of the concept(s) you select in the space provided.

Concepts

A. Aptitude-treatment interaction
B. individualized educational program
C. hearing impairment
D. P.L. 94-142
E. physical/health impairment
F. least restrictive environment
G. trainable mentally retarded
H. speech disorder
I. educable mentally retarded

J. acceleration
K. specific learning disability
L. severely mentally retarded
M. language disorder
N. giftedness
O. enrichment
P. behavior disorder
Q. visual impairment

Descriptive Statements

_____ 1. Sometimes Ted misses part of a unit because of his frequent visits to the physical therapist.

_____ 2. Melinda is aphasic, and so she often has difficulty understanding directions.

_____ 3. The chemistry teacher noticed something curious when he was averaging the scores of students for their report cards: the boys had better grades in the lab section of the class, and the girls had better grades in the lecture and discussion section.

_____ 4. Jane goes twice a week to the high school for a calculus class and spends the rest of her class time here at the junior high.

_____ 5. Betty seems to be doing fine. She's in the regular classroom all day now, with the exception of second period, when she leaves to see her specialist.

_____ 6. Today we're meeting with Ron's parents to finalize and record the details of what we will all specifically be doing with him this term, and what objectives will be met.

_____ 7. I provide this group of three students with special equipment for science experiments that they conduct once a week.

_____ 8. Cedric just tore up another one of his English compositions. His perfectionism is really interfering with his production, since nothing he writes is acceptable to him.

_____ 9. I think it's great that there are federal guidelines about the "mainstreaming" of children into regular public school classrooms.

_____10. The district has just acquired 50 large-print copies of all the texts. I've already requested a set for James.

_____11. My uncle lives and works here. His job is to sort paper for recycling.

_____12. Right now we're working on simple addition so that our students will be able to do their own grocery shopping when they are living on their own.

_____13. I'm very careful to look right at Janet frequently when I'm talking to the entire group, so that she'll be able to see my lips as an additional cue to what's being said.

_____14. Dominic is always asking perceptive questions, is very quick to learn concepts and principles, and uses new words well in advance of the other students.

_____15. Davey has so much difficulty in spelling, but he's at grade level in reading comprehension and math.

_____16. Her intellectual functioning prevents her from being able to take care of herself.

_____17. Freda's stuttering interferes with the expression of her ideas.

MULTIPLE-CHOICE SELF-TEST

Select the response that best answers the question or completes the statement. Place the letter of the chosen answer in the space provided.

_____ 1. Which aspect of the "mainstreaming" law (P.L. 94-142) guards against the inappropriate placement of cultural minority group members in special education classes?
A. The selection committee is required to include at least two minority group members.
B. The one criterion for inclusion in a special education class must be the result of a standardized testing procedure.
C. More than one criterion for categorization as a special education child must be used.
D. Language differences or deviations cannot be used for placement purposes.

_____ 2. Exceptional learners are typically different from regular classroom learners in
A. about three or four areas.
B. usually only a particular area.
C. all respects.

_____ 3. Which of the following is the best reason to compare the behavior of a student you suspect has a specific learning disability with that of other children in the class?
A. To help the child's parents understand the problem
B. To explain to the school psychologist the "average" behavior of the child
C. To prevent the teacher from identifying as a problem a behavior that is typical for the child's particular age
D. To protect the teacher legally

_____ 4. Usually the most efficient strategy the teacher can use to treat a specific learning disability is to
A. find the underlying cause of the observed problem.
B. change the specific observable problem behavior of the child.
C. plan a complete, individualized program for the child in all basic curriculum areas.
D. recommend that the child receive a battery of tests covering ability to function in reading and mathematics.

_____ 5. Which of the following descriptions of a learning disabled child's behavior would be most useful in assessment and instruction?
A. "Ann can never pay attention."
B. "Ann can't pay attention in large-group settings."
C. "Ann can only pay attention about 50 percent of the time."
D. "Ann can only pay attention to her seatwork for about 5 out of 15 minutes."

_____ 6. Mildred often shows a lack of attention, reluctance to participate in oral classroom activities, shyness, and achievement and attention levels in small-group activities higher than in large-group activities. Her teacher will probably suspect that she
A. may have a mild hearing loss.
B. probably is just not listening and concentrating.
C. is not receiving enough attention at home.
D. is educably mentally retarded.

_____ 7. Terman's longitudinal study of the gifted reveals that as a group those with IQs over 140, as compared with those with an average IQ, are
A. physically inferior in health.
B. more prone to emotional problems.
C. less popular with peers.
D. all of the above.
E. none of the above.

_____ 8. Approximately what percentage of school-age children have an exceptionality that requires the teacher's special attention?
A. less than 1 percent
B. 2 percent
C. 8 percent
D. 20 percent

_____ 9. Learners with which type of exceptionality will you most frequently have in your class?
A. Visual impairment
B. Hearing impairment
C. Behavior disorder

    D.   Educable mentally retarded

    E.   Specific learning disability

_____10. The causes of behavioral disorders are usually
   A. genetic.
   B. neurological.
   C. environmental.
   D. unknown.

_____11. Which of the following is <u>not</u> advisable for the instruction of educable mentally retarded students?
   A. Carefully sequenced instruction
   B. Adequate time for completion of work
   C. Moderate rates of success
   D. Uncomplicated learning tasks
   E. Overlearning

_____12. How can the classroom teacher most help a consulting speech-language specialist?
   A. Record the conditions in which speech problems occur
   B. Immediately point out to the student any speech problems that occur
   C. Treat the student exactly like the other children in the classroom
   D. Arrange for weekly meetings

_____13. The aptitude-treatment interaction approach examines the relationship between student characteristics, or aptitudes, and
   A. the teaching method considered to be the best for increasing student achievement.
   B. teacher aptitudes in order to attempt to provide an optimal match.
   C. their preferences for particular courses.
   D. two or more methods or treatments for fostering a given kind of achievement

_____14. Chastain studied ATIs in foreign language instruction. He found that
   A. students' verbal ability interacted with the method of instruction.
   B. students of all types in the audiolingual method achieved the same as students of all types in other methods.
   C. students' anxiety interacted with the method of instruction.
   D. students did better in one method, but liked the other method of instruction better.

_____15. Dowaliby and Schumer studied the relationship between student anxiety and teaching method. They found that
   A. students low in anxiety performed better in lecture situations.
   B. students high in anxiety performed better in group discussion situations.
   C. students low in anxiety performed better in group discussion situations.
   D. most students performed better in lecture situations.
   E. most students were moderate in anxiety, and so performed better in small-group discussion situations.

_____16. Ms. Chang, the physics teacher, has noted that the more outgoing students in her class do well on tests covering the lab experiments, whereas the more quiet and shy students do better on tests covering the lecture material . Her observations are an example of

A. student characteristics interacting with teaching method.
B. student characteristics interacting with teacher characteristics.
C. student preferences correlating with student ability.
D. test material correlating with both teacher and student characteristics.

PROJECTS AND ACTIVITIES

1. Write to your local member of Congress or the Bureau of Education for the Handicapped, Department of Education, Washington, D.C., requesting a copy of the complete text of Public Law 94-142. Carefully read the document, noting the criteria for categorization of a child as a special education student.

2. Ask a school psychologist in your district if you may observe the meeting(s) between teacher, parent, and student in the formulation of an Individualized Educational Program. If attendance at such a meeting is not possible, ask if you may see several IEPs for students with the names deleted from the records you review.

3. Visit a classroom that has a member with a speech disorder. Note specifically how consistently the particular problem behavior occurs and under what conditions.

4. Interview teachers of second-grade mathematics/eighth-grade civics/algebra/etc. about how they modify their instruction for particular types of students.

5. Conduct a survey of students' opinions about types of teachers and their most effective teaching methods. For example, you might find students who feel they learn more in situations where the teacher primarily lectures than in situations where student discussion is the focus. Some students may prefer teachers whose style is quite "unstructured," whereas other students may feel very unsure of themselves in such situations and may achieve more and feel more comfortable with teachers who have a very rigid and planned approach to teaching. From the data you gather in your survey, develop hypotheses about how best to match student characteristics and styles with teacher characteristics, styles, and teaching methods.

SUGGESTIONS FOR TERM PAPERS

1. Developing alternative curricula for students who vary in anxiety/authoritarianism/verbal ability/etc.

2. Some hypotheses about types of students for whom certain teaching activities might not be effective (for example, pupils who do not respond to positive reinforcement; students who do poorly in open classroom environments; etc.)

3. Designing a reading/math/spelling/etc. curriculum for a student who is speech/hearing/visually impaired

4. Formulation of an Individual Educational Program for a student observed in the second/fourth/sixth/etc. grade at _____ school

5. Implementation of P.L. 94-142 by the _____ School District

6. An historical overview of the treatment of special education students in the United States

CHAPTER 11   THE DEFINITION AND VARIETIES OF LEARNING

OBJECTIVES

The student should be able to

o define learning

o identify examples of respondent, contiguity, operant, observational, and cognitive learning

o give an example of contingent reinforcement

o describe how observational learning can lead to the acquisition of new responses, or inhibit or disinhibit already acquired responses

o distinguish between the emphasis of behavioral and cognitive psychologists

REMINDER

This chapter provided a definition of learning and a discussion of the basic varieties of learning: respondent, contiguity, operant, observational, and cognitive. You'll recall that learning was defined as a change in behavior as a result of experience. This definition excluded changes in behavior resulting from physiological, mechanical, or maturational processes, and focused on changes in behavior that are due to the establishment of relationships between stimuli and responses. Such relationships are established either on the basis of contiguity between stimulus and response, or because of the consequences of a behavior, or as a result of observing other persons, or as an outcome of thinking, that is, cognitive processes.

DEFINITIONS OF KEY CONCEPTS

The following key concepts were discussed in this chapter. In your own words, write the definition of each concept in the space provided.

1. Learning _____

_____

_____

2. Maturation _____

_____

_____

3. Respondent learning _____

_____

_____

4. An unconditioned stimulus _____

_____

_____

5. An unconditioned response _____

_____

_____

6. A conditioned stimulus _____

_____

_____

7. A conditioned response _____

_____

_____

8. Contiguity learning _____

_____

_____

9. Operant conditioning _____

_____

_____

10. The consequences of a behavior _____

_____

_____

11. A reinforcer _____

_____

_____

12. Operant level _____

_____

_____

13. Contingent reinforcement _____

_____

_____

14. Observational learning _____

_____

_____

15. Inhibition _____

_____

_____

16. Disinhibition _____

_____

_____

17. Cognitive learning _____

_____

_____

APPLICATION OF KEY CONCEPTS

The terms listed below refer to important concepts that were discussed in this chapter. Carefully read each descriptive statement, and identify the concept or concepts each statement implies. Place the corresponding letter(s) of the concepts(s) you select in the space provided.

Concepts

A. observational learning   H. consequence of a behavior

B. inhibition
C. respondent learning
D. conditioned stimulus
E. learning
F. unconditioned stimulus
G. contingent reinforcement

I. conditioned response
J. unconditioned response
K. masturation
L. disinhibition
M. cognitive learning
N. operant level

Descriptive Statements

_____ 1. I think I can play the character more realistically after watching the drama teacher go through one of the scenes.

_____ 2. Angie, I thought you understood that you were going to do at least two of your arithmetic problems before going to PE.

_____ 3. The second-grade class gets very excited and happy whenever they spot the film projector in the room, because it usually means they're going to see a movie. Seeing the film projector is an example of this.

_____ 4. In item 3 above, the excitement and happiness of the class is an example of this.

_____ 5. After a month of practicing, she was able to play the Beethoven piano sonata without making a mistake.

_____ 6. During recess, it looked as if two of the boys were arguing over the basketball, but when Larry caught my eye, they stopped.

_____ 7. My eyes blink whenever someone throws a ball at me.

_____ 8. In item 7 above, blinking of the eyes is an example of this.

_____ 9. In item 7 above, the ball thrown at the speaker is an example of this.

_____ 10. The coach told him to try out for the basketball team next year when he is a little taller.

_____ 11. On the average, Jill talks out of turn six times a day. But tomorrow, I start with a program to lessen that unacceptable behavior.

_____ 12. Whenever Paul gives an incorrect answer, his teacher explains to him why it was wrong.

_____ 13. After seeing the way the referees called the plays, I'm going to be more aggressive in the next game.

_____ 14. Oh . . . I see! That's how you solve quadratic equations.

_____ 15. You can see that she is becoming an excellent driver.

MULTIPLE CHOICE SELF-TEST

Select the response that best answers the question or completes the statement. Place the letter of the chosen answer in the space provided. For items 1-5, write <u>A</u> if the statement describes an instance of learning, and <u>B</u> if the statement does not describe an instance of learning.

_____ 1. After being in Mr. Washington's mathematics course, Jose begins to hold his chalk in the same way as Mr. Washington does.

_____ 2. Jose could not see the stars at all when he first went outside, but after a while he could see them clearly.

_____ 3. After sitting in his chair for three hours of the seminar, Jose could no longer sit up straight.

_____ 4. To improve his ability in calculus, Jose works on calculus problems every morning for an hour; by the end of the year, he can solve every problem in the book.

_____ 5. After taking Mr. Washington's course, Jose has begun to think seriously about majoring in mathematics.

_____ 6. Under the contiguity model of learning, we could expect that students would learn to spell <u>hippopotamus</u> by saying the word and then spelling the word correctly.
   A. True
   B. Only if they received a reward for correct spelling
   C. Only if they heard other children saying "hippopotamus" and spelling the word correctly
   D. Only if saying the word was pleasing, so that this feeling would become associated with its correct spelling

_____ 7. On the day before she gives a surprise quiz to her students, Ms. Sharp invariably says, "Now make sure you understand these points." She is always amazed at her students' excellent performance on these unannounced tests. An educational psychologist would explain the phenomenon by referring to
   A. contiguity-learning theory.
   B. respondent-learning theory.
   C. observational-learning theory.
   D. cognitive-learning theory.

Use the following information in answering items 8, 9, and 10. Peter had a long history of not paying attention in history class. His teacher, Ms. Glass, decided to perform a small experiment to see whether she could modify Peter's attending behaviors. In order to be able to judge whether her experimental treatment had any effect, she recorded the number of times Peter looked at her or the chalkboard during each history class for a week. The second week, every time Peter made an attending response (looking at the teacher or the chalkboard), Ms. Glass made a remark like "It's nice to know you're paying attention" or smiled at Peter. The third week, Ms. Glass recorded the number of times Peter attended in class. The graph of the number of attending responses for each class period appears below:

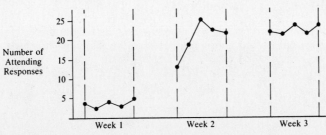

_____ 8. In this little experiment, the operant is
        A. Ms. Glass's remarks and smiles.
        B. the chalkboard and the teacher.
        C. Peter's attending responses.
        D. Peter's increased motivation to pay attention.

_____ 9. The baseline measure is the recording of attending responses during
        A. Week 1.
        B. Week 2.
        C. Week 3.
        D. Week 3 vs. Week 1.
        E. Week 2 vs. Week 1.
        F. Week 3 vs. Week 2.

_____ 10. In this experiment, Ms. Glass's remarks and smiles
        A. served as the negative reinforcer.
        B. should have been recorded to give another baseline measure.
        C. are an example of observational learning.
        D. were contingent on attending responses.
        E. were the unconditioned stimulus.

For each of the following types of behavior (items 11-14), write A if the statement is an example of respondent behavior, and B if the statement is an example of operant behavior.

_____ 11. John gets tense whenever he runs into Joe, who never fails to come across with a cutting remark.

_____ 12. John calls Mary for a date because he knows she will admire his knowledge of wines.

_____ 13. John's mouth begins to water as soon as the waiter gives him the menu.

_____ 14. John just plain feels good when Mary thanks him sincerely for a wonderful evening.

_____ 15. Megan's biology teacher always seems to be particularly enthusiastic when she speaks of vertebrates and their development. Megan, too, seems to show a more receptive attitude about this subject matter in the biology club activities. We might predict this behavior on the basis of which model of learning?
        A. Respondent
        B. Operant
        C. Observational
        D. Contiguity

_____ 16. Which of the following effects would result solely from observational learning?
        A. Inhibition of an unconditioned response
        B. Reinforcement of an already acquired response
        C. Acquisition of a new intellectual insight
        D. Learning of a new behavior

_____ 17. Which of the following choices is the best definition of learning?
        A. Relatively permanent contiguity between the stimulus and response
        B. Relatively permanent acquisition of knowledge

    C.   Relatively permanent change in a behavioral tendency that is the result of experience
    D.   Relatively permanent experience, which is coded in the central processes of the brain

_____18.   Johnny is arranging flowers for a still life picture in art class. A spider emerges and bites his hand. The next day, on a field trip to collect wild flowers, Johnny won't pick any flowers. This event might best be explained by what we know of
    A.   operant conditioning.
    B.   imitation learning.
    C.   classical conditioning.
    D.   contiguity learning.

For each of the following types of behavior (items 19-25), write

<u>R</u> if the statement describes an example of respondent learning
<u>C</u> if the statement describes an example of contiguity learning
<u>O</u> if the statement describes an example of operant learning

_____19.   Because he has a phobia for heights, Josh begins to have a rapid heartbeat as soon as he gets into an elevator going to the cocktail lounge on the twentieth floor of the hotel.

_____20.   Mary begins to relax the minute she enters the classroom of Professor Coleman, who has never had anything but praise for Mary's work.

_____21.   Heidi is reminded of her old flame, Nicholas, because the movie <u>Nicholas and Alexandra</u> is being shown on TV tonight.

_____22.   Rachel has learned that Thor likes her better if she just keeps quiet and listens to him.

_____23.   As the weekend of her mother's visit approaches, Corrine begins to have a sinking feeling in her stomach.

_____24.   Introduced to a girl named Alexandra, Heidi begins to think again about her old boyfriend, Nicholas.

_____25.   Knowing that Professor Coleman is especially fond of research papers with short but highly pertinent bibliographies, Mary writes her paper in just that way.

PROJECTS AND ACTIVITIES

    1.   This is a demonstration of respondent learning you can perform by yourself. Sit in a dimly lit room in front of a table with a mirror, a lamp, and a bell on it. (A bell that rings when the button on top is depressed works well.) The room should be lighted just enough to allow you to see yourself clearly in the mirror. You'll notice that your pupils constrict when you turn the table lamp on, and dilate when the lamp is turned off. Turning on the lamp is the unconditioned stimulus, and pupil constriction is the unconditioned response. Practice this a few times to adjust the lighting in the room for maximum pupil constriction and dilation. Now, with the lamp off, ring the bell and notice the effect on your pupil size. There is no effect; ringing the bell is a neutral stimulus. Next, ring the bell just before turning on the lamp. Continue this procedure of ringing the bell right before turning on the

lamp for several trials - about 5 or 10 minutes. Now, ring the bell, but do not turn on the lamp. <u>Your pupils will constrict!</u>

In this experiment, the unconditioned stimulus (turning on the lamp) elicited the unconditioned response (pupil constriction). The sound of the bell, which had previously been a neutral stimulus, became a conditioned stimulus through several associations with the unconditioned stimulus. Ringing the bell then was able to elicit the conditioned response, pupil constriction.

2.   This is an activity that will help you unravel the factors involved in learning. Two or three times over a period of a week, work with a very young child, teaching the child how to write the first letter of his or her name. At the end of your last session, think about what this task required of the child. What parts do you think were due to learning? Did muscular control develop as a result of practice? What maturational processes do you think were required for the child to be successful?

SUGGESTIONS FOR TERM PAPERS

1.   The irrelevancy of respondent conditioning when applied to humans

2.   An analysis of children's fear responses to school, and their possible interpretation in terms of learning theory

3.   The effects of Seconal /caffeine/Dexedrine/marijuana/nicotine/etc. on learning

4.   Areas in the second-grade biology/mathematics/physical education/etc. curriculum where observational learning can be effectively used

5.   The effects of mass media on children's/adolescents' behavior

CHAPTER 12   OPERANT CONDITIONING: A PRACTICAL THEORY

OBJECTIVES

The student will be able to

o describe the two basic kinds of reinforcement and of punishment, and give examples of each kind

o define four basic types of partial reinforcement schedules and give an example of each

o construct a program to modify behavior using contingency-management procedures

o identify examples of the Premack principle, stimulus control, discrimination, and generalization

o describe how the use of extinction, reinforcement of other behavior and of low response rates, and punishment leads to the elimination of a response

o give examples of eliminating a response by use of time out and response cost

REMINDER

In this chapter you learned about concepts in, and the application of principles from, operant-conditioning theory. These included positive and negative reinforcers, both of which increase the probability of a response; primary and secondary reinforcers, which satisfy unlearned and learned needs, respectively; types of partial reinforcement schedules; contingency management, which uses behaviors with a high probability of occurrence as reinforcers for behaviors with a low probability of occurrence; stimulus control in operant learning, including stimulus discrimination and stimulus generalization; and elimination of response by means of extinction techniques, differential reinforcement of other behavior and of low response rates, and two types of punishment, including time out and response cost. Concluding the chapter was a discussion of ethical issues raised by the use of operant-conditioning techniques, and the possible merger of humanistic and behavioral concerns.

DEFINITIONS OF KEY CONCEPTS

The following key concepts were discussed in this chapter. In your own words, write the definition of each concept in the space provided.

1. Positive reinforcers _____
_____
_____

2. Negative reinforcers _____
_____
_____

3. Primary reinforcers _____
_____
_____

4. Secondary reinforcers _____
_____
_____

5. Continuous reinforcement _____
_____
_____

6. Intermittent reinforcement _____
_____
_____

7. Ratio schedule of reinforcement _____
_____
_____

8. Interval schedule of reinforcement _____
_____
_____

9. Fixed-ratio schedule of reinforcement _____
_____
_____

10. Token reinforcement system _____

_____

_____

11. Variable-ration schedule of reinforcement _____

_____

_____

12. Fixed-interval schedule of reinforcement _____

_____

_____

13. Variable-interval schedule of reinforcement _____

_____

_____

14. Contingency management _____

_____

_____

15. The Premack principle _____

_____

_____

16. Successive approximations _____

_____

_____

17. Stimulus control _____

_____

_____

18. Stimulus discrimination _____

_____

_____

19. Stimulus generalization _____

_____

_____

20. Extinction _____

_____

_____

21. Differential reinforcement of other behavior _____

_____

_____

22. Differential reinforcement of low response rates _____

_____

_____

23. Punishment I _____

_____

_____

24. Punishment II _____

_____

_____

25. Time out _____

_____

_____

26. Response cost _____

_____

_____

27. Behavioral humanism _____

_____

_____

28. Intrinsic reinforcement _____

_____

_____

APPLICATION OF KEY CONCEPTS

The terms listed below refer to important concepts that were discussed in this chapter. Carefully read each descriptive statement, and identify the concept or concepts each statement implies. Place the corresponding letter(s) of the concept(s) you select in the space provided.

Concepts

A. intrinsic reinforcement
B. positive reinforcement
C. stimulus control
D. extinction
E. punishment I
F. secondary reinforcer
G. intermittent reinforcement
H. fixed-interval schedule of reinforcement

I. continuous reinforcement
J. variable-interval schedule of reinforcement
K. negative reinforcement
L. punishment II
M. fixed-ratio schedule of reinforcement
N. contingency management
O. successive approximations
P. Premack principle
Q. response cost

Descriptive Statements

_____ 1. Mr. McNeill sometimes calls on me when I raise my hand, and sometimes he doesn't.

_____ 2. The coach keeps me in the game longer when I do well during practice.

_____ 3. I usually practice the clarinet only on Monday and Wednesday nights because band practice is on Tuesday and Thursday after school.

_____ 4. It was really exhilarating to finally be able to clear 16 feet with the pole vault!

_____ 5. I started my pole-vaulting at 14 feet last month, and for every inch higher I gave myself a glass of beer.

_____ 6. Sam, I know that I've been letting you go to art class early, but today you'll have to wait and go at the regular time, because you have to learn that you can't hit boys who are smaller than yourself.

_____ 7. I've found that if I don't say anything to Marcie about her always taking the hall pass, she doesn't seem to do it as often.

_____ 8. Mr. Eisley gives us a quiz once a week, but we never know on what day it will be.

_____ 9. Mr. Gripley just ignores me when I ask a question, unless I raise my hand first and he calls me by name.

_____10. This course will have only a midterm and a final examination.

_____11. Jane, you'll have to stay in from recess for talking to Robert during the exam.

_____12. For every three programmed-workbook sections that we successfully complete, our teacher gives us one hour a week of "free time" during which we do what we want.

_____13. My dad gives me a dollar for every A and B I get on my report card.

_____14. Every time I show my creative writing teacher a modified draft of the short story I'm writing for the literary magazine, she tells me how well I'm doing in the course.

_____15. If Mr. Bloom sees any of the students littering during lunch time, he makes them pick up all the papers on the floor in the cafeteria.

_____16. After Manuel does his vocabulary work, I let him watch television.

_____17. When you can play the three Brahms piano sonatas perfectly, I'll buy you a new grand piano.

_____18. If I can just keep from being too noisy and jumpy in class, I'll never have to go to the principal's office again.

MULTIPLE-CHOICE SELF-TEST

Select the response that best answers the question or completes the statement. Place the letter of the chosen answer in the space provided.

_____1. When the appropriate reinforcer is offered,
   A. we label it as a positive reinforcer.
   B. undesirable behaviors are immediately extinguished.
   C. all students will respond positively.
   D. the probability of a response is increased.

_____2. An example of a primary reinforcer is
   A. money.
   B. food.
   C. praise.
   D. movies.
   E. gold stars.

_____3. If every response of a given type is reinforced,
   A. we have a fixed schedule.
   B. we have an intermittent schedule.
   C. we can expect dramatic behavioral changes.
   D. we have continuous reinforcement.

_____4. When responses are reinforced on a certain average ratio, but each individual reinforcement comes after a different number of correct responses, we call it a
   A. median-ratio schedule.
   B. fixed-intermittent schedule.

    C.   variable-ratio schedule.
    D.   variable-interval schedule.
    E.   fixed-average schedule.

_____ 5.   Behaviors that have been reinforced by a variable-ratio schedule
    A.   are diffult to extinguish.
    B.   cannot be changed by another schedule.
    C.   are easily extinguished.
    D.   are known as fixed behaviors.

_____ 6.   When reinforcement is provided on a fixed-interval schedule,
    A.   a period of decreased responding occurs after each reinforcement.
    B.   a stable and uniform rate of responding occurs.
    C.   a period of increased responding occurs after each reinforcement.
    D.   no change in the rate of responding is observable.

_____ 7.   Supose that a language instructor, by operating a master console, can listen in to a student's pronunciation of audiotaped lessons in a language laboratory without the student's fore-knowledge. The instructor might randomly choose which students to listen to, and say something to, at any time. In what looks like an effort to ensure reinforcement, the students respond at
    A.   various levels, producing a scalloped effect.
    B.   relatively uniform rates, with no scalloping effect.
    C.   a low level, with the behavior being quickly extinguished.
    D.   an increasing rate as the period of time is increased.

_____ 8.   Learning the word <u>fruit</u> and responding with that word to bananas, peaches, plums, pears, and strawberries reflects
    A.   learning a generalization.
    B.   discrimination learning.
    C.   learning to differentiate.
    D.   Gestalt learning.

_____ 9.   The decrease in the rate of occurrence of a response as a result of nonreinforcement is called
    A.   response acquisition.
    B.   stimulus control.
    C.   extinction.
    D.   generalization.

_____10.   Sending a student to the principal, yelling at the student, and praising or rejecting him or her may be equivalent behaviors from the student's point of view if
    A.   ambiguous cues have preceded each action.
    B.   it is the teacher's attention that the student is trying to elicit.
    C.   generalized learning is low.
    D.   extinction has reduced the behavior to its operant or baseline level.

_____11.   Generalization consists of making a particular response to
    A.   any similar stimuli.
    B.   any dissimilar stimuli.
    C.   discriminatory stimuli.
    D.   similar, but not identical, stimuli.

_____12. A small child runs toward his grandmother, even though she is just one of a large group of older people. This is an example of
A. discrimination.
B. classical conditioning.
C. feedback.
D. generalization.

_____13. When he gets near the end of a classroom assignment, Matt starts jumping up an down and doesn't finish his work. His new teacher praises him for any amount of work done and ignores his jumping around. The teacher's behavior is most likely based on an understanding of
A. differential discrimination.
B. the differential reinforcement of other behavior.
C. contiguity.
D. shaping.

Use the following information in answering items 14, 15, and 16: David always pinches Linda during spelling. David's teacher asks for advice on this problem.

_____14. Teacher X suggests that for five days David be pulled out of recess shortly after it begins. Teacher X's advice is an example of applying
A. positive reinforcement.
B. negative reinforcement.
C. punishment.
D. classical extinction.

_____15. Teacher Y suggests that David be released from spelling if he doesn't pinch Linda for five minutes. Teacher Y's advice is an example of applying.
A. positive reinforcement
B. negative reinforcement.
C. punishment
D. classical extinction.

_____16. Teacher Z suggests that David be given extra spelling work for his misconduct. Teacher Z's advice is an example of applying
A. positive reinforcement.
B. negative reinforcement.
C. punishment.
D. classical extinction.

_____17. In general, the time interval between a desirable response and its reinforcement should be
A. as short as possible.
B. of any duration up to about 10 minutes.
C. of any duration up to about an hour.
D. of any duration, as long as the person knows it will certainly be forthcoming eventually.
E. as long as possible without permitting the person to forget that he or she has made the response to be reinforced.

_____18. Sarah is trying very hard not to bite her fingernails. Her mother is trying to help Sarah reach her goal. Therefore, even though Sarah isn't completely free of this bad habit, her mother took her out for lunch yesterday because she is not biting her nails as frequently as she did in the past. Sarah's mother is using the

technique of
A. response cost.
B. differential reinforcement of other behavior.
C. differential reinforcement of low response rates.
D. extinction.

For each of the following example (items 19--30), mark the item with

A, if it could represent a positive reinforcement
B, if it could represent punishment of Type I
C, if it could represent punishment of Type II
D, if it could represent negative reinforcement
E, if it could represent response cost

_____19.   A traffic ticket given for parking in a "No Parking" zone

_____20.   Stopping the projector in the middle of an exciting movie because of the students' noisiness

_____21.   Winning a big pot through successful bluffing in a poker game

_____22.   An A of a term paper

_____23.   The arrival of the end of the hour in a boring class

_____24.   The teacher's being interrupted while she is telling you how good your painting is

_____25.   Someone's stopping smoking in a stuffy room

_____26.   Finding letters from friends in your mailbox

_____27.   The arrival of a person who is always criticizing you

_____28.   The departure of the person who is always criticizing you

_____29.   A beer barrel's becoming empty

_____30.   Losing points on an exam for copying your neighbor's answer

_____31.   In contingency contracting, how much should the teacher let the student know about the "terms" of the contract?
A. As little as possible
B. What the student should do, but not what he or she will receive
C. What the student will receive, but not exactly what he or she should do to receive it
D. What the student should and what he or she will receive

_____32.   The presently accepted conclusion concerning the effectiveness of punishment is that it can reduce the frequency of behavior
A. only if a warning is given.
B. only temporarily.
C. permanently.
D. only in ways that are unjustifiable.

PROJECTS AND ACTIVITIES

1.   Try training a dog (or any similar animal), using the technique of successive approximations.   Pick a behavior that the animal spontaneously engages in only occasionally—rolling-over behavior might be a good one to practice with. Initially, reinforce the dog with praise, petting, or food (be careful not to satiate him) whenever he approximates rolling over. Gradually provide reinforcement only as the behavior more and more closely resembles rolling over. Finally, withhold reinforcement until the dog rolls over on command.

2.   Reinforcers must be positively valued by an individual or group if they are to be effective. Try cataloging a given group of students' likes and dislikes by developing and administering a questionnaire. The catalog will tell you what behaviors can be used as reinforcers for other behaviors; that is, you will be determining in advance how Premack's principle may be used in a classroom.

3.   Imagine you are in the following setting. You teach a seventh-grade literature class. One student, Sue, is particularly withdrawn. She never offers an answer to your questions and seldom interacts with the other students in discussion groups, although she does good work. You decide that one way to modify Sue's behavior, so that it becomes somewhat more socially acceptable, is to enter into a contingency contract with her. Design this contract, with particular concern for the criteria of good ethics in operant conditioning. Be certain to comment briefly on each of the nine points that go into the contract. Also, address the problem of how you will know when Sue has achieved the terminal behavior specified in the contract.

4.   Compare and contrast punishment I and punishment II (not including the notions of time out and response cost) in terms of administrability and effectiveness in a classroom. Do you think it is possible to completely eliminate punishment in the classroom? Justify your response in terms of the principles of operant conditioning discussed in this chapter.

SUGGESTIONS FOR TERM PAPERS

1.   An analysis of the maintenance of disruptive behaviors and a personalized program for modification

2.   The ethics of using behavior modification with children

3.   Skinner, operant conditioning, and totalitarianism

4.   Pro's and con's of using punishment in classrooms

5.   Observation of children's preferences in classroom environments for application of Premack's principle of reinforcement

6.   Humanistic concerns and behavior modification

7.   Modification of a personal habit (for example, overeating, nail bitng) using principles of operant conditioning

CHAPTER 13   THE COGNITIVE PROCESSING OF INFORMATION

OBJECTIVES

The student should be able to

o construct a model of memory and explain each of the components

o define four kinds of arousing stimuli and give a classroom example of how each type could be used to evoke an orienting response

o include an advance organizer in a lesson plan

o define and give an example of schemata

o construct a mnemonic device for learning some curricular material

o give an example of how imagery can be used to enhance the associations connected with some material to be learned

o list and describe four techniques that help students retrieve information from long-term memory

REMINDER

Chapter 13 focused on how memory works and how learning from meaningful verbal material takes place. An information-processing model was presented, including a discussion of orienting responses--investigative responses to psychophysical, emotional, discrepant, and manding stimuli--and short-term and long-term memory. You will recall that retrieval from long-term memory is more efficient when meaningfulness is enhanced through the use of mediators, advance organizers, hierarchical structuring, organization, and appropriate schemata. You also learned about mathemagenic behaviors, that is, those behaviors that "give birth to learning," as well as four techniques that capitalize on mathemagenic processes associated with increased student retention: active recitation by students, use of physical activity in teaching, overlearning, and employment of mnemonic devices such as imagery, the method of loci, and the keyword method.

DEFINITIONS OF KEY CONCEPTS

The following key concepts were discussed in this chapter. In your own words, write the definition of each concept in the space provided.

1. Short-term sensory store _____

_____

_____

2. Short-term memory _____

_____

_____

3. Working memory _____

_____

_____

4. Long-term memory _____

_____

_____

5. Orienting responses _____

_____

_____

6. Psychophysical stimulus properties _____

_____

_____

7. Emotional stimulus properties _____

_____

_____

8. Discrepant stimulus properties _____

_____

_____

9. Manding stimuli _____

_____

_____

10. Propositions _____

_____

_____

11. Propositional networks _____

_____

_____

12. Mediation _____

_____

_____

13. An advance organizer _____

_____

_____

14. Schemata _____

_____

_____

15. Mathemagenic behaviors _____

_____

_____

16. Recitation _____

_____

_____

17. Overlearning _____

_____

_____

18. Mnemonic devices _____

_____

_____

19. Imagery _____

_____

_____

20. The method of loci _____

_____

_____

21. The keyword method _____

_____

_____

APPLICATION OF KEY CONCEPTS

The terms listed below refer to important concepts that were discussed in this chapter. Carefully read each descriptive statement, and identify the concept or concepts each statement implies. Place the corresponding letter(s) of the concept(s) you select in the space provided.

Concepts

A. emotional stimulus
B. short-term memory
C. working memory
D. advance organizer
E. orienting response
F. discrepant stimulus
G. psychophysical stimulus
H. long-term memory

I. recitation
J. manding stimulus
K. overlearning
L. mnemonic device
M. imagery
N. schemata
O. method of loci

Descriptive Statements

_____ 1. Mr. Loper will do almost anything to get his students' attention--this week he's role playing five different Shakespearean characters, and at the end of the class his students guess which character he had been that day.

_____ 2. If I can have your attention immediately, we'll begin.

_____ 3. I just close my eyes and imagine I'm walking to school. For every street I cross I "insert" a part of my speech. That way I can learn it in the right order.

_____ 4. "Twelve time six is?" "Seventy-two!" "Twelve time seven is?" "Eighty-four!"

_____ 5. My roommate frequently walks around the house saying lists of Russian vocabulary words.

_____ 6.   Today we will talk about the formation of fossils--their chemical substance, types of imprinting, and the conditions under which they are formed and preserved.

_____ 7.   When Stewart dropped his books, the whole class turned to look at him.

_____ 8.   The class was speechless when Mr. Cervantes came to school in shorts. He always dresses so formally.

_____ 9.   I could just barely overhear my name as the teacher and principal were talking in the hall.

_____ 10.   Let's see, now, what page did I just say that problem was on?

_____ 11.   When I see the word "lead" in print I automatically think of a major part in a play, whereas my roommate thinks of a metal. I guess that's because I'm a drama major and she's studying the physical sciences.

_____ 12.   I can remember the cranial nerves (olfactory, optic, ocular, trochlear, trigeminal, abducent . . .) by recalling a catchy phrase: On old Olympus' towering tops, a . . .

_____ 13.   I was able to thread the movie projector in class today without asking one of the students to help, but I still practiced threading it several times after class just to make sure I've got the hang of it.

_____ 14.   Just think of Rasputin as a seven-foot vodka sponge, with his hands on the throat of Mother Russia.

_____ 15.   I'll never forget the scene where Rhett Butler carries Scarlett O'Hara upstairs in "Gone With the Wind." It's indelibly etched in my mind--I've seen the movie so many times!

_____ 16.   My roommate laughed when he overheard me softly talking to myself when I was doing my statistics homework. I guess saying the steps to solve the problems helps me remember them.

MULTIPLE-CHOICE SELF-TEST

Select the response that best answers the question or completes the statement. Place the letter of the chosen answer in the space provided.

_____ 1.   According to the information-processing approach, stimulus inputs enter short-term sensory store, then progress to the
A.   enhanced association stage.
B.   long-term memory.
C.   coding system.
D.   short-term memory.

_____ 2.   Which of the following is the best example of an orienting response?
A.   Bobby looking up as someone walks through the door
B.   Tommy reading a novel
C.   Betty looking both ways before crossing a street

D. Sally watching a movie on television

3. Which of the following is the best example of a psychophysical stimulus-property change made by a teacher?
A. Assigning a reading lesson that is known for its exciting content
B. Reading to the class in the voices of the characters in the reading lesson
C. Calling out the name of the student who is to read a portion of the lesson

4. Which of the following is least likely to be one of the kinds of phenomena that can arouse an orienting response?
A. A color illustration in an otherwise black-and-white book
B. A frequently recurring phrase such as "and all that" in a lecture
C. An emotional word such as fantastic! in an otherwise dispassionate discourse
D. A man wearing a Scottish kilt at an American social gathering

5. Research on what is retained from school and college courses would lead you to expect that, of the following, the best retained kind of achievement would be the ability to
A. name specific parts of a complex structure.
B. identify technical terms.
C. interpret the data from an experiment.

6. According to the information-processing approach, the problem of being able to remember things that one has learned is
A. primarily a problem of storage and only slightly a problem of retrieval.
B. about equally a problem of storage and a problem of retrieval.
C. only slightly a problem of storage and primarily a problem of retrieval.

7. What type of representation of information is considered the most important by current theorists?
A. assertive
B. verbal
C. visual
D. propositional

8. A recent study found that young children learning to read were able to remember words such as murder, gold, mother, and toy better than words such as table, box, and paper. This is probably due to
A. the rehearsal strategies used.
B. differences in the richness of association of words.
C. mnemonic devices.
D. overlearning.

9. Ms. Grady is teaching the alphabet to kindergartners. She says, "And here's O. She is a fat lady who has no insides." Ms. Grady is using techniques based on
A. imagery.
B. verbal mediators.
C. rehearsal.
D. overlearning.

10. Research shows that the percentage of learned material retained by students is correlated with the intelligence of the students
A. very highly and positively-- about .75.
B. moderately and positively--about .30.

C. about zero.
D. moderately and negatively--about -.30.
E. very highly and negatively--about -.75.

_____11. Experiments have shown that the speed with which material is learned is correlated with the speed with which it is forgotten
A. positively.
B. about zero.
C. negatively.

_____12. The meaningfulness of information or stimuli is positvely related to the
A. number of associations a person can make to that information.
B. arbitrariness of the information.
C. freedom from structure of the information.
D. unfamiliarity of the information.

_____13. Mediation can best be illustrated by the activity of
A. resolving a conflict between which of two kinds of dessert to have by having a little of each.
B. using color as a way of increasing attention value.
C. putting two apparently unrelated words, such as squirrel and window, into a meaningful sentence.
D. determing the average difficulty of a set of tasks by averaging the percentages of those failing each task in the set.

_____14. Which of the following statements is the best example of schemata?
A. Human beings walk on two legs.
B. Chapter 12 introduces three new concepts.
C. After the second street light, turn left.
D. That smell just reminded me of Sunday morning donuts.

_____15. Which of the following is the best example of a mathemagenic behavior?
A. Engaging in repeated drill and practice of computational skills in mathematics
B. Deriving the proofs or rationales of mathematical formulas
C. Applying formulas to real-life problems
D. Reciting out loud when memorizing

_____16. In the learning of verbal material, overlearning is said to commence
A. after the first perfect response.
B. when errors are near zero.
C. when the subject gets a majority of the responses correct.

_____17. Which part of the brain is related to visual coding?
A. Right hemisphere
B. Left hemisphere
C. Both hemispheres equally
D. Depends on the handedness of a person

_____18. Which of the following ways of coding information does not enhance retrieval?
A. Systematic ordering of loci
B. Use of the working memory
C. Use of imagery
D. Logical organization

PROJECTS AND ACTIVITIES

1. Write out a list of nonsense syllables (of the form consonant-vowel-consonant) 20 items long--for example, CAJ, XOP, BYK--and have a few of your friends learn the list in serial order. Keep a count of the number of learning trials it takes each of your "subjects" to produce one perfect ordering of the list. Then ask them to recall the list in order 10 minutes later, one hour later, one day later, and one week later. Plot the data to see how a basic memory curve looks.

2. Have three different friends from those who participated in your first experiment (or three pupils, if you are a student teacher) learn a small set of nonsense syllables, say, 8 to 12 items. Have subject 1 study the list until he or she can recite it one time without making errors. Have Subject 2 study the list unitl he or she can recite it one time without error, then ask him or her to keep studying the list for half again as many trials as it took to learn it initially. Have Subject 3 study the list until he or she can recite it one time perfectly, and then ask him or her to keep studying the list for the same number of trials as it took to learn it initially.

Ask the subjects who were in the overlearning conditions how they felt going over the material they had already learned. Test all three of your subjects for recall one hour, one day, and one week after learning. Did overlearning improve recall?

3. Develop five mnemonic devices that can be used by students in your subject matter area. For example, a good mnemonic device for teaching children how to read musical notes is:

every	good	boy	does	fine
(E)	(G)	(B)	(D)	(F)

SUGGESTIONS FOR TERM PAPERS

1. Some suggestions for programming more mathemagenic processes into chemistry/civics/botany/etc.

2. Ways to provide multiple associations for important ideas in the teaching of third-grade reading/anatomy/Russian/etc.

3. The students' side of boredom: What puts them to sleep

4. How to incorporate advance organizers and mediators into written curriculum materials

5. How the great mnemonists work

6. Why forgetting is useful

7. Hemispheric dominance and cognitive functioning

CHAPTER 14   SOCIAL LEARNING THEORY

OBJECTIVES

The student should be able to

o compare and contrast a social learning view with an operant view of learning

o state the four phases involved in learning from models

o discuss how characteristics of both models and learners can affect what behavior is learned

o identify instances of vicarious reinforcement and punishment and note the consequences to the learner's behavior

o distinguish between "learning" and "performance"

o plan a program for a particular student to help that student regulate his or her own behavior.

REMINDER

In Chapter 14 you learned about social learning theory, a theory that combines ideas from operant conditioning and cognitive psychology. You read about how much of students' learning occurs from observing the behavior of others and the consequences of that behavior. You will recall that learning to match the performance of models involves four phases--the attentional, retention, reproduction, and motivational phases. The chapter concluded with a discussion of how teachers can help students regulate and control their own behavior by observing, judging, and determining the consequences for their own behavior.

DEFINITIONS OF KEY CONCEPTS

The following key concepts were discussed in this chapter. In your own words, write the definition of each concept in the space provided.

1.   Observational learning _____

_____

_____

2.   The attentional phase _____

_____

_____

3.   The retention phase _____

_____

_____

4.   The reproduction phase _____

_____

_____

5.   The motivational phase _____

_____

_____

6.   Vicarious reinforcement _____

_____

_____

7.   Vicarious punishment _____

_____

_____

APPLICATION OF KEY CONCEPTS

The terms listed below refer to important concepts that were discussed in this chapter. Carefully read each descriptive statement, and identify the concept or concepts each statement implies. Place the corresponding letter(s) of the concept(s) you select in the space provided.

Concepts

A.   attentional phase
B.   vicarious reinforcement
C.   motivational phase
D.   retention phase
E.   vicarious punishment
F.   reproduction phase

Descriptive Statements

_____ 1. Hilda got to be hall monitor yesterday for being the first one to finish page 32 in our workbook, so today I'm going to work quickly so I can finish first.

_____ 2. To remember how to play the left-hand part of "Chopsticks" on the piano, I just close my eyes and imagine where my sister puts her fingers when she plays that part.

_____ 3. Since Amy knows this part of the dance routine so well, I'd like all of you to carefully watch her perform it again. Just watch now.

_____ 4. I wouldn't do that if I were you. You heard what happened to Paul yesterday, didn't you? He had to pick up all the litter in the front and side yards.

_____ 5. Think of what I showed you yesterday about curving your back to the right in order to clear the bars. Now you all try that jump.

MULTIPLE-CHOICE SELF-TEST

Select the response that best answers the question or completes the statement. Place the letter of the chosen answer in the space provided.

_____ 1. Which of the following is not one of the phases involved in learning from models?
A. Attentional
B. Symbolic representational
C. Retention
D. Reproduction
E. Motivational

_____ 2. Factors that affect the likelihood that a model will be attended to are characteristics of the
A. model only.
B. learner only.
C. stimuli to be attended to.
D. model and learner.
E. model, learner, and stimuli to be attended to.

_____ 3. From the results of the study by Swanson and Henderson on training

A. modeling the behavior yourself for the child.
B. describing the behavior for the child and then having the child enact the behavior.
C. exposing the child to a model, then having the child enact the behavior.
D. encouraging the child to choose the learning method the child prefers.

_____ 4. During the student's initial enactment of a newly acquired behavior, teachers can be particularly helpful by providing
A. reinforcement for the correct aspects of a performance.
B. reinforcement for correct aspects and punishment for incorrect aspects of a performance.
C. reinforcement for correct aspects and corrective feedback for incorrect aspects of a performance.

_____ 5. In which of the following ways does social learning theory not incorporate an operant view?
   A. Covert cognitive activity affects the learner's behavior.
   B. Behavior acquired through observation is enacted if it's reinforced.
   C. Behavior acquired through observation is less likely to occur if it's punished.
   D. Consequences to one's own overt behavior will affect later enactment of the behavior.

_____ 6. Learning of the behavior of a model occurs
   A. if the viewer observed the model being reinforced.
   B. if the viewer has been provided with a positive incentive after viewing the model.
   C. after the viewer is exposed to the model's performance of the behavior.

_____ 7. Performance of the behavior of a model occurs
   A. if the viewer observed the model being reinforced.
   B. if the viewer has been provided with a positive incentive after viewing the model.
   C. after the viewer is exposed to the model's performance of the behavior.

_____ 8. If you asked students to collect their own data about how frequently they are inattentive during lab sections, you would expect that
   A. no prediction can be made about the students' future behavior.
   B. no change in the students' behavior will occur.
   C. inattention will increase because of the time the students must allow to record their behavior.
   D. inattention will decrease as a result of self-evaluation and self-determined reinforcement.

_____ 9. To be most effective, a teacher who wants students' performance to reflect high standards should attend to
   A. reinforcement of the students' high standards.
   B. modeling of the high standards.
   C. modeling of the high standards, coupled with reinforcement when the students meet the high standards.
   D. matching of the students' own self-expectation with their behavior.

_____ 10. The viewing of televised violence and children's aggressive behavior are
   A. postively correlated.
   B. negatively correlated.
   C. unrelated.
   D. causally related.

_____ 11. Social learning theorists view the observed consequences of behavior as
   A. determiners of learning.
   B. motivators of learning.
   C. direct causes of learning.
   D. unrelated to learning.

PROJECTS AND ACTIVITIES

1. As an exercise to aid in understanding the practical importance and power of social learning theory, select one session of your educational psychology class to carefully observe

your instructor as a model. Monitor your own behavior, noting when you are in the attending, retention, reproduction, and motivational phases of learning through observation. Think about how the active behavior of both the model and the student are required to explain the learner's acquisition of a response. During the next meeting of your class, repeat the same exercise, but apply only the principles of an operant view to explain your acquisition of new behaviors. Which view best accounts for your learning, or are both required?

2. Go to the library and read several of Albert Bandura's articles describing his experimental work. If possible replicate, that is, reproduce the procedures of, the basic design of the experiment(s) with students of the age you will be working with in the future. If children or adolescents are not available, then role-play the procedure with other students in your class. Think about those characteristics of the model and those of the learner that affect what and how well new behaviors are learned.

SUGGESTIONS FOR TERM PAPERS

1. The influence of operant conditioning on social learning theory

2. The influence of cognitive psychology on social learning theory

3. The power of self-observation and self-regulation in changing one's own behavior

4. A training program to increase teachers' effectiveness as models during third/fifth/etc. grade reading/spelling/math/geography/etc.

5. The effect of teachers' standards on students' performance at the elementary/junior high/high school level

6. The effects of televised violence on children's aggression.

7. Pros and cons of television censorship.

CHAPTER 15   IMPROVING THE TRANSFER OF LEARNING

OBJECTIVES

The student should be able to

o define transfer of learning

o contrast the concepts of identity of substance and identity of procedure

o give an example of negative transfer

o demonstrate stimulus predifferentiation when teaching a new topic

o predict the amount of transfer likely to occur under different conditions of stimulus similarity and response similarity

o implement six guidelines to improve the positive transfer of learning

o differentiate in writing between teaching for substantive transfer and procedural transfer

o monitor your own metacognitive thoughts during your learning of the material in this chapter

o identify instances of expert and novice problem-solving strategies

REMINDER

This chapter introduced you to traditional and contemporary views regarding the transfer of learning. Since the goal of teaching is to have your students show evidence of learning in situations outside of school, you read about how positive transfer occurs when teachers provide a variety of explanations, use different examples, provide practice, differentiate among similar stimuli, teach rules with wide generalizability, and provide real-life situations for training. You'll recall that experts and novices approach problem solving differently, and that some skills used by experts are teachable by helping students effectively use metacognitive strategies during learning. These strategies include self-monitoring, self-questioning, problem identification, dismissal of irrelevant information, and visualization during problem solving. Chapter 15 also taught you to differentiate between teaching for substantive transfer and for procedural transfer--two approaches that are complimentary, not mutually exclusive.

DEFINITIONS OF KEY CONCEPTS

The following key concepts were discussed in this chapter. In your own words, write the definition of each concept in the space provided.

1. Transfer of learning _____

   _____

   _____

2. Theory of identical elements _____

   _____

   _____

3. Doctrine of formal discipline _____

   _____

   _____

4. Identity of substance _____

   _____

   _____

5. Identity of procedure _____

   _____

   _____

6. Transfer value of principles _____

   _____

   _____

7. Negative transfer _____

   _____

   _____

8. Metacognition _____

   _____

   _____

9. Cognitive-skill training _____

_____

_____

10. Stimulus predifferentiation _____

_____

_____

APPLICATION OF KEY CONCEPTS

The terms listed below refer to important concepts that were discussed in this chapter. Carefully read each descriptive statement, and identify the concept or concepts each statement implies. Place the corresponding letter(s) of the concept(s) you select in the space provided.

Concepts

A. identity of substance
B. identity of procedure
C. doctrine of formal discipline
D. transfer value of principles

E. stimulus predifferentiation
F. negative transfer of learning
G. metacognition

Descriptive Statements

_____ 1. An elementary school student who has learned that a singular-number subject must take a singular-number verb uses a plural-number verb in a sentence with a plural-number subject.

_____ 2. Our typing teacher told us today that to be effective secretaries we must learn to take dictation at a rate of at least 90 words per minute.

_____ 3. If you don't bother to vote in your class elections, you may not take the time or have the interest to vote in state and federal elections when you're older.

_____ 4. Learning physiology helps you understand not only how your body functions, but also how to keep your body as healthy as possible.

_____ 5. I keep forgetting that this year's teacher doesn't like us to ask questions while she's explaining something, because our teacher last year always encouraged us to ask questions at any time.

_____ 6. Although a sonnet may resemble other poetry written in iambic pentameter, it is important to know its unique characteristics.

_____ 7. My parents keep telling me how important it is that I study mathematics. They say it will "improve my mind."

_____ 8. I just identified the ten important points in this chapter. I figure I'll need to review them one more time from my notes before I feel confident that I can paraphrase them.

MULTIPLE-CHOICE SELF-TEST

   Select the response that best answers the question or completes the statement.
Place the letter of the chosen answer in the space provided.

_____ 1. Given the two signs above, we might analyze the situation as
             A. stimuli different, responses similar.
             B. stimuli different, responses different.
             C. stimuli similar, responses different.
             D. stimuli similar, responses similar.

_____ 2. $(\underline{X} + 2)(\underline{X} + 4)=0$;   = square; <u>E pluribus unum</u> means "one from many."
             In this situation, what is the relation of stimuli and responses?
             A. Stimuli different, responses similar
             B. Stimuli different, responses different
             C. Stimuli similar, responses different
             D. Stimuli similar, responses similar

_____ 3. The doctrine of formal discipline would support the value of
             A. studying logic as a way to improve reasoning power in all fields.
             B. studying Sanskrit as a way of improving ability to read Sanskrit.
             C. discipling a child in order to help her correct her chonic tardiness.
             D. learning Archimedes' law.

_____ 4. A teacher wants ot maximize the substantive transfer value to students of
             learning to become proficient in recognizing trees of various kinds; therefore,
             the teacher will give them practice in
             A. analyzing the shapes of leaves into basic geometric figures.
             B. learning the Latin names of the major families of trees.
             C. translating the Latin names into English names, and vice versa.
             D. naming trees on a visit to an arboretum.

_____ 5. Teaching students the general formula for solving quadratic equations, namely,

             $x = \dfrac{-b \pm \sqrt{b^2 - 4\,ac}}{2a}$, is an example of teaching for
             A. formal discipline.
             B. identical elements.
             C. procedural transfer.
             D. stimulus-response transfer.

_____ 6. Tim has learned that he can get an A on his literature papers if he waits until the
             night a paper is due and then writes a "free-flowing, personal" essay. When he
             applies this knowledge to his drama papers, however, he receives a D. All other
             things being equal, this is an example of
             A. no transfer.

       B. positive transfer.
       C. negative transfer.
       D. interfering transfer.

_____ 7. Sara has learned how to conjugate the verb to plant. When she is given the verb to pick, you would predict
       A. strong positive transfer.
       B. slight positive transfer.
       C. strong negative transfer.
       D. slight negative transfer.

_____ 8. In her fifth-grade science lesson, Alice learned Bernoulli's principle, that is, the faster a fluid (liquid or gas) flows over a surface, the lower the pressure of the fluid on the surface. As an example, her teacher demonstrated that a playing card could be lifted easily by blowing across the card parallel to the surface on which it lay. What would you predict about the correctness of Alice's explanation when she is asked to explain how an airplane wing lifts a plane off the ground (which we know to be an application of Bernoulli's principle)?
       A. Strong positive transfer
       B. Slight positive transfer
       C. Strong negative transfer
       D. Slight negative transfer
       E. Nothing, because no prediction is possible

_____ 9. "Students should study geometry so that they can develop their ability to reason logically." This statement would be offered by someone adhering to
       A. the narrow form of Thorndike's theory of identical elements.
       B. the broad form of Thorndike's theory of identical elements.
       C. the theory of formal discipline.
       D. a theory of generalization training.

_____ 10. As the basis of the broad form of Thorndike's theory of identical elements, you should teach
       A. as much subject matter as possible.
       B. students to discriminate between stimulus conditions.
       C. generally applicable principles and procedures.
       D. students to like geometry.

_____ 11. Traditional theories of transfer focused on similarity of elements across learning situations, whereas contempory views of transfer focus on
       A. similarity of responses.
       B. thought processes of people who demonstrate ability to generalize.
       C. the learning demands of the particular situations.
       D. the actual content of what is to be transferred.

_____ 12. Research indicates that students who are taught metacognitive strategies show
       A. superior reading ability, but no change in comprehension.
       B. no consistent increase in achievement.
       C. increased self-monitoring, but a baseline level of achievement.
       D. increased comprehension ability.

_____ 13. Which of the following is not a metacognitve skill?
       A. Self-questioning
       B. Maintained focus

      C.   Verbatim recitation
      D.   Paraphrasing

_____14. Teachers interested in teaching for transfer should avoid
      A.   exposing students to a vast array of knowledge domains.
      B.   modeling problem solving strategies.
      C.   fostering in-depth student experience with a knowledge domain.
      D.   demonstrating how to classfiy problems by category.

PROJECTS AND ACTIVITIES

1. Initiate a tutoring session with a young child who is just learning to print the alphabet. Focus on teaching the child the difference between a small b and a small d. Be sure to keep notes about the child's errors, his or her comments, and the approximate amount of time spent in learning how to print these two letters. Schedule a second session to teach your student how to print a small p and small q. Again keep notes of what happened during the session. Did it take less time for the child to master the letters p and q? What do you think was the role of transfer in the second learning situation?

2. Examine an existing curriculum unit of your choosing for its transferability. Does the unit provide for stimulus predifferentiation? Does it contain instances of identity of substance and identity of procedure? If not, what revisions of the unit would you make to ensure positive transfer of learning?

3. Choose a subject area and design a one-hour lesson in a way that meets the following criteria. First, design the lesson so that what is taught in the initial stages can be transferred to what is to be taught in the later stages. Second, explicitly identify how you would assess the degree to which learning of the initial parts of the lesson was achieved and how well this learning transferred to the later parts of the lesson.

4. Incorporate at least five of the guidelines for enhancing metacognition skills in your own studying and learning of educational psychology. Do this consciously for at least three weeks, keeping a record of specific strategies you used. For example, jot down questions that might be asked by your instructor or peers, what points were particularly difficult for you, how you related new information to your existing knowledge, how often you asked a collegue for help in understanding a given point, and so on. Did conscious attention to sharpening your own metacogntive skills lead to increased comprehension? Which skills did you previously use in your learning? Which new skills will you use as you approach other learning situations? Do you behave more like an expert or a novice problem solver?

SUGGESTIONS FOR TERM PAPERS

1.   Some specific suggestions for incorporating principles of positive transfer into a fifth-grade reading/elementary school art/language arts/etc. curriculum

2.   A critical analysis of a unit of instruction in geometry/music/creative writing/etc. in order to examine its potential for positive and negative transfer

3.   A historical overview of the doctrine of formal discipline and its relevance to current teaching practices

4.   Implementing a cognitive-skills training program for junior high school students

5.   The case of real-life learning situations in academic programs

CHAPTER 16   THE INFLUENCE OF MOTIVATION ON LEARNING

OBJECTIVES

The student should be able to

o define <u>motivation</u>

o compare and contrast <u>states</u> and <u>traits</u>

o name at least five terms for concepts closely related to motivation

o describe the concepts of underachievement and overachievement

o explain Maslow's theory of motivation

REMINDER

Intellectual ability alone cannot account for the differences in the academic performance of students. Motivation must also be taken into account. In this chapter you learned that the concept of motivation is needed to explain why students with similar abilities perform differently, and why an individual student's performance on the same task is different at different times and under different circumstances. You also read about how motivation determines what makes a reinforcer, accounts for goal orientation, and is linearly related to the time spent in various activities.

DEFINITIONS OF KEY CONCEPTS

The following key concepts were discussed in this chapter. In your own words, write the definition of each concept in the space provided.

1. Motivation _____

_____

_____

2. Traits _____

_____

_____

3. States _____

_____

_____

4. Interest _____

_____

_____

5. Need _____

_____

_____

6. Value _____

_____

_____

7. Attitude _____

_____

_____

8. Aspiration _____

_____

_____

9. Incentive _____

_____

_____

10. Overachievement _____

_____

_____

11. Underachievement _____

_____

_____

12. Psychogenic needs _____

_____

_____

13. Self-actualization _____

_____

_____

APPLICATION OF KEY CONCEPTS

The terms listed below refer to important concepts that were discussed in this chapter. Carefully read each descriptive statement, and identify the concept or concepts each statement implies. Place the corresponding letter(s) of the concept(s) you select in the space provided.

Concepts

A. state
B. trait
C. incentive
D. attitude
E. value
F. aspiration

G. underachievement
H. need
I. interest
J. overachievement
K. psychogenic need

Descriptive Statements

_____1. Since Cindy became a stamp collector almost a month ago, she's read four books on the subject and collected several unique stamps.

_____2. Everybody always says how calm, gentle, and kind he is.

_____3. When I grow up, I'm going to be a musician like my mother.

_____4. It's really important for people to be considerate of each other--you know, polite and kind to each other. That's why I try to act that way.

_____5. All of his teachers agree that he is a very capable student--if he would only put his mind to it instead of playing around.

_____6. I'm always very cautious and conservative about supporting a candidate. I don't trust any of them!

_____7. I just can't seem to help myself. I have this real desire to buy clothes all the time.

_____8. Knowing that I'll get straight A's this quarter keeps me working on this last assignment.

_____ 9. I looked in her cumulative file and saw that her IQ is a little below average, yet she's always gotten A's and B's on her report cards.

_____ 10. I've never been so excited about anything in my life as I am about this date tonight.

_____ 11. I was dying of thirst after the game, so I literally ran to the beer keg.

MULTIPLE-CHOICE SELF-TEST

Select the response that best answers the question or completes the statement. Place the letter of the chosen answer in the space provided.

_____ 1. For a teacher, motivating students is <u>least</u> defensible on the grounds that
    A. we want students to regard their school work as somehow "relevant."
    B. motivation can serve as both an objective in itself and a means for furthering achievement of toher educational objectives.
    C. we want to avoid the negative extrement at which students become so frustrated and dissatisfied that they want to drop out of school.
    D. only highly motivated students succeed.

_____ 2. Motivation is a diffuse concept and is often tied to other factors. Which of the following is <u>not</u> a factor that directly influences the energy and direction of behavior?
    A. Interest
    B. Need
    C. Value
    D. Intellect

_____ 3. A value is
    A. an incentive that arouses instrumental activity.
    B. an orientation toward a whole class of goals as important in one's life.
    C. an emotional matter, having directionality, an object, and cognitive elements.
    D. a hope or longing for a certain kind of achievement.

_____ 4. The concept of motivation is <u>not</u> needed to account for which of the following facts about behavior and learning?
    A. The goal orientation of behavior
    B. What is reinforcing
    C. The benefits of "overlearning"
    D. The persistence of behavior

_____ 5. The relationship between time spent in a particular activity and motive strength is
    A. curvilinear.
    B. linear.
    C. scattered.
    D. circular.

_____ 6. Daphne is in a high school English class. She likes reading contemporary novels. However, she is not particularly interested in romantic poetry. We would predict that she would most likely spend

A. about an equal amount of time reading both types of literature.
B. more time reading poetry, since it is more difficult for her.
C. more time reading novels, since she likes them.
D. an unpredictable amount of time reading either poetry or novels.

_____ 7. Student overachievement or underachievement can best be accounted for by
A. motivation.
B. the inaccuracy of measures of intelligence or aptitude.
C. acute awareness of the operational procedures of the system.
D. subject matter content.

_____ 8. Some theories of motivation rely on two factors; Murray (1938), however, offered a long list of what he labeled
A. psychological needs.
B. psychosexual needs.
C. psychogenic needs.
D. hierarchical motivational needs.

_____ 9. Which of the following is not included among the sets of needs listed by Maslow?
A. Safety
B. Love and belonging
C. Esteem
D. Self-actualization
E. Social awareness

_____ 10. Maslow's list of needs was arranged in order of
A. increasing complexity.
B. decreasing complexity.
C. increasing priority.
D. decreasing priority.

_____ 11. Which of the following phrases best describes motivation?
A. Explains activity, but not inactivity
B. Refers to the factors that increase and decrease the energy of students' activity
C. Takes into account the effects of intelligence, environment, and habit on human experience
D. Is a difficult concept to study because it is determined by factors of which the student is not conscious

_____ 12. Arousal describes
A. the general state of excitability of an organism.
B. a momentary belief about the likelihood that a particular outcome will follow a particular set.
C. goal objects.
D. an expected reinforcer

PROJECTS AND ACTIVITIES

1. To understand something about the power of motivation (and perhaps to help you lose some weight), fast for a full day. If you customarily take your dinner with other people, continue to do so, but don't eat. Keep track of your thoughts. See how many times between

6 and 10 o'clock you have food fantasies. How many times did food predominate in your thoughts? As you fast, think about Maslow's notion that basic needs must be satisfied before one can even attempt to satisfy higher needs.

2. College counseling offices or testing centers administer low-cost interest inventories to their students. Make an appointment to take one or more of these tests. You might want to specifically ask for the Allport-Vernon-Lindzey Study of Values. If you're curious about your measured vocational interests, ask to take the Kuder Preference Record, Vocational or the Strong Vocational Interest Blank. When you receive the results, think about how motives, interests, and values guide the decisions you make in your life.

SUGGESTIONS FOR TERM PAPERS

1. The concepts of overachievement and underachievement in the educational system

2. Characteristics of the self-actualized individual

3. Trait and state motives in elementary/junior high/senior high school students

4. Level of aspiration and student achievement

5. Student perserverance as a predictor of achievement.

CHAPTER 17   PERSONALITY FACTORS IN MOTIVATION

OBJECTIVES

The student should be able to

o describe how achievement imagery is measured and give an example of an achievement-oriented story

o contrast the behavior of individuals motivated to succeed and those motivated to avoid failure

o describe the attribution of reasons for success and failure by internal and external locus of control

o contrast the concepts of "origin" and "pawn"

o describe the affiliation and approval-dependent motives and their associated classroom behavior

o plan an achievement-training program and an attribution-training program

REMINDER

This chapter focused on students' needs for affiliation, power, approval, and especially achievement. Achievement motivation may be of two types: automomous and social. Achievement motivation also originates from two sources: the need to succeed and the need to avoid failure. You learned that students vary in their attribution of reasons for success and failure. Students who attribute their successes and failures to their own behavior have an internal locus of control, whereas those who attribute their successes and failures to chance or task difficulty have an external locus of control. Finally, you learned how to discover students' predominant motive and attributional patterns and how to improve the achievement motivation of students by direct training to change behavior or to change how students think about their behavior. An understanding of students' achievement motivation is important because of the relationship with important variables, such as persistence, risk taking, and quality of performance.

DEFINITIONS OF KEY CONCEPTS

The following key concepts were discussed in this chapter. In your own words, write the definition of each concept in the space provided.

1. Thematic Apperception Test _____

_____

_____

2. Autonomous achievement motivation _____

_____

_____

3. Social achievement motivation _____

_____

_____

4. Achievement motivation _____

_____

_____

5. Internal locus of control _____

_____

_____

6. External locus of control _____

_____

_____

7. Learned helplessness _____

_____

_____

8. An "origin" _____

_____

_____

9. A "pawn" _____

_____

_____

10. Affiliation motives _____

_____

_____

11. Power motives _____

_____

_____

12. Need for approval _____

_____

_____

APPLICATION OF KEY CONCEPTS

The terms listed below refer to important concepts that were discussed in this chapter. Carefully read each descriptive statement, and identify the concept or concepts each statement implies. Place the corresponding letter(s) of the concept(s) you select in the space provided.

Concepts

A. motivation to succeed
B. motivation to avoid failure
C. "pawn"
D. affiliation motive
E. internal locus of control
F. power motive
G. "origin"
H. need for approval
I. external locus of control
J. autonomous achievement motivation
K. social achievement motivation
L. learned helplessness

Descriptive Statements

_____ 1. I worked several hours on that homework assignment last night because I didn't want to be called on today and not know the answer in front of the whole class.

_____ 2. It's really frustrating talking to Ellen because she'll never give you a straight answer—you know, she'll never tell you her opinion without qualifying it a dozen different ways. I think she's afraid she might offend me or something.

_____ 3. I don't even want to study anymore. It doesn't make a difference anyway. I just never catch on.

_____ 4. Even though calculus is very difficult for me, I know that if I practice working the problems over and over again, I'll finally master it.

_____ 5. Albert likes to get good grades in school, but his main interest seems to be talking to everybody during study period.

_____ 6. Laurence always tries to monopolize the conversation and dominate the decisions made by our group.

_____ 7. I've got to keep practicing my scales. Deborah still has a higher singing range than I.

_____ 8. That was the dumbest test I've ever taken—no wonder I didn't do well. I thought the test was going to be multiple-choice and instead the teacher gave us all those true-false questions.

_____ 9. Once I started working on solving the quadratic equation problems, I couldn't stop. I got so interested in the orderliness of the computational steps required that I just wanted to keep working them until I had them all correct.

_____ 10. I'm really excited that I broke my own swimming record from last year, even though there were others in the competition who were much faster than I.

MULTIPLE-CHOICE SELF-TEST

Select the response that best answers the question or completes the statement. Place the letter of the chosen answer in the space provided.

_____ 1. As part of a battery of psychological tests, Jane was shown a picture of a man standing by his car. The scene appears to be a superhighway, the car's hood is up, and the man has his thumb out to hitch a ride. She was asked, "Does this suggest anything to you?" Would this situation qualify as one that might appear in the Thematic Apperception Test?
   A. Yes
   B. Yes, but only if it is assumed that Jane knows someone who looks like the man pictured
   C. No, because the stimulus does not allow Jane to project her fantasies
   D. No, because Jane was not directly told to fantasize about the scene

_____ 2. Ted, one of your better students, is known to be high in achievement motivatin. Therefore, you would expect him to do especially well with tasks that
   A. require only a small amount of organization.
   B. are not interrupted.
   C. demand long periods of performance without external reinforcement.

_____ 3. When can failure at a task be motivating to approach the task again?
   A. When $M_s > M_{af}$
   B. When $M_s < M_{af}$
   C. When $M_s = M_{af}$
   D. Almost never

_____ 4. In which type of class would you expect the various research findings about achievement motivation to hold best?
   A. An all-female class
   B. An all-male class
   C. A class consisting of both males and females

_____ 5. Research has shown that regular classroom teachers

A. cannot be trained to improve students' achievement motivation.
B. can be trained to produce improved student achievement motivation, which, in turn, results in improved performance.
C. can be trained to produce improved student achievement motivation, but that this improvement does not alter their students' performance.

_____ 6. At about what age does social achievement motivation become more prevalent than autonomous achievement motivation?
A. Five
B. Seven
C. Ten
D. Thirteen
E. Eighteen

_____ 7. When Jennifer's teacher asked her why she did so poorly on her homework assignment, Jennifer said it was probably because she hadn't tried as hard as she could. We can assume that this student's achievement motivation is
A. low.
B. moderate.
C. high.

_____ 8. Some findings of research on achievement motivation have been surprising. For instance, students who are more highly motivated to avoid failure than to succeed will
A. decrease their work output with success.
B. work persistently and at a high level in programmed instruction.
C. be challenged to increase their efforts when met with failure.
D. do better when exposed to a system of strict grading.

_____ 9. One major problem in using the concepts of motivation to avoid failure and motivation to succeed in everyday teaching is that
A. these variables are not very often related to performance.
B. students' motivational patterns are constantly changing.
C. measurement techniques for assessing these variables are not readily available.

_____ 10. A good way for a teacher to help a child high in external attribution is to
A. reinforce and model internal attribution.
B. reinforce and model external attribution.
C. help the student understand that sometimes luck contributes to success or failure.
D. provide situations of low difficulty so that the student doesn't experience failure.

_____ 11. To what do students generally attribute their school successes and school failures, respectively?
A. External factors and internal factors
B. Internal factors and external factors
C. Both internal and external factors equally

_____ 12. Sam is more likely than Sally to explain an A grade in terms of
A. luck.
B. ease of test.
C. ability.

_____13. Why do students with an internal locus of control for failure often just give up trying to learn?
A. Low effort is more socially acceptable than low ability.
B. Low ability is more socially acceptable than low effort.
C. Low ability is highly correlated with internal locus of control.
D. Students accurately estimate their low ability.

_____14. Coleman (1966) found that white children are more likely than black children to believe that their school success was due to
A. effort.
B. ability.
C. luck.

_____15. The attribution training programs to increase achievement motivation focus on
A. increasing skill level.
B. moving toward greater external locus of control.
C. improving actual accomplishment.
D. modeling and reinforcement of internal attributions.

_____16. You observe that Peter is always saying things like "I know I can do better than that" and "Maybe if I try it this way I can do it without help." Which of the following is a good description of Peter?
A. Origin
B. Need actualizer
C. Motivated by the approval of others
D. Pawn

_____17. A student who is high in affiliative needs will be more likely to
A. have higher task persistence than a student with high achievement motivation.
B. be chosen as a work partner by a student who has high affiliative needs.
C. do a great many problems in an allotted time.
D. choose a partner with high achievement motivation.

_____18. Ms. Kilner knows that Millie has low need for achievement and high need for affiliation. To best promote harmonious relations between Millie and her partner, Ms. Kilner should assign a student who is
A. high in need achievement.
B. good at the task.
C. friendly.
D. low in affiliation need.

_____19. In classes in which volunteering is not encouraged explicitly by the teacher, which type of student would probably receive a higher grade, all other things being equal?
A. Males with high power needs
B. Males with low power needs
C. Females with high power needs
D. Females with low power needs

_____20. The approval-dependent student would most likely exhibit which of the following?
A. High achievement motivation, but poor performance
B. Verbal aggression toward others

      C.   Overcompensatory independence
      D.   High affiliative needs, but has few good friends

PROJECTS AND ACTIVITIES

1.   Go through a magazine and pick out a picture that seems ambiguous. Using the four Thematic Apperception Test questions presented in the text (p.388), ask a few friends or students to respond to your picture. If you know the students well (or their teacher can help you), select one student who really strives for excellence, one student who seems unconcerned about academic success, and one student who seems to be very anxious about academic work. If you are questioning friends, select them using the same criteria. See whether the kinds of stories they make up about the ambiguous picture gives you any insight into their motivational patterns.

2.   A technique for finding out how a class regards the achievement and affiliative motives of each of its members is to give students a questionnaire asking them which of their classmates they would like to work with in a group situation when the goals of the group differ. Possible items would include: "Pick the three students in your class whom you'd like to be with in a group when you want the flow of the group discussion to go smoothly and in a friendly manner." "Pick the three students in your class whom you'd like to be with in a group when you want your group to get done the job it has been assigned to do."

Administer your questionnaire and see whether there is consensus among the class about those members who have higher affiliation needs and those members who have higher achievement needs.

SUGGESTIONS FOR TERM PAPERS

1.   Achievement motivation in women/minorities/handicapped students

2.   A review of achievement-motivation training for low-income students

3.   Need for achievement and capitalism

4.   Achievement imagery in children's stories

5.   Teaching the approval-dependent student

6.   Implementing an attribution-training program at the elementary/secondary level

7.   The development of social achievement motivation

TECHNICAL NOTE E

DETERMINING MOTIVATION TO SUCCEED AND MOTIVATION TO AVOID FAILURE

The text discusses two types of motivated students: those who want to succeed, and those who are frightened of failure. We have already discussed the kinds of predictions that have been made about the tasks that each type of student prefers to engage in. The theoretical model behind that research is interesting, and is presented here.

The basic question is, How can we differentiate a student motivated by fear of failure from one motivated by desire to do well? The approach taken by Atkinson (1964) considered (a) anxiety level (measured by a paper-and-pencil self-report test of anxiety) as a person's tendency to avoid failure, or M_{af}; (b) the probability of success for particular tasks, or P_s; and (c) the incentive value of a task, or I_s, which equals $1 - P_s$ (see Weiner, 1972).

All in all, a student's tendency to avoid failure T_{af} is a function of his or her enduring motive to avoid failure M_{af}, the probability of success P_s, and the incentive value of success I_s. Symbolically,

$$T_{af} = M_{af} \times P_s \times I_s$$

which is really the measure of how aversive a task would be, or how much anxiety would be aroused before the task is performed.

Now suppose the tendency to succeed T_s is also seen as a function of (a) the motive to succeed M_s measured with the TAT, as was described in Chapter 17; (b) the probability of success P_s; and (c) the incentive value of the task I_s. The symbolic equation for estimating the tendency to succeed is

$$T_s = M_s \times P_s \times I_s$$

RESULTANT ACHIEVEMENT MOTIVATION

Resultant achievement motivation may be defined as T_s minus T_{af}. When P_s and I_s are held constant, as they are for any single task, then resultant achievement motivation becomes M_s minus M_{af}.

We have reasons for this little excursion into symbolic equations. By substituting hypothetical values for the symbols, we obtain interesting results. Table E-1 presents two sets of hypothetical data. The top half of the table presents a case in which the motive to achieve is high (say, 10 units on an arbitrary scale) and the motive to avoid failure is low (say, 3 units). By considering the different values of P_s and Is, we can see that the tendency to undertake a particular task (which is simply $T_s - T_{af}$ is greatest when the probability of success is .5. The data indicate that tasks of intermediate difficulty should be most

153

attractive to people high in achievement needs and low in their concern with failure, that is, where $M_s > M_{af}$.

The bottom half of Table E-1 presents a different situation. Here M_s is low (3 units) and M_{af} is high (10 units). For various values of P_s and I_s, the resultant tendency to approach a task becomes least negative when the task is very easy or very hard. The tendency to approach a task is most negative when the task is of intermediate difficulty. This is exactly the opposite of what we found when $M_s > M_{af}$.

The data from these two hypothetical cases point out that when $M_s > M_{af}$, tasks of medium difficulty are most positively motivating. When $M_{af} > M_s$, tasks of easy or difficult levels are least negatively motivating. The application of these data to predictions about school behavior is given in Chapter 17 of the text.

Table E-1
Hypothetical Data for Determining Tendency to Approach a Task

		Tendency to Succeed (T_s)				Tendency to Avoid Failure (T_{af})				Tendency to Approach Task
	M_s	P_s	I_s	$=$	T_s	M_{af}	P_s	I_s	$=$	T_{af}	$T_s - T_{af}$
High achievement motivation and low anxiety	10	.9	.1	=	.90	3	.9	.1	=	.27	.63
	10	.7	.3	=	2.10	3	.7	.3	=	.63	1.47
	10	.5	.5	=	2.50	3	.5	.5	=	.75	1.75
	10	.3	.7	=	2.10	3	.3	.7	=	.63	1.47
	10	.1	.9	=	.90	3	.1	.9	=	.27	.63
High anxiety and low achievement motivation	3	.9	.1	=	.27	10	.9	.1	=	.90	− .63
	3	.7	.3	=	.63	10	.7	.3	=	2.10	−1.47
	3	.5	.5	=	.75	10	.5	.5	=	2.50	−1.75
	3	.3	.7	=	.63	10	.3	.7	=	2.10	−1.47
	3	.1	.9	=	.27	10	.1	.9	=	.90	− .63

REFERENCES

Atkinson, J.W. (1964) An introduction to motivation. Princeton, N.J.: Van Nostrand.

Weiner, Bernard (1972) Theories of motivation. From mechanism to cognition. Chicago, Ill.: Markham.

CHAPTER 18   ENVIRONMENTAL FACTOR IN MOTIVATION

OBJECTIVES

The student should be able to

o define intrinsic and extrinsic motivation

o develop a motivational contract

o construct a token economy system

o name the conditions that give rise to frustration and state three or more behaviors that often follow frustrating experiences

o write a lesson plan that makes use of suspense, curiosity, and discovery

o explain a set of rules for a new learning game in any subject matter area

o define and give examples of the five bases of social power

REMINDER

Chapter 18 distinguished between intrinsic and extrinsic motivation, cautioning the teacher to use extrinsic rewards to induce student engagement, but to withdraw those rewards as soon as intrinsic rewards appear. You read that frustration is motivating, and typically results in aggressive behavior. Therefore, the chapter provided some ideas on how behavior modification approaches, such as the use of token economies and motivational contracting, can control and redirect student frustration and aggression. The chapter also discussed techniques that teachers can use to increase student motivation. These include use of verbal praise; use of suspense, discovery, and curiosity to arouse students; and use of stimulation and games. An examination of the classroom and school concluded the chapter.

DEFINITIONS OF KEY CONCEPTS

The following key concepts were discussed in this chapter. In your own words, write the definition of each concept in the space provided.

1. Intrinsic motivation _____
   _____
   _____

2. Extrinsic motivation _____
   _____
   _____

3. An incentive _____
   _____
   _____

4. Discontinued reinforcement _____
   _____
   _____

5. Frustrated behavior _____
   _____
   _____

6. Token economies _____
   _____
   _____

7. Motivational contracts _____
   _____
   _____

8. Social rewards _____
   _____
   _____

9. Epistemic curiosity _____
   _____
   _____

10. "Ethos" _____

_____

_____

11. Reward Power _____

_____

_____

12. Coercive Power _____

_____

_____

13. Legitimate power _____

_____

_____

14. Referent Power _____

_____

_____

15. Expert Power _____

_____

_____

APPLICATION OF KEY CONCEPTS

The terms listed below refer to important concepts that were discussed in this chapter. Carefully read each descriptive statement, and identify the concept or concepts each statement implies. Place the corresponding letter(s) of the concept(s) you select in the space provided.

Concepts

A   token economy
B. frustration
C. intrinsic motivation
D. discontinued reinforcement
E. motivational contract
F. incentive
G. extrinsic motivation
H. referent power

I.   "ethos'
J.   epistemic curiosity
K. functional autonomy
L. expert power
M. social reward
N. legitimate power
O. coercive power
P. reward power

Descriptive Statements

_____ 1. I've had a course in public speaking, so I think I should represent our committee at the hearing.

_____ 2. As the president of the PTA, I'd like to congratulate you all on the success of the candy drive last month.

_____ 3. I'm going to continue doing two chemistry problems a week so that I can keep up the A grade I have in the class.

_____ 4. I could tell that Lynn was really irritated when Mac didn't call; she was so sure he would.

_____ 5. So, if I do all the homework problems right for a week, Ms. Snyder, I get to be in the group that goes to tutor the third graders.

_____ 6. What's this all about--he said we'd get to cut up frogs today, so why is he getting out his lecture notes?

_____ 7. Bobby has put that puzzle together three times now; I just don't understand why he keeps working on it.

_____ 8. The morale of this faculty is at an all-time low over this particular issue.

_____ 9. Paul, sit down this minute and keep still! All right, you'll stay in during recess to practice.

_____ 10. I've noticed that Heather will do anything Barb asks her to do--Heather just idolizes Barb.

_____ 11. I got so interested in the history of early California after seeing that movie that I'm going to take some courses to learn more about it.

_____ 12. Julio's able to work quite independently on his biology assignments now; in fact, I think he actually enjoys doing them.

_____ 13. I'd like to turn in these points for a pass to leave early today.

_____ 14. He really wants to be class president--that's why he campaigning so hard.

_____ 15. There is just no pleasing Mr. Ebeling. He's never satisfied with the work any of us do. He says we don't come up to his standards and he's not about to lower them.

_____ 16. The substitute teacher said the class was very helpful to her while I was gone, so I'm taking them on an unscheduled field trip to the zoo as a surprise.

_____ 17. It was great receiving the honor award at our student body assembly.

MULTIPLE-CHOICE SELF-TEST

Select the response that best answers the question or completes the statement. Place the letter of the chosen answer in the space provided.

_____ 1. Which of the following is the best argument that "pure" behaviorists might give to refute the idea that material reinforcement spoils the child?
A. Extrinsic motivation is stronger than intrinsic motivation and can be used more effectively to change behaviors.
B. There is no such thing as intrinsic motivation; behavior is a consequence of extrinsic motivation.
C. It is easy to modify the behavior of a spoiled child.
D. Intrinsic motivation often develops as an outcome of initial reinformcement from extrinsic sources.

_____ 2. The best definition of an incentive is that it is
A. a reinforcer.
B. a contingency.
C. expectation of reinforcement.
D. a contingency ratio of reinforcement.

_____ 3. What is the usual effect on students' motivation of judiciously using and monitoring a reward system?
A. Always effective
B. Effective most of the time
C. Rarely effective
D. Never effective

_____ 4. Which type statement of teacher verbal reward is most likely to undermine student motivation?
A. Those that provide information
B. Those that attempt to control
C. Those that increase feelings of competence
D. Those that lead to an internal orientation

_____ 5. Which of the following is not a source of frustration?
A. Expectations are not satisfied because of nonoccurrence of reinforcement of response to a stimulus.
B. Expectations are not satisfied because of prevention of response to a stimulus.
C. The stimulus that produces a response leading to reinforcement increases in frequency of occurrence.
D. Response to a stimulus produces negative reinforcement, that is, the stimulus is removed.

_____ 6. When a teacher notices signs of frustration on the part of students, he or she should monitor events in the classroom for evidence that
A. excessive numbers of reinforcers are being used.
B. students are being kept from completing a task that leads to reinforcement.
C. student behavior has not been brought under stimulus control.
D. punishment is causing students to act aggressively.

_____ 7. The tokens or points in a token economy are
A. neutral stimuli.
B. neutral reinforcers.
C. incentives.
D. controlling stimuli.

_____ 8. Cohen's study demonstrated that impressive gains in achievement among delinquent boys can be obtained. In his work he used
A. a contracting system.
B. a frustration-reduction system.
C. a token economy.
D. intrinsic reinforcers only.

_____ 9. The easiest and most natural of the motivational devices available to a teacher is
A. the fair use of grades.
B. criticism.
C. the use of his or her influence power.
D. praise.

_____ 10. Approximately what percentage of all new classroom tasks and activities did Brophy find were not introduced by teachers?
A. 10
B. 20
C. 30
D. 40
E. 50

_____ 11. Which of the following types of praise is most effective?
A. Rewards for participation, but not necessarily performance
B. Praise that fosters competition between students
C. Global positive reactions to student behavior
D. Praise that attributes success to effort and ability

_____ 12. When the average teacher takes the time and trouble to write comments (believed to be encouraging) on student papers,
A. student morale is improved, but there is no measurable effect on student achievement.
B. they apparently have an effect upon student effort.
C. the eventual outcome of that effort appears to be directly related to student abilities.
D. the student develops a positive orientation to the teacher.

_____ 13. Familiar names and examples should be used when the teacher is attempting to
A. build interest in learning something new.
B. develop ability to apply something already learned.
C. minimize the attractiveness of competing incentives.
D. whet the students' appetites.

_____ 14. Unique and unexpected contexts, rather than familiar names and examples, should be used when the teacher is attempting to
A. illustrate new routines or skills.
B. improve ability to apply things already learned.
C. minimize the unpleasant consequences of student involvement.
D. provide social rewards.

_____ 15. In Coleman's study of the status systems of high schools, male students were asked, "How would you most like be remembered in school?" Most responded that they would prefer to be remembered as
A. a brilliant student.
B. most popular.
C. an athletic star.

D. a wit.

_____16. Coleman found that the greater the emphasis on high grades among students in a given high school, the greater the tendency for students who made A's to
A. have lower IQs within that school.
B. have about average IQs within that school.
C. have higher IQs within that school.

_____17. Coleman interpreted the results of his study as indicating that the subcultures of high schools tend to
A. encourage academic achievement.
B. discourage academic achievement.
C. have no effect on academic achievement.

PROJECTS AND ACTIVITIES

1. It was stated in the chapter that both intrinsic and extrinsic motivation derive from an interaction of environmental and personal variables. Briefly outline a progam showing how you might foster in a student intrinsic motivation for a particular social behavior, for example, for showing positive attitudes toward a given subject matter or relating positively to fellow students.

2. Set out a plan for developing a token economy in whatever area or grade you are specializing in. Determine the number of points to be earned in order to achieve certain services or activities. Determine the worth of the services or activities on the basis of how much students value them. Set yourself a limit of $100 for materials that can be used as tokens in your reinforcement system. (If you get a good system outlined, perhaps your school administration will contribute the $100!)

3. Observe the interaction of a teacher with his or her students for about one hour. During that time period, record as many examples of the use of social power as you can observe. In other words, when does the teacher invoke power to reward or coerce? When do the students acknowledge his or her expert or legitmate power? Social influence of this type is very subtle and hard to indentify, so be sure to restudy the section on power in Chapter 18 before trying this exercise.

SUGGESTIONS FOR TERM PAPERS

1. The foolishness of external reinforcement systems

2. Ethical considerations in using token economies

3. Normative aspects of the educational system that frustrate students

4. How teachers can make more use of their expert and referent power

5. Development of academic games in fifth-grade music/ninth-grade alegbra/contemporary literature/etc.

6. Arousal techniques in the teaching of art history/spelling/English composition/etc.

7. The impact of the computer revolution on teaching

CHAPTER 19 LECTURING AND EXPLAINING

OBJECTIVES

The student should be able to

o compare and contrast the advantages and disadvantages of the lecture method versus the discussion method of teaching

o list the functions of the introduction, body, and conclusion of a lecture or explanation

o illustrate the use of the rule-example-rule technique, explaining links and structural support

o write a description of component, sequential, material-to-purpose, chained, connective, and classificatory relationships in a lecture or explanation

o create an advance organizer for a lecture

o cite evidence on the relationship of humor to lecture effectiveness

o summarize the teaching objectives for which the lecture method is appropriate and inappropriate

o implement a model for organizing explanations

o describe four ways in which a teacher can maintain attention during a lecture

REMINDER

Chapter 19 examined the advantages and disadvantages of the lecture and discussion methods of teaching. You learned that the appropriateness of either method can be evaluated only when instructional goals and objectives are considered. You read about the essential components of a lecture and an explanation, and techniques to help you improve the effectiveness of both. An effective lecture gains student attention and exposes the lesson's aim and crucial content in the introduction. The body of the lecture provides a logical organization of material through the speaker's use of component, sequential, material-to-purpose, and connective relationships of the ideas presented. The lecture's conclusion summarizes what students should know and be able to do, and indicates the content of the next lecture. You will recall that among the valuable techniques to use in a lecture or explanation are the rule-example-rule pattern, explaining links, physical activity, and inserted questions.

DEFINITIONS OF KEY CONCEPTS

The following key concepts were discussed in this chapter. In your own words, write the definition of each concept in the space provided.

1. Teaching methods _____

_____

_____

2. Teaching techniques _____

_____

_____

3. The lecture method of teaching _____

_____

_____

4. Explanations _____

_____

_____

5. The equalization effect _____

_____

_____

6. Motivational cues _____

_____

_____

7. Clarity of aims _____

_____

_____

8. Advance organizers _____

_____

_____

9. Student opportunity to learn _____

_____

_____

10. Transitional statements _____

_____

_____

11. Discountinuity in a lecture _____

_____

_____

12. Component relationships in a lecture _____

_____

_____

13. Classification hierarchy _____

_____

_____

14. Sequential relationships in a lecture _____

_____

_____

15. Material-to-purpose (relevance) relationships in a lecture ___

_____

_____

16. Chaining _____

_____

_____

17. Connective relationships in a lecture _____

_____

_____

18. A model for organizing explanations _____

_____

_____

19. The rule-example-rule technique _____

_____

_____

20. Explaining links _____

_____

_____

21. Interlecture structuring _____

APPLICATION OF KEY CONCEPTS

The terms listed below refer to important concepts that were discussed in this chapter. Carefully read each descriptive statement, and identify the concept or concepts each statement implies. Place the corresponding letter(s) of the concept(s) you select in the space provided.

Concepts

A. interlecture structuring
B. classification hierarchy
C. clarity of aims
D. transitional statement
E. explanation
F. rule-example-rule technique
G. equalization effect

H. student opportunity to learn
I. advance organizer
J. motivational cue
K. chaining
L. explaining link
M. discontinuity

Descriptive Statements

_____ 1. The purpose of today's lecture is to introduce you to the main functions of the circulatory system of the body.

_____ 2. Animals may be classified into two general groups according to their eating habits--carnivorous and herbivorous. Meat- and insect-eating animals belong to the former group, and animals that feed on grasses and plants belong to the latter.

_____ 3. I know he's going to ask us all about the vascular reflexes on the test. He didn't talk about that much in class, so I'm really concentrating on that chapter in my studying.

_____ 4. You've just heard how novelists may use the first-person or the third-person point of view in their writing. Now we're going to examine how the use of the first person gives a biographical perspective to the novel.

165

_____ 5. We're currently experiencing a marked shift in geographic distribution of the population. The latest census figures indicated that people are moving from urban areas to either suburban or rural areas. In fact, the biggest influx has been to the "Sunbelt" states in the Southwest. So you can see that population distribution is changing.

_____ 6. I really dislike coming to this class. It seems like half the time he just talks off the top of his head about stuff that isn't even remotely related to the lecture.

_____ 7. To understand the origins of the Anglican Church in England, we must examine the events in the life of Henry VIII that lead to his excommunication by the pope.

_____ 8. Next time we shall continue with our discussion of the nervous system, focusing on the chemical processes of breaking down ingested food.

_____ 9. Today we'll be talking about the natural resources of Chile--where they are found and how they are refined--so that we can use this information to understand how those resources directly influence the economic structure of the country.

_____ 10. Please pay very close attention, because now we move to the crux of Descartes' argument.

_____ 11. The plants closer to the window are growing better than those in the corner, because plants require nourishment--sunlight, water, and food--in order to thrive.

_____ 12. That was a really unfair test question. He didn't talk about that at all in class and it wasn't in the text.

_____ 13. The reason we will not loose strength is that we have our own oil supply and, therefore, are only partially dependent on other nations' energy resources.

MULTIPLE-CHOICE SELF-TEST

Select the response that best answers the question or completes the statement. Place the letter of the chosen answer in the space provided.

_____ 1. Which of the following considerations can be used to support the lecture over the textbook as a method of instruction?
A. Clarity of content
B. Availability of information to students
C. Flexibility
D. In-depth coverage of information

_____ 2. The lecture has probably maintained its status as a teaching method because it is
A. generally the best method of promoting student interest.
B. directly related to a strong theory of learning.
C. so comfortable that teachers expect to lecture more than to teach by other methods.
D. more efficient administratively.

_____ 3. Dubin and Taveggia's (1968) review of empirical studies of the last 40 years

showed that, in terms of student achievement on final examinations, the lecture method is
A. superior to other teaching methods.
B. better than the tutorial method, but not better than the discussion method.
C. less effective than the lecture-discussion approach.
D. about as effective as any other teaching method.

_____ 4. The equalization effect in research on teaching methods refers to
A. general intelligence variables.
B. the students' efforts to learn.
C. the trade-off between interests and anxiety in learning.
D. the need to control for time devoted to a given topic.

_____ 5. Which of the following is not a purpose of the introduction of a lecture?
A. Providing motivational cues to students
B. Promoting student attention
C. Cognitive preparation of the teacher
D. Establishing teacher-student relations

_____ 6. A statement at the beginning of a lecture that provides an organizational framework for the content is called
A. an advance organizer.
B. an explaining link.
C. a cognitive structure.
D. an introduction.

_____ 7. If the nature of the topic is unknown to your students, you will want to use the introduction of a lecture for
A. establishing teacher-student relations.
B. prompting student attention.
C. exposing essential content.
D. arousing their need for affiliation.

_____ 8. The amount of time the lecturer spends in providing content he or she wants the students to learn is called
A. the ration of effectiveness.
B. time on target.
C. effective temporality.
D. the temporal characteristic.

_____ 9. Relationships in the lecture's content that are characterized by chronological, cause-effect, building-to-climax, and topical sequences are termed
A. component relationships.
B. sequential relationships.
C. material-to-purpose relationships.
D. transitional relationships.

_____ 10. When a lecturer is making a comparison between two or more things, he or she should proceed
A. by making explicit the bases of comparison.
B. by stopping the lecture and asking questions.
C. to list all the differences.
D. in his or her customary manner so as not to confuse the students.

_____11. "You have seen the novelist's use of character development during the first five chapters; now we will address the turning point that occurs in Chapter Six." What in a lecture is this an example of?
A. A classification hierarchy
B. A relevance relationship
C. Chaining
D. A transition signal

_____12. How does teacher digression during a lecture affect student achievement of content?
A. Not at all, because some students like digressions and some do not
B. Postively, because students need a short break to assimilate all the prior material
C. Negatively, because digressions interrupt the flow of the lesson

_____13. Which of the following should be avoided by teachers in their explanations?
A. Use of examples
B. Use of determinate quantifiers
C. Use of approximations

The text presents a model for organizing an explanation into four steps. Using that model, indicate the correct order of usage of the components of an explanation, given in items 14-17.
A. Step 1
B. Step 2
C. Step 3
D. Step 4

_____14. Specify the relationship between the "things" identified.

_____15. Make sure you understand the question that is being asked.

_____16. Show how the relationship is an instance of a more general relationship or principle.

_____17. Identify the "things" involved in the relationship to be explained.

PROJECTS AND ACTIVITIES

1. Tape a friend's lecture or talk. Listen to it to determine whether such things as rule-example-rule patterns, advance organizers, transitional statements, and connective and component relationships were used. Determine also whether explanations followed the model presented in the text. Would you have handled that lecture differently? How?

2. Take a chapter in a text that you may use in your teaching. Outline it, and specify the component relationships, classfication hierarchy, sequential relationships, relevance relationships, chaining, and connective relationships that could be used to help you present the material.

SUGGESTIONS FOR TERM PAPERS

1. The lecture: Pro and con

2. Note-taking during a lecture: Its effects on retention

3. Designing the perfect lecture: Techniques, devices, and activities to be incorporated

4. When to use the lecture method and when to use the discussion method of teaching

5. The use of humor in lectures

6. Student attitudes toward the lecture method

CHAPTER 20 TEACHING SMALL GROUPS

OBJECTIVES

The student should be able to

o list the advantages and disadvantages of small-group teaching according to particular educational objectives

o distinguish between high- and low-consensus fields of study

o list the teaching functions to be performed before, during, and after a discussion

o compare and contrast different communication networks

o describe four ways to improve student particpation in discussions

o identify four intellectual and two social-emotional pitfalls from observation of a discussion

o establish a role-playing situation with students

o describe the relationship between teaching objectives and various seating arrangements

REMINDER

In this chapter you read about how to teach small groups most effectively. You will remember that there are three steps to be taken in teaching small groups: those that precede the discussion with students, those that take place during the discussion, and those that follow the discussion. Initially, the teacher must be concerned with choosing a topic, establishing common ground, refining objectives, and deciding on a particular communication network and seating arrangement. Concerns during a discussion include the extent of teacher involvement and the structure of the discussion. The teacher's activity after the discussion has taken place includes making notes, keeping records, and evaluating the discussion in terms of intellectual and social-emotional pitfalls. Finally, the chapter concluded with a discussion of two additional teaching techniques that can be used with small groups: role-playing and cooperative learning.

DEFINITIONS OF KEY CONCEPTS

The following key concepts were discussed in this chapter. In your own words, write the definition of each concept in the space provided.

1. Small-group teaching _____

_____

_____

2. High-consensus fields _____

_____

_____

3. Low-consensus fields _____

_____

_____

4. "Intelectual agility" _____

_____

_____

5. The discovery method _____

_____

_____

6. Extemporaneous speech _____

_____

_____

7. Communication networks _____

_____

_____

8. Logical fallacies _____

_____

_____

9. The cognitive map approach _____

_____

_____

10. Intellectual pitfalls _____
_____
_____

11. Biasing the discussion _____
_____
_____

12. Social-emotional pitfalls _____
_____
_____

13. The next-in-line phenomenon _____
_____
_____

14. Group cohesiveness _____
_____
_____

15. Role-playing _____
_____
_____

16. Cooperative learning _____
_____
_____

APPLICATION OF KEY CONCEPTS

The terms listed below refer to important concepts that were discussed in this chapter. Carefully read each descriptive statement, and identify the concept or concepts each statement implies. Place the corresponding letter(s) of the concept(s) you select in the space provided.

Concepts

A. role-playing
B. communication network
C. group cohesiveness

H. logical fallacy
I. social-emotional pitfall
J. discovery method

D. next-in-line phenomenon
E. "intellectual agility"
F. high-consensus field
G. biasing the discussion

K. low-consensus field
L. extemporaneous speech
M. intellectual pitfall
N. cooperative learning

Descriptive statements

_____ 1. I was so nervous while Brad was speaking, because I knew I had to talk next, that I didn't pay attention to him at all.

_____ 2. Today I'm going to talk about the digestive system, which is composed of the organs that act both mechanically and chemically on ingested food. The alimentary canal, a major component of the digestive system, is made up of the mouth, pharynx, esophagus, stomach, small intestine . . .

_____ 3. That was one of the best class sessions our group has ever had. Everyone was so engrossed. Even when we'd go off the track a bit, someone would always bring us back to focus on the question.

_____ 4. Mrs. Jones, although this discussion is fruitful, I feel I need to point out that your interpretation of the book is traditional, Western, and capitalistic. Now, if we brought to bear a Marxist-Leninist interpretation . . .

_____ 5. OK, why don't you be the white employer, and I'll be a young black woman who has no previous experience in sales. Ready?

_____ 6. Wasn't that one of the best movies we've ever seen, class? Those people who agree, come over here and we'll talk about the best parts. Those who don't can continue on page 15 of your Skilpak.

_____ 7. We divided our group into two teams to debate the issue, with our teacher acting as the moderator.

_____ 8. I don't know why you're all being so quiet. Now come on and discuss this, and show me by what you say that you've read chapter 13. Erica, what was the main point of Chapter 13?

_____ 9. Do I have to switch to that group? It's not that I don't like the members, but I've gotten so attached to the one I'm already in.

_____10. Now, Bill, Stan, Jo, and Rachel, you all tackle the problem of revising the senior dress code and report back to all of us next Monday on your findings and recommendations.

_____11. Will all the people who've read Steinbeck's short story come sit in this section of the room? That's right, move the chairs around so you can see each other. Why don't we start by talking about what you thought of the story, you know, how you liked it or disliked it.

_____12. During lab, the teacher didn't tell us what materials and chemicals we needed; he said we should try to find the right combinations of substances to solve the problem ourselves.

_____13. I just can't be persuaded by her ideas. I don't know why exactly. I think it's her southern accent that keeps me from listening to what's being said. I find it so grating.

MULTIPLE-CHOICE SELF-TEST

Select the response that best answers the question or completes the statement. Place the letter of the chosen answer in the space provided.

_____1. An important dimension of a topic under discussion that affects the way small-group teaching should proceed is
   A. meaningfulness.
   B. controversiality.
   C. sequential organization.
   D. objectivity.

_____2. Which of the following is a low-consensus field of study at the high school level?
   A. Physics
   B. Geometry
   C. Auto mechanics
   D. Social studies

_____3. Which of the following pairings is generally most beneficial for learning?
   A. Tutoring, low-consensus field
   B. Discussion, low-consensus field
   C. Lecture, low-consensus field
   D. Discussion, high-consensus field

_____4. Member satisfaction in centralized communication networks is usually
   A. very low.
   B. very high.
   C. indeterminate.
   D. a function of the ability of the group members.

_____5. McKeachie and Kulik (1975) compared the lecture method with group discussion. They concluded that
   A. the lecture is more efficient than group discussion for promoting understanding of concepts.
   B. group discussion is more efficient than the lecture for promoting understanding of concepts.
   C. no differences exist between the lecture and group discussion methods in terms of effectiveness for promoting understanding of concepts.

_____6. In most discussion groups it is found that the various members of the group tend to participate
   A. about equally.
   B. quite unequally, with a few members participating much more than others.
   C. quite unequally, with half the members participating and half the members being relatively quiet.
   D. not much at all if the teacher is the group leader.

_____7. In general, the teacher's role in teaching by the discussion method should be one of
   A. speaking fairly frequently, that is, about as much as the more active students speak.

174

B. speaking as much as the average student does.
C. speaking only when necessary to avoid various pitfalls.

_____ 8. If in a group discussion the students accept an outright error of fact, the teacher should probably
A. change the topic to one the students are more familiar with.
B. ignore the mistake and proceed.
C. remain silent.
D. intervene to correct the error.

_____ 9. Confusing what is accidental with what is essential is termed
A. a logical fallacy.
B. an error of inadequacy.
C. a digression.
D. a social-emotional pitfall.

_____ 10. One type of intellectual pitfall in discussion groups is
A. member nonparticipation.
B. the possibility of mismatched participants.
C. sticking to a dead topic.
D. the possibility of ego involvement.

_____ 11. In which of the following communication networks does the teacher have the most control over the flow of messages between group members?
A. Circle
B. Chain
C. A "Y"
D. Wheel
E. All channel

_____ 12. For which goal is the traditional straight-row seating arrangement best suited?
A. Small-group work
B. Role-playing
C. Discussion between students
D. Independent student work

_____ 13. Which type of seating arrangement is most preferred by college students for elective coursework?
A. Straight row
B. Horseshoe
C. Modular
D. Square or rectangle

_____ 14. Which of the following is probably the most basic advantage of the role-playing technique?
A. It's fun; therefore, it encourages participation.
B. It is highly motivating.
C. It provides a secure and nonthreatening situation.
D. The emotional cost to participants is extremely high.

_____ 15. If you were to set up a role-playing situation for your students, you'd want to make sure that participants
A. lead the interaction to a logical outcome.

B. have ample time to rehearse before role-playing before the entire class.

C. have all been assigned roles congruous with their own unique personalities.

D. continue with the interaction until enough material has been provided for a useful discussion.

PROJECTS AND ACTIVITIES

1. See if you can find a small discussion group in operation. (It could be school-or nonschool-related.) Give each member of the group a different letter of the alphabet, and keep track of who talks to whom and for how long (for example, A B: 40 seconds; B Group: 2.5 minutes, etc.). Try to determine the communication structure of the group, and who were its dominant and who its passive members. How would you judge the groups's efficiency?

2. Plan, organize, and actually carry out a role-playing session with some of your classmates. Perform the roles of a parent angry about lack of homework for his or her child; a teacher feeling failure because of the non-responsiveness of a particular student; a shy student trying to explain why he's embarrassed when called upon in class; an administrator justifying a set of strict rules and regulations for the school; etc. Were the discussions following the role-playing valuable? What objectives were met? Was the role-playing a unique or especially effective way to meet those objectives?

3. Read Table F-1, based on Stephen and Mishler (1952), in Technical Note F, which follows, and see if it accurately represents participation rates in discussions. You can check this table by making a simple frequency count of who participates in discussion groups of various sizes. These findings are supposed to have wide generalizability over a great number of settings and topics of discusssion. If they appear to hold up, you should think carefully about group size when planning a discussion.

SUGGESTIONS FOR TERM PAPERS

1. Implications of communication networks for education

2. Conformity and independence in school discussion groups

3. Costs and benefits of teaching by the discovery method

4. Finding low-consensus areas in high-consensus fields of study

5. A teachers' guide to using role-playing techniques with elementary/secondary students

6. Effects of seating arrangement on student participation

TECHNICAL NOTE F

EFFECT OF GROUP SIZE ON FREQUENCY OF PARTICIPATION BY GROUP MEMBERS

The text mentioned that the participation rates of individuals in a group seem to be quite lawful, depending on the size of the group. A constant ratio of responses by the next most frequently contributing member in the group appears to be maintained. The number of responses actually given is determined by how much the most frequently responding individual participates. This sounds more complicated than it really is. Let us look at the data on this interesting phenonomenon.

When eight-person groups are studied, the curve shown in Figure F-1 is obtained. When the leader is a <u>teacher</u>, a generally higher rate of participation occurs (teachers tend to talk too much), and the constant ratio holds for the third through the eighth rank. When the leader is a <u>student</u>, the ratio appears to hold for the second through the eighth rank. The constant ratio in groups of eight is about .667. That is, the number of participations by the second-ranked participant is 67 percent of the number made by the first-ranked participant; the number of participations by the third-ranked participant will be about 67 percent of the number made by the second-ranked individual, and so on. If the fifth-ranked individual participated 100 times, the sixth-ranked individual would have participated 67 times.

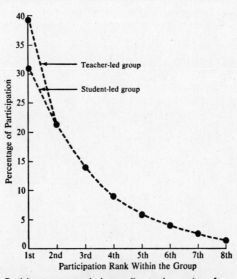

Figure F-1
Relative participation of eight members of a college discussion group.

Teacher-led group

Student-led group

Percentage of Participation

Participation Rank Within the Group

Participants were ranked according to the number of participations each originated during 14 meetings.

Source: Adapted from Stephan and Mishler (1952).

177

Expectancies about the way groups often perform are based on observations by Stephan and Mishler (1952) of constant ratios in many different groups. From these data we can compute Table F-1 and note that the last-ranked person in groups of 4 to 12 persons will participate very infrequently in larger groups, and much more frequently in smaller groups.

Table F-1
Effect of Group Size on Individual Participation

Group Size	Constant Ratios	Estimated Number of Times Participated, by Rank in Group											
		1	2	3	4	5	6	7	8	9	10	11	12
4	.589	100	59	35	21								
5	.611	100	61	38	23	14							
6	.623	100	62	39	24	15	10						
7	.661	100	66	44	29	19	13	9					
8	.667	100	67	45	30	20	13	9	6				
9	.668	100	67	45	30	20	14	9	6	4			
10	.694	100	70	48	35	23	16	11	8	6	4		
11	.710	100	71	51	36	26	18	13	9	7	5	4	
12	.727	100	73	53	39	28	21	15	11	8	6	4	3

Note: Group size participation ratios and estimated number of contributions by members are based on the leader's participating 100 times.

The quietest, most reticent group member may make 10 percent (21 contributions) of the total contributions in a four-person group, but in a group of 12, he or she may make less than 1 percent of the total contributions. Clearly, group size is something to be considered when teachers form groups and monitor participation rates.

You should be able to check out these constant ratios by simple monitoring of group discussions. If the group size were 10, you would expect the second most frequently participating member of the group to participate about 70 percent as often as the most frequently participating group member. Similarly, in groups of 5, you would expect the quietest individual to participate approximately 61 percent of the time that the fourth-ranked individual participated. These are interesting data that you can verify yourself by simply counting the frequency of participation in group discussions.

REFERENCE

STEPHAN, F. F., and MISHLER, E. G. (1952) The distribution of participation in small groups: An exponential approximation. American Sociological Review, 17: 598-608.

CHAPTER 21 INDIVIDUAL INSTRUCTION

OBJECTIVES

The student should be able to

o state when and for what objectives individual instruction is the most appropriate teaching method

o use the SQ3R technique to increase study efficiency

o list 10 kinds of behavior that will probably help students study better

o construct a Keller plan program of individual instruction

o write a learning contract with a student

o describe and illustrate the ways in which a tutor can diagnose, remedy, and support

o write a frame for programmed instruction

o summarize the research on computer-assisted instruction

REMINDER

Chapter 21 discussed the objectives of individual instruction and the various forms it can take. You read about the types of individual instruction that can be implemented by a single teacher in a school, including homework, independent study, self-directed study, and mastery learning. You learned about the Keller plan, which is a system of instruction that requires students to pace their own mastery of material with the guidance of the teacher and tutors. The chapter also discussed those approaches to individual instruction that require a substantial reorganization of the school. These approaches include programmed instruction and computer-assisted instruction.

DEFINITIONS OF KEY CONCEPTS

The following key concepts were discussed in this chapter. In your own words, write the definition of each concept in the space provided.

1. Individualized instruction _____

_____

_____

2. Ability grouping _____

_____

_____

3. Homogeneous grouping _____

_____

_____

4. Independent study _____

_____

_____

5. Self-directed study _____

_____

_____

6. SQ3R _____

_____

_____

7. A multiple correlation coefficient _____

_____

_____

8. A partial correlation coefficient _____

_____

_____

9. A contract _____

_____

_____

10. The Keller plan _____
_____
_____

11. Mastery learning _____
_____
_____

12. Diagnostic tests _____
_____
_____

13. Tutoring _____
_____
_____

14. Programmed instruction _____
_____
_____

15. A frame in programmed instruction _____
_____
_____

16. Computer-assisted instruction _____
_____
_____

APPLICATION OF KEY CONCEPTS

The terms listed below refer to important concepts that were discussed in this chapter. Carefully read each descriptive statement, and identify the concept or concepts each statement implies. Place the corresponding letter(s) of the concept(s) you select in the space provided.

Concepts

A. ability grouping
B. multiple correlation coefficient
C. Keller plan
D. tutoring
E. linear program of instruction
F. computer-assisted instruction
G. programmed instruction

H. contracting
I. frame of programmed instruction
J. diagnostic test
K. branching program of instruction
L. SQ3R
M. partial correlation coefficient

Descriptive Statements

_____ 1. I study best when I examine subtopics of a chapter, then make up questions from those subtopics, read the chapter, answer aloud the questions I raised, and finally review the chapter.

_____ 2. It's much easier for me and for my students to divide our class into three distinct groups for reading. That way neither the brighter students nor the slower students seem to get as frustrated and bored.

_____ 3. I've found that students' popularity, as ranked by their peers, combined with their participation in extracurricular activities, correlates about .40 with their overall high school grade-point average.

_____ 4. This quarter Mr. Hansen is teaching his class differently than in the past—students have to get a score of at least 75 percent on the quiz at the end of each chapter before going on to the next chapter. We also meet with the upper class student tutors in addition to attending the regular class lectures.

_____ 5. With the influence of age upon both height and weight eliminated, the correlation between the two is about .85 for elementary school children.

_____ 6. Stan, I think it's your turn for spelling practice at the teletype terminal—here are the earphones.

_____ 7. I like using these materials, but the problem I see with them is that the faster students have to wade through all the frames, which are often redundant.

_____ 8. These programmed materials are effective because they allow the faster students to skip certain frames if they've correctly answered prior key frames.

_____ 9. He told me that my test profile showed that I really understand the digestive, reproductive, and circulatory systems, but I'm weak in my understanding of the nervous system, so I'm going to read the section on the nervous system in another text that he recommended.

_____ 10. Dorothy volunteered to spend two periods a week helping a third grader with his math. The teacher explained that her job is to keep checking on his progress, encouraging him, and trying different solutions until one works.

_____ 11. A student receives a frame of content, responds, and is immediately reinforced in this system of instruction.

_____12. OK, I can expect you to turn in this report, based on library research and interviews, in two weeks.

_____13. The federal government is divided into three branches: the legislative, the executive, and the judiciary. The branches of government are the legislative, the executive, and the _____.

MULTIPLE-CHOICE SELF-TEST

Select the response that best answers the question or completes the statement. Place the letter of the chosen answer in the space provided.

_____ 1. A criticism of ability grouping as an intermediate step toward individual instruction is that
A. although it copes with stable individual differences, it does not deal with momentary individual differences between students.
B. true individual instruction requires a one-to-one relationship between student and teacher that is logistically impossible in ability-grouped classes.
C. although it deals with student differences in academic achievement, it does not take into account family characteristics and ethnicity in the assignment of students to groups.
D. it gives students assigned to the lower groups a less favorable self-concept, thereby actually depressing their achievement.

_____ 2. Which of the following components of a Personalized System of Instruction (PSI) have been found to account most for resultant higher achievement?
A. Ten-unit format
B. Use of proctors
C. Delayed feedback
D. Unit mastery requirement

_____ 3. The correlation between self-reported desirable student study habits and GPA is
A. very positive (around .85).
B. moderately positive (around .55).
C. around zero.
D. moderately negative (around -.55).
E. very negative (around -.85).

_____ 4. Research findings indicate that teaching by the Keller plan as compared with traditional course formats
A. increases student achievement.
B. decreases student achievement.
C. has no effect on student achievement.

Items 5-9 refer to the following situation. Mr. Pinne is using a mastery approach in teaching his class this term. Ms. Alvarez is using a more conventional approach in teaching her class. For each of the statements below, place an A in the space provided if the statement is a description of behavior more likely to be observed in Mr. Pinne's class, and place a B in the space provided if the statement is a description of behavior more likely to be found in Ms. Alvarez's class.

_____ 5. Tony is planning to take his test Friday so that he can begin a new chapter on the following Monday.

_____ 6. Bart has an appointment to see his tutor tomorrow to discuss a problem he's been having with his assignment.

_____ 7. Charlotte is finding it more and more difficult to keep up with the other students in her class.

_____ 8. Chuck got only half the problems correct on his last test, so he'll have to spend more time covering the material.

_____ 9. Olivia sometimes gets very bored in class because she has already learned what the teacher is talking about.

_____ 10. In a frame of programmed instruction, a response is followed by
  A. information.
  B. a cue.
  C. a control.
  D. an operant.
  E. an incentive.

_____ 11. When instructional time is not taken into account, comparisons of programmed instruction with conventional teaching have typically found that
  A. programmed instruction is more effective than conventional teaching.
  B. conventional teaching is more effective than programmed instruction.
  C. there is no highly consistent difference in the effectiveness of the two methods.

_____ 12. Student overt responses to frames of programmed instruction are sometimes unnecessary. However, overt responses are facilitative of learning when
  A. the student is a slow learner.
  B. reinforcement is not provided on a continuous schedule.
  C. the programmed material is easy, since students become bored if they do not overtly respond.
  D. the programmed material is technical or unfamiliar.

_____ 13. One major advantage of computer-assisted instruction (CAI) over programmed instruction is that under CAI
  A. student motivation is higher.
  B. the teacher's role is an easier, more manageable one.
  C. students' responses can be stored, retrieved, and analyzed more easily.
  D. the cost per student is less in a moderate- to large-sized school district.

_____ 14. CAI is not capable of doing which of the following?
  A. Carrying on a dialogue
  B. Writing sentences
  C. Responding with humor
  D. Drilling

_____ 15. When CAI was used to supplement regular classroom instruction, it was found to
  A. have no effect on student achievement.
  B. increase student achievement.
  C. take away valuable "live teacher" time for instruction.
  D. depersonalize teacher-student interaction.

_____ 16. Studies examining the effectiveness of the PSI method of instruction have found

it superior to conventional methods on all variables but
A. retention test scores.
B. final examination scores.
C. student course ratings.
D. student withdrawal rates.

_____ 17. What type of corrrelation has been found between homework time and achievement?
A. Moderate and positive
B. High and positive
C. Moderate and negative
D. High and negative
E. No consistent relationship

_____ 18. Homework time and achievement are related
A. correlationally.
B. causally.
C. correlationally and causally.
D. not at all.

PROJECT AND ACTIVITIES

1. See if you can get an opportunity to work with a student an any grade level who needs remedial work in any subject matter. Schedule a few tutoring sessions on a particular problem with the student. Plan how you will ask diagnostic questions, how you can give practice, how you can provide longer-term prescriptions, and how you can encourage the student's achievement. Carry out your plans and monitor the student's progress in the particular problem area.

2. Go to your college library and check out a programmed textbook or a set of programmed instructional materials. (These are available in almost every subject-matter area, including educational psychology and educational measurement.) Go through the program until you have achieved one of the objectives of that program. What can you do in your own teaching to remove the boredom inherent in small-stepped programmed instruction? What parts of the curriculum you teach would you recommend be supplemented with programmed instruction? Why?

3. This activity will help you separate myth and reality in educational innovation. Try to find a school in your vicinity that uses computer-assisted instruction. Examine the programs, talk to the teachers, and talk to the students. What are the teachers' attitudes toward computers in their classrooms? Did they volunteer for the new program or were they drafted? How much retraining did they receive? What are the students' attitudes? Try to determine how much of the innovation is rhetoric and how much is of educational value.

SUGGESTIONS FOR TERM PAPERS

1. Building a mastery model for the teaching of art history/social studies/physics/etc.

2. Independent study and contracting systems in the elementary/junior/high/high school

3. The rise, fall, and realities of programmed instruction

4. The present status of computer-assisted instruction

5. Will computers replace teachers?

6. The teacher as manager in computer-taught classrooms

CHAPTER 22 OPEN AND HUMANISTIC APPROACHES TO TEACHING

OBJECTIVES

The student should be able to

o list five principles of humanistic education

o implement an affective exercise in the classroom

o state the relationships between humanistic approaches and student achievement and student attitude

o describe the teacher's role in a humanistic classroom

o explain the objectives and intended outcomes of open education

REMINDER

In Chapter 22 you read about the objectives and principles of open and humanistic education. This movement is based on the idea that students are capable of self-direction and self-evaluation in a facilitative, nonthreatening environment. You'll recall that the teacher's role is as a facilitator of learning who determines the classroom climate and helps students both learn and explore their feelings. The chapter concluded with an evaluation and analysis of the effectiveness of open education.

DEFINITIONS OF KEY CONCEPTS

The following key concepts were discussed in this chapter. In your own words, write the definition of each concept in the space provided.

1. Humanistic or open approaches to teaching _____

_____

_____

2. Self-actualization _____

_____

_____

3. Confluent education _____

_____

_____

4. Facilitator of learning _____

_____

_____

5. Integrated-day plans _____

_____

_____

6. Project AWARE _____

_____

_____

7. Affective education _____

_____

_____

APPLICATION OF KEY CONCEPTS

The terms listed below refer to important concepts that were discussed in this chapter. Carefully read each descriptive statement, and identify the concept or concepts each statement implies. Place the corresponding letter(s) of the concept(s) you select in the space provided.

Concepts

A. confluent education
B. facilitator of learning
C. integrated-day plans
D. self-actualization
E. affective education

Descriptive Statements

_____ 1. I think that your idea of starting a school newspaper is a good one, and since I don't have enough background to help you, why don't you arrange for an interview with the editor of the newspaper here in town. She would probably have a lot of good ideas for you.

188

_____ 2. I've enrolled my daughter in a special program that helps youngsters develop self-reliance and respect for others.

_____ 3. I'm stressing to parents how important it is for their children to address emotions in the school curriculum as well as the academic part.

_____ 4. In this school you frequently see very young children freely moving from one activity to another, such as water play, art, and music.

_____ 5. If you would just stop telling her what to do, she'd find her own way. I'm convinced that people "naturally" do what's best for themselves.

MULTIPLE-CHOICE SELF-TEST

Select the response that best answers the question or completes the statement. Place the letter of the chosen answer in the space provided.

_____ 1. Evaluation in a humanistic classroom should be done by
A. the teacher.
B. standardized testing.
C. no one, since there is no evaluation.
D. the students themselves.

_____ 2. Humanistic teachers argue that learning is easiest, most meaningful, and retained best when the classroom environment is
A. nonthreatening.
B. full of love and happiness.
C. completely unstructured.
D. moderately structured.

_____ 3. Which of the following is not involved in the teacher role as a classroom facilitator?
A. Setting the mood or climate of the class
B. Eliciting concerns and clarifying purposes
C. Selecting the appropriate learning activities
D. Meeting the unique needs of the class

_____ 4. In practice, humanistic teaching methods most closely resemble a combination of
A. lecture and small-group discussion methods.
B. independent study and programmed instruction.
C. large-group discussion and independent study.
D. discussion and individual-instruction methods.

_____ 5. Which of the following is not a principle of humanistic education?
A. Wanting and knowing how to learn
B. Emphasis on feelings
C. Peer evaluation
D. Self-direction

_____ 6. In a humanistic or open classroom, who is responsible for student learning and the choice of appropriate learning activities?
A. Teacher
B. Parents

      C. Students
      D. Teacher and students

_____ 7. How effective are humanistic approaches in terms of enhancing academic achievement?
      A. No consistent effect on achievement
      B. Increased achievement
      C. Decreased achievement

_____ 8. What effect does open education have on achievement motivation?
      A. No consistent effect on motivation
      B. Increased motivation
      C. Decreased motivation

_____ 9. What effect does open education have on student self-concept?
      A. No consistent effect on self-concept
      B. Increased self-concept
      C. Decreased self-concept

PROJECTS AND ACTIVITIES

1. Schedule a visit to a school that adheres to an open education or integrated-day policy. Observe the students at work and play. Think about whether they are getting enough academic instruction, whether or not their attitudes toward school are positive, and whether they have only the semblance of freedom or real freedom. Talk to some students and get their opinions about their class. If you can, repeat this observation in a traditional classroom, and compare and contrast what you have seen and heard.

2. Try to find a school or classroom that claims to be part of the humanistic movement in education. (Very often free schools, or alternative schools, are set up to implement this kind of philosophy.) See whether you can observe the program and activities in that classroom or school. Do students seem more motivated? Is the teacher more a facilitator of learning, or does the teacher take more traditional, direct instructional roles? From what you observed, what would you not want to incorporate into your own teaching? How can you incorporate aspects of teaching that you like into your own teaching?

SUGGESTIONS FOR TERM PAPERS

1. Open education and the corruption of academic values

2. Open education and the "bright new future of America"

3. Why we need a curriculum for the development of feelings

4. The need for humanistic education in a nuclear world

5. The educational writings of A. S. Neill/Carl Rogers/Abraham Maslow/John Holt/etc.

6. An evaluation of humanistic education

CHAPTER 23 CLASSROOM TEACHING: PLANNING AND MANAGEMENT

OBJECTIVES

The student should be able to

o state five reasons for the prevalence of classroom teaching

o identify the teacher behaviors of structuring, soliciting, and reacting

o describe how the classroom recitation pattern differs across socioeconomic levels

o distinguish between noninteractive and interactive phases of teaching

o list the ways teachers spend most of their planning time

o describe techniques for use in changing a situation in which students show too little behavior of a desirable kind and too much behavior of an undesirable kind

o define and illustrate the five teaching behaviors identified by Kounin as correlated with student work involvement

o write a plan for controlling for and reducing teacher bias

o implement a plan for providing variety and flexibility in classroom teaching

REMINDER

Classroom teaching combines parts of all the teaching methods you read about in previous chapters—lecturing and explaining, discussion, individual instruction, and humanistic approaches. This chapter specifically dealt with the planning phases of classroom teaching, where the teacher must prepare for the interactive phases of classroom teaching. These decisions concern control and management of the class, preparation of the material to be taught, control of biases toward particular students, and provisions for variety and flexibility.

DEFINITIONS OF KEY CONCEPTS

The following key concepts were discussed in this chapter. In your own words, write the definition of each concept in the space provided.

1. Classroom teaching _____

_____

_____

2. Recitation _____

_____

_____

3. Structuring _____

_____

_____

4. Soliciting _____

_____

_____

5. Responding _____

_____

_____

6. Reacting _____

_____

_____

7. The preinteractive phase _____

_____

_____

8. The "integrated ends-means model" _____

_____

_____

9. Withitness _____

_____

_____

10. Overlappingness _____
_____
_____

11. Momentum _____
_____
_____

12. Smoothness _____
_____
_____

13. Group alerting _____
_____
_____

14. Bias in teacher-student interaction _____
_____
_____

15. Variation in classroom teaching _____
_____
_____

16. Style in classroom teaching _____
_____
_____

17. Method in classroom teaching _____
_____
_____

18. Flexibility in classroom teaching _____
_____
_____

APPLICATION OF KEY CONCEPTS

The terms listed below refer to important concepts that were discussed in this chapter. Carefully read each descriptive statement, and identify the concept or concepts each statement implies. Place the corresponding letter(s) of the concept(s) you select in the space provided.

Concepts

A. variation in classroom teaching
B. style in classroom teaching
C. method in classroom teaching
D. flexibility in classroom teaching
E. preinteractive phase of teaching
F. responding
G. overlappingness
H. momentum

I. smoothness
J. reacting
K. structuring
L. soliciting
M. group alerting
N. withitness
O. "integrated ends-means model"

Descriptive statements

_____ 1. I've been talking, now, long enough--why don't some of you say what you think about it?

_____ 2. I try to make sure that I ask my second graders about an equal number of higher- and-lower order questions.

_____ 3. All right, we've talked about computing the area of a right triangle; let's go on to computing the area of an isosceles triangle.

_____ 4. I realized that while the students were manipulating the clay we were really working on their fine motor coordination. I hadn't planned that objective, but it worked out so well!

_____ 5. Why do you think Miss Busbe always moves her hand like that when she paces in front of the board?

_____ 6. I like it when the teacher shows us movies--they're a lot more fun than just reading or listening about things.

_____ 7. And who remembers the "last straw" that sparked the beginning of the First World War?

_____ 8. I'm preparing for a more mastery-oriented approach to teaching my class this year.

_____ 9. Old Mrs. Clements seems to have eyes in the back of her head. Every time I get ready to do something, she catches me.

_____ 10. That's a great idea, Ed. What a unique solution to the problem posed.

_____ 11. When Mr. Smothers lectures, you really feel like you don't know what's going to pop up next or who will be called on.

_____12. I want to compliment you, Ms. Forsyth, on the way the children seem to move from area to area in the classroom as they study different subject matter.

_____13. I think the answer to your question is that they didn't have effective leadership to band them together into a functioning group.

_____14. Wow! Did you see how that teacher was able to deal with Billie's bloody nose while helping Margaret pin the rip in her dress?

_____15. I'm exhausted. I don't think we let up for a minute as we studied that unit.

MULTIPLE-CHOICE SELF-TEST

Select the response that best answers the question or completes the statement. Place the letter of the chosen answer in the space provided.

_____1. What is the most common teaching method found at all grade levels?
A. Seat work
B. Individual instruction
C. Small-group instruction
D. Explanations and lectures
E. Classroom teaching

_____2. What is the unique component of classroom teaching?
A. Structuring
B. Discussion
C. Recitation
D. Questioning

_____3. Several studies of the structure-solicit-respond-react model of classroom teaching indicate that there is much similarity of classroom moves across
A. grade levels, but not across subject matter areas.
B. subject matter areas, but not across grade levels.
C. both subject matter areas and grade levels.
D. neither subject matter areas nor grade levels.

_____4. Which of the following is not a plausible explanation for the prevalence of the classroom recitation method of teaching?
A. Adaptable
B. Reinforcing to students
C. Reinforcing to the teacher
D. Teacher lack of knowledge about other methods
E. Rigid school organization

_____5. Glass and Smith's (1979) review of class size and achievement studies suggests that in order to boost achievement, class size should
A. remain the same, about 25 to 30.
B. increase to about 40.
C. decrease to about 15.

_____6. Which of the following examples of teacher behavior would not be found during the preinteractive phase of teaching?
A. Selecting or writing a test to evaluate student achievement

B. Administering a test to evaluate student achievement
C. Formulating teaching objectives
D. Arranging for a field trip

_____ 7. During the preinteractive phase, a teacher must be concerned with a hierarchy of planning needs. The first need to consider is
A. control of biases.
B. planning for variety and flexibility.
C. establishment of classroom control.
D. planning of lessons and activities.

_____ 8. What area do teachers consider first in their preinteractive planning time?
A. Subject matter
B. Educational objectives
D. Strategies and activities
E. Instructional processes

_____ 9. Which of the following sources of pressure most influences teacher decision-making regarding topics to cover?
A. Other teachers' opinions
B. Principal's opinions
C. Textbook material
D. District test

_____ 10. What is the correlation between achievement and aggression for both boys and girls?
A. High and positive   (+.80)
B. Moderate and positive   (+.40)
C. Nonexistent   (0.00)
D. Moderate and negative   (-.40)
E. High and negative   (-.80)

_____ 11. If Toby were observed constantly tapping his fingertips on his desktop, which category of disruptive behavior would this probably be classified as?
A. Peer affinity
B. Attention seeking
C. Critical dissension
D. Challenge of authority

_____ 12. Jennifer and Milly always sit next to each other during study hall, talking and disrupting the class. To eliminate their "too much" kind of problem behavior, the teacher should
A. reinforce Jennifer whenever she talks to anyone other than Milly during study hall.
B. have a talk with both the girls, explaining to them that it is unfair to disturb the other students.
C. make sure that Jennifer and Milly do not sit next to each other in study hall.
D. constantly remind them that there is a rule of no talking during study hall.

_____ 13. Kounin (1970) has examined several types of teacher managerial skills. Which of the following statements would be made by a teacher who is competent in handling overlappingness?
A. "Pay special attention this point, because it will be brought up again and again."

B.   "Tomorrow, there will be a surprise for you that I'm sure you'll all enjoy."
C.   "Andy, we haven't heard much from you about this. What do you think?"
D.   "Greg, get down from that desk immediately, and you girls in the corner, please wait until recess to wrestle."

_____14.   Mrs. Alcott typically calls on the higher-achieving students in her class when she asks higher-order questions ancd calls on the lower-achieving students in her class when she asks lower-order questions. Mrs. Alcott's behavior would be classified as an example of
A.   method in classroom teaching.
B.   style in classroom teaching.
C.   variation in classroom teaching.
D.   flexibility in classroom teaching.

_____15.   Research indicates that, in general, variety and flexibility in teaching are
A.   positively associated with student achievement to a moderate degree.
B.   negatively associated with student achievement to a mild degree.
C.   unrelated to student achievement.

_____16.   From your knowledge of the results of Clifford and Walster's (1973) study of student attractiveness and teacher judgments, you would probably want to
A.   always attend more to attractive-looking students.
B.   always attend more to less attractive-looking students.
C.   check to see if you have any unconscious biases on the basis of student attactiveness.
D.   arrange classroom seating of attractive-looking students next to less attractive-looking students.

_____17.   What was the resolution of the American Psychological Association regarding the use of corporal punishment with children in public or private institutions?
A.   Opposed to the use of corporal punishment
B.   Should be used judiciously and in moderation
C.   Can have positive effects if applied systematically by behavioral experts
D.   Supported the use of corporal punishment

PROJECTS AND ACTIVITIES

1. Find a classroom at any age level that you can observe. Identify one student in the classroom who shows "too much" of a certain behavior, and one student who shows "too little" of a certain behavior. (For example, a student who talks too much and a student who hardly participates.) Try to keep track of the frequency of their behaviors during your observation. Recommend to the teacher a plan for modifying the behavior of those students. Observe again one week later, recording the frequency of behavior of the target students. Did their behavior change? Did the teacher follow your recommendations? What would you do differently in similar circumstances?

2. This activity is a check for bias in teaching. Count the number of boys and girls in a classroom you're observing. Compute percentages. Count the number of times the teacher calls on boys or girls. Again, compute percentages. Is the percentage of communications sent to boys from the teacher roughly equal to the percentage of boys in the class? Or does the teacher show a systematic sex bias? You can repeat this procedure using other dimensions, for example, seating patterns of students -- front/back, left/right; ratings of physical attractiveness of students; ethnicity of students, etc.

SUGGESTIONS FOR TERM PAPERS

1. Techniques for ensuring variety in the teaching of third-grade science/spelling/botany/etc.

2. Ethical issues in controlling student behavior through operant techniques

3. Systematic bias of the schools in the education of American Indians/Chicanos/blacks /Asians/etc.

4. A case for decreasing class size

5. An historic overview of the classroom recitation method

6. Is teacher lesson planning essential?

CHAPTER 24 CLASSROOM TEACHING: SEATWORK AND THE RECITATION

OBJECTIVES

The student should be able to

o name and describe the four major dimensions of classroom recitation

o compute "academic learning time"

o list and implement five ways to increase academic learning time

o state the relationship various forms of teacher structuring behaviors have with student achievement

o state the relationship between teacher use of higher-and-lower order questions, redirecting and probing, and student achievement

o state the relationship between positive and negative teacher reactions to students' response and student achievement

REMINDER

Chapter 24 focused on teacher behaviors that occur during the interactive phase of classroom teaching. Teaching strategies used widely during this phase are seatwork and recitation. You read that a most important variable during seatwork is academic learning time, that is, the time students are actively engaged with material of low difficulty. The second major teaching strategy you read about is recitation, which consists of the teacher's structuring and soliciting behavior, followed by student response and teacher reaction to that response. You learned how teacher interactive behaviors such as signal giving, organization, question asking, wait time, and praise are related to student outcomes. The chapter concluded with an emphasis on the importance of the appropriate combination, sequencing, and pacing of these behaviors in classroom teaching.

DEFINITIONS OF KEY CONCEPTS

The following key concepts were discussed in this chapter. In your own words, write the definition of each concept in the space provided.

1. Classroom seatwork _____
   _____
   _____

2. Classroom recitation _____
   _____
   _____

3. Academic learning time _____
   _____
   _____

4. Monitoring _____
   _____
   _____

5. Signal giving _____
   _____
   _____

6. Discontinuities _____
   _____
   _____

7. Lower-order questions _____
   _____
   _____

8. Higher-order questions _____
   _____
   _____

9. Wait time I _____
   _____
   _____

10. Wait time II _____

_____

_____

11. "Call-outs" _____

_____

_____

12. Redirecting _____

_____

_____

13. Probing _____

_____

_____

14. Acceptance of student ideas _____

_____

_____

APPLICATION OF KEY CONCEPTS

The terms listed below refer to important concepts that were discussed in this chapter. Carefully read each descriptive statement, and identify the concept or concepts each statement implies. Place the corresponding letter(s) of the concept(s) you select in the space provided.

Concepts

A. probing
B. lower-order question
C. signal giving
D. monitoring
E. acceptance of student ideas
F. discontinuity
G. wait time I

H. classroom seatwork
I. higher-order question
J. academic learning time
K. redirecting
L. wait time II
M. "call-out"

Descriptive statements

_____ 1. You remember what Rachel just said. I think that's a very unique way of looking at this question and deserves further discussion.

_____ 2. Jean, can you tell us the names of the bones found in the leg?

_____ 3. I've found that my students always have a lot to say--you just have to be patient and give them a chance to think for a moment before calling on a student for an answer.

_____ 4. I like to walk around and check each student's work as they go along. That way I can give help to those who need it.

_____ 5. I allow 55 minutes for reading because I know not everybody will be attending the entire time. I figure that on the average students are working about 30 of those 55 minutes.

_____ 6. That's a good answer, Seth, but do you think you could be a bit more specific? . . . That's right. Now, why do you think that happened? . . . Good, that's true. What do you think would prevent a recurrence of that same situation? . . . Yes. Do you think that will be in our lifetime or many more years away?

_____ 7. What did Mr. Hibdon just say? I thought he was talking about food chains, but then he said something about weather. It's confusing when he does that.

_____ 8. James, I know you're anxious to tell the answer, but from now on, please wait until I call on you, OK?

_____ 9. I like the way Mrs. Washington usually pauses before commenting on what I have to say. It makes me feel like she thinks what I have to say is important.

_____ 10. If there are no more questions about succulents, let's talk about another type of plant family--one called the bromeliad. A typical bromeliad that you've probably all seen is a pineapple.

_____ 11. Maybe, Alice, you could tell us how well you thought the composer worked in the two major themes during the last movement of his symphony. Do you think he was effective?

_____ 12. Red just said the answer is 1066. Ginny, what year was the Battle of Hastings fought?

_____ 13. Joey, did Mr. Stiver say our group was to start answering the questions on page 58 or page 68? I didn't hear him.

MULTIPLE-CHOICE SELF-TEST

Select the response that best answers the question or completes the statement. Place the letter of the chosen answer in the space provided.

_____ 1. From Berliner's (1979) research on academic learning time, one would conclude that
   A. students attend during about one-half of the time allocated to a given lesson.
   B. students spend the overwhelming majority of engaged time working with materials of high difficulty.
   C. most teachers allow about the same amount of time for second-grade reading instruction.
   D. the amount of time allocated for instruction in a given subject area varies across teachers and classrooms.

_____ 2. Research by Fisher et al. (1978) on the effects of academic learning time (ALT) on student achievement in reading and mathematics found which of the following relationships?
A. Student achievement increased as the amount of ALT increased.
B. Student achievement decreased as the amount of ALT increased.
C. As the amount of ALT increased, student achievement increased to a point, then decreased as the amount of ALT continued to increase.
D. As the amount of ALT increased, student achievement remained about the same.

_____ 3. The classroom recitation method is a repeated chain of four events; however, some of these links may be omitted. Which two events in the chain are considered essential parts of the classroom recitation method?
A. Teacher structuring and teacher reaction
B. Student response and teacher reaction
C. Teacher solication and teacher reaction
D. Teacher solication and student response

_____ 4. Which of the following teacher moves is not an example of structuring behavior?
A. Inserted questions
B. Signal giving
C. Emphasizing words to be learned
D. Verbal markers of importance

_____ 5. Which of the following pairs of student classroom activities would most likely be associated with higher achievement?
A. Use of games and textbooks
B. use of textbooks and workbooks
C. use of games and workbooks

_____ 6. In which type of classroom activity do students show the highest rates of "engagement"?
A. Reading a textbook
B. Writing in a workbook
C. Participating in a teacher-led group
D. Completing a teacher-made worksheet.

_____ 7. If a beginning teacher asked you about the relationship between the number of questions asked during recitation and student achievement, on the basis of your knowledge of research, you'd reply that the evidence is
A. in favor of teachers asking more questions.
B. in favor of teachers asking fewer questions.
C. inconsistent, and therefore no recommendations can be made.
D. too complex to allow for a recommendation to be made.

_____ 8. In general, it has been found that teachers' use of higher-order questions is associated with
A. decreased student achievement.
B. more complex student cognitive behavior.
C. more positive student attitudes.
D. no change in student behavior.

_____ 9. You have observed that a teacher trainee working with lower-SES students asks lower-order questions about 80% of the time and higher-order questions about 20% of the time. On the basis of research examining the relationship between type of teacher questions and student achievement, you would predict
A. nothing, because the research findings have been too inconsistent.
B. that students in the trainee's class would show gains in achievement.
C. that students in the trainee's class would show no gains in achievement.
D. that student attitude, but not achievement, would show gains.

_____ 10. Without any other information, which of the following students would you predict is the most likely to receive a negative teacher reaction?
A. Jeff, who has about a 3.0 grade-point average
B. Carmella, who has about a 3.0 grade-point average
C. Roger, who has about a 2.0 grade-point average
D. Linda, who has about a 2.0 grade-point average

_____ 11. What is the effect of asking higher-order questions on student achievement?
A. Positive
B. Negative
C. No effect

_____ 12. What is the best way to call on students to answer questions?
A. Ask the question, then call on a student by name.
B. Call on a student by name, then ask the question.
C. Use a random order of calling on students so that they won't know in advance whose turn it is.
D. There is no best way.

_____ 13. Why should teachers prevent a high frequency of student-initiated questions and comments?
A. The students will deliberately try to get the teacher "off the track."
B. The less able students will dominate the session.
C. The more able students will dominate the session.
D. It shows a lack of respect for the authority of the teacher.

_____ 14. Most reactions by teachers to student answers or comments are
A. positive.
B. negative.
C. neutral.

PROJECTS AND ACTIVITIES

1. Using the concepts of teacher structuring, teacher solicitation, student response, and teacher reaction, observe a class in any subject at any grade level from sixth grade through high school. See if you can recognize these patterns as they occur. What was their frequency per 15-minute block of time? Was the sequence of these events repetitive? Was there variety in the kinds of structuring moves made by the teacher? How does your own teaching compare with what you have observed?

2. Study the taxonomy of objectives in the cognitive domain, which was discussed in Chapter 4. Try to have in mind the six kinds of cognitive objectives that were defined. Now, observe a classroom and tally the questions asked by the teacher according to the cognitive processes required by the question. Your tally sheet might look like this:

Cognitive Process	Frequency of Question Type	Total
Knowledge	𝍦 𝍦 𝍦 ///	18
Comprehension	𝍦 /	6
Application	//	2
Analysis	//	2
Synthesis		0
Evaluation	/	1

Were the "memory-type" questions more prevalent than the "thinking-type" questions? Approximately what percentage of the questions asked were higher-order (for example, "What kind of plan would you design to modify the situation?" "What do you think was the author's purpose in writing the novel?" "Is this the most efficient way to approach the problem; what other hypotheses can you suggest?"). Is this percentage appropriate, or would you recommend a modification?

3. Observe in an elementary classroom during either reading or mathematics period for at least one week. Using Table 24-1 in your text as a guide, estimate the average time in minutes per day allocated to the subject, percent of time students are engaged, minutes per day students are engaged in the given subject area, percent of time students are engaged in material of low difficulty, and academic learning time per day. If possible, repeat the procedure at the same grade level, but with a different class. Compare your results. Think about the impact of academic learning time on student achievement over the entire school year. Do you think time allotment and engagement variables are powerful contributors to individual differences in achievement? Are these variables more easily changed than student characteristics such as intelligence, cognitive style, and motivation? What are the implications for your teaching?

SUGGESTIONS FOR TERM PAPERS

1. A review of the effects of teacher questioning on student learning

2. The teaching behaviors that are related to student achievement and attitudes

3. An evaluation of alternatives to traditional classroom teaching

4. Computing the academic learning time for a second/fifth/eighth/etc. grade class

5. Implementation of a plan to increase academic learning time

6. To praise or not to praise . . .

7. The importance of teacher organization

CHAPTER 25   BASIC CONCEPTS IN MEASUREMENT AND EVALUATION

OBJECTIVES

The student should be able to

o define the terms test, reliability, validity, standards, and norms

o state the pros and cons of criterion-referenced and norm-referenced approaches to student evaluation

o implement one simple procedure to improve test reliability

o distinguish between content, construct, and criterion validity

o contrast formative and summative evaluations

REMINDER

Chapter 25 deals with basic concepts used in educational measurement and evaluation: testing, reliability, and validity. Tests may be of two types--norm-referenced (interpreted in light of the test performance of other individuals) or criterion-referenced (interpreted in light of some established objective or standard). Reliability, you will recall, is a test characteristic that indicates the stability of a student's test performance over different testings or time spans. Reliability also refers to the precision of a test measurement on a single occasion. Validity is a test characteristic that indicates the degree to which a test measures what it purports to measure. You learned that teachers must be concerned with at least three types of test validity. Content validity refers to the logical match between a test and the subject matter area it should sample; construct validity refers to how well a test measures the ability it is intended to measure; and criterion validity refers to the degree to which a test predicts how well students will do in a particular course, school, or job. The chapter concluded with a discussion of formative and summative evaluation procedures.

DEFINITIONS OF KEY CONCEPTS

The following key concepts were discussed in this chapter. In your own words, write the definition of each concept in the space provided.

1. A test _____

_____

_____

2. A behavior sample _____

_____

_____

3. Evaluation _____

_____

_____

4. A test standard _____

_____

_____

5. Norm-referenced tests _____

_____

_____

6. Criterion-referenced tests _____

_____

_____

7. Test reliability _____

_____

_____

8. Test-retest reliability _____

_____

_____

9. Internal-consistency reliability_____

_____

_____

10. The standard error of measurement _____

_____

_____

11. A confidence band _____

_____

_____

12. Validity _____

_____

_____

13. Content validity _____

_____

_____

14. Construct validity _____

_____

_____

15. Criterion validity _____

_____

_____

16. Formative evaluation _____

_____

_____

17. Summative evaluation _____

_____

_____

APPLICATION OF KEY CONCEPTS

The terms listed below refer to important concepts that were discussed in this chapter. Carefully read each descriptive statement, and identify the concept or concepts each statement implies. Place the corresponding letter(s) of the concept(s) you select in the space provided.

Concepts

A. test standard
B. confidence band

G. formative evaluation
H. test-retest reliability

C. summative evaluation
D. standard error of measurement
E. behavior sample
F. construct validity

I. criterion-referenced test
J. criterion validity
K. content validity
L. norm-referenced test

Descriptive statements

_____ 1. I like to use this test because I've found that it fairly consistently ranks students in the same order from one test-making session to another.

_____ 2. That test Ms. Blakely gives students to decide who can be in her creative writing class is really accurate--most of the students selected do quite well and show considerable writing promise by the end of the term.

_____ 3. The team of experts that was here last week examining the administrative organization of the new special education department made quite a few recommendations about changes we could make to operate more efficiently.

_____ 4. Mr. Williamette is a really tough grader--he gives us these really hard tests and then grades us on the percentage of the questions we got right. Because of his criteria, a third of the class will probably fail the course.

_____ 5. I don't think this a very good test. The reliability is about .50. I bet there is a lot of inaccuracy in any single student's score.

_____ 6. Her real score in this area is somewhere between 74 and 90.

_____ 7. I got the highest grade in our class on that test, so I automatically got an A.

_____ 8. The end-of-year report indicated that the special program offering college courses for sixth through ninth graders wasn't yielding the gains in student achievement that were initially sought.

_____ 9. This test needs experimental verification of the claim that it measures children's anxiety.

_____10. I'm observing and recording the students' playground behavior every Monday morning and every Wednesday afternoon for the next month. This schedule should allow me to view fairly representative behavior.

_____11. When I was preparing this test, I was very deliberate about including items that were representative of the material covered in the class and in the text.

_____12. It's clear to students that they have to be able to answer 15 of the 20 test items on an objective correctly before they can move onto the next objective.

MULTIPLE-CHOICE SELF-TEST

Select the response that best answers the question or completes the statement. Place the letter of the chosen answer in the space provided.

_____ 1. Which of the following is an example of giving a test score meaning by comparing

it with a standard?
A. Henry scored 57.3 on the MPQ test of gardening.
B. Mathilda was 27 points below the cutoff for Global College.
C. Hortense was 196th in a class of 200.
D. Isadora's score was better than that of 95 percent of all the students who took the test.

_____ 2. The relationship between reliability and the standard error of measurement for a particular test is such that when reliability goes
A. up, the standard error of measurement goes down.
B. up, the standard error of measurement goes up.
C. down, the standard error of measurement goes down.
D. up, the standard error of measurement can go up, down, or remain the same.

_____ 3. When the items in a test are tied closely to the instructional materials a student was exposed to, the test is said to have
A. construct validity.
B. convergent validity.
C. content validity.
D. criterion validity.

_____ 4. If your classroom test of student ability in geometry correlates about .10 with the citywide test of geometry ability, which kind of validity of your test is in doubt?
A. Construct validity
B. Content validity
C. Criterion validity
D. Predictive validity

_____ 5. Which of the following most accurately expresses the teacher's role in evaluation?
A. Role is bigger in formative evaluation than in summative evaluation.
B. Role is bigger in summative evaluation than in formative evaluation.
C. Role is the same in both.

_____ 6. The type of test that tells you most about what a person knows and doesn't know is
A. norm-referenced, using the immediate peer group.
B. norm-referenced, using a distant peer group.
C. criterion-referenced.
D. one that is reliable.

_____ 7. Most teacher-made tests have
A. small errors of measurement.
B. large errors of measurement.
C. high reliability.
D. power-construct validity.

_____ 8. If you are primarily interested in measuring students' competency in a particular subject area, which type of test approach would be most useful to you?

A. Norm-referenced
B. Criterion-referenced
C. Student-referenced
D. Teacher-referenced

_____ 9. The PTA subcommittee found that student attitudes toward music are more positive when the school band plays popular selections than when "classic" marching band selections are played. The music department will incorporate this information into next year's programs. This is an example of
  A. parent-teacher cooperation.
  B. content validity.
  C. summative evaluation.
  D. formative evaluation.

PROJECTS AND ACTIVITIES

1. Ask a teacher for a test that was recently given and the curriculum content that it covered. Check the test for content validity and then compute the test's mean, standard deviation, reliability, and standard error of measurement (see Technical Note H). Judge the degree to which the test is really content-valid. Does it have sufficient reliability for the teacher's purposes? How wide a confidence band is needed to interpret an indvidual student's score?

2. Try to identify an innovation in a school. It could be a new curriculum, a television instructional system, or a system of teaching. Plan and conduct a small, informal evaluation of the innovation. What sources of information do you need? Whom should you interview? What should you observe? Should anyone be tested? Who could use the information? Will the information result in a better program?

SUGGESTIONS FOR TERM PAPERS

1. Development of content-valid tests in science/social studies/metal shop/etc.

2. The development of a criterion-referenced testing system

3. Current models of evaluation

4. The case for criterion-referenced measurement

5. Why use norm-referenced measurement?

6. The history of testing in American public education

TECHNICAL NOTE G

THE STANDARD DEVIATION, VARIANCE, RELIABILITY, AND STANDARD ERROR OF MEASUREMENT

COMPUTING THE STANDARD DEVIATION AND VARIANCE

The scores on a test can spread over a considerable range, or their distribution can be narrow, with most scores near the mean, or average. Figure G-1 presents examples of these two kinds of distributions. the preferred measure of this kind of variability or dispersion in scores is the <u>standard deviation</u>. It has special meaning for certain distributions called <u>normal curves.</u> Such distributions have the bell shape shown in Figure G-1. They are mathematically defined abstractions that approximate the actual distribution of many variables, such as the height of adult white females in the United States. Often test scores have distributions that are fairly normal.

The standard deviation is a statistic that, for curves that are normal or approximately normal, marks off the distribution of scores into intervals that contain a known percentage of the cases. In both distributions shown in Figure G-1, the interval between the mean and 1 standard deviation above the mean contains 34 percent of the cases. Similarly, the interval between the mean and 1 standard deviation below the mean contains 34 percent of the cases. When a particular score falls anywhere within 1 standard deviation of the mean, we know it is grouped with about 68 percent of the other scores in that normal distribution. If a score falls 2 standard deviations below the mean, it is exceeded by about 98 percent of the scores in that normal distribution. If a score falls 1 standard deviation above the mean, it is exceeded by about 16 percent of the scores and exceeds 84 percent of the scores. All this information is known because of the mathematical properties of normal distributions. The percentage of cases associated with various standard-deviation distances from the mean, as determined by mathematicians, is given in Figure G-1.

Here is a numerical example. Suppose a student receives a score of 33 points on the test whose distribution is displayed on the left in Figure G-1. Since we know that the mean is 29 and the standard deviation is 2, we know that this student is 2 standard deviations above the mean. Because the standard deviation marks off interpretable percentages of cases in the distribution, we can estimate that this student's score falls at about the 98th percentile, exceeded by only about 2 percent of the scores in that distribution. Now, suppose that the same score is received by a student whose test comes from the distribution presented on the right in Figure G-1. The mean is the same as in the first distribution, but the variability of scores is more than twice as great. The test score does not quite reach the point that is 1 standard deviation above the mean. This score certainly falls lower than the 84th percentile, and we can estimate that it is at about the 80th percentile, exceeded by about 20 percent of the scores. Thus we see that, even when the mean is the same, the same score has very different meanings, depending upon the dispersion of scores in the distribution in which it occurs. In one case the score of 33 is practically the best score one could obtain; in another case it is above average, but hardly exceptional.

The standard deviation, along with the mean, provides some of the most important information you can obtain about a test. The mean tells you about the central tendency of the distribution, and the standard deviation tells you about the viability of the scores. The smaller the standard deviation, the more closely the scores are clustered around the mean. Knowing the standard deviation and the mean, and assuming that the scores are approximately normally distributed, you can tell almost immediately the percentile rank of a score. You can accurately estimate (or use tables provided in most testing and statistics books) how this score compares with other scores in the distribution. For example, suppose you learn that a friend received a score of 390 on the verbal part of the Graduate Record Examination. Since the Graduate Record Examination has a mean of 500 and a standard deviation of 100, we know immediately that the person's score is more than 1 standard deviation below the mean. Therefore, the score of 390 is almost at the 16th percentile, exceeded by over 84 percent of the scores received by other students.

Although information of this kind is often important, it still tells us nothing about what that particular test taker knows or what he or she can do. The interpretation of score by reference to the mean and standard deviation is a norm-referenced approach to evaluation.

Figure G -1
Two distributions of test scores with the same mean and different standard deviations.

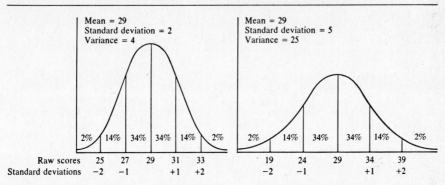

The text noted that the standard deviation could be computed. We shall use a short-cut formula developed by Diedrich (1964), which Sabers and R. D. Klausmeier (1971) found to be accurate to within 2 percent of the more formal procedure when applied to classroom tests.

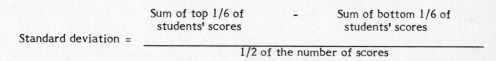

In a class of 30 students, this means summing the top five scores, subtracting from that total the sum of the bottom five scores, and then dividing that difference by 15. This is not a difficult formula to apply.

Another useful measure of variability is the variance. The variance is the square of the standard deviation. Once we estimate the standard deviation, we need only square that value to obtain the variance. The variance has some beneficial statistical properties that the standard deviation does not possess. Thus both measure of variability are often used to indicate the dispersion of a set of scores.

COMPUTING INTERNAL-CONSISTENCY RELIABILITY

The standard deviation and variance are important statistics to describe the spread of scores in a frequency distribution. In addition, these statistics help us understand internal-consistency reliability. For a test in botany, Table G-1 pesents the total test scores and a breakdown of those scores into the score on the odd-numbered items and the score on the even-numbered items. The logic of dividing a test into odd and even halves is to give us something like the test-retest situation we really want in order to estimate reliability. By thinking of the odd-numbered items as one test and the even numbered items as another test, we obtain two parallel forms of the test. The correlations between rank orderings of students on these two equivalent tests, that is, on the odd and even halves, is what we can then use as an estimate of reliability. The way we shall obtain a simple and quick estimate of that correlation is with the formula

$$\text{Reliability} = 2 \left(1 - \frac{\text{Variance of the scores on the odd items} + \text{Variance of the scores on the even items}}{\text{Variance of the scores on the total test}} \right)$$

In Table G-1, the estimates of the standard deviation are obtained by the formula presented above. The variances of the two halves of the test and the total test are obtained by squaring these standard deviations. These variances are substituted into the formula for reliability. We can then judge the degree to which our test is giving us reliable information. In this case, the rliability of the test is .65--hardly high enough to give us confidence if we have important decisions to make. The kind of confidence we can actually have about scores is easily calculated, and it is called the standard error of measurement.

COMPUTING THE STANDARD ERROR OF MEASUREMENT

The score of a student on any test is composed of "error" as well as the "true" amount of the ability we are measuring. The formula for estimating the error in a score, the standard error of measurement, is

$$\text{Standard error of measurement} = \text{Standard deviation for the total distribution} \sqrt{1 - \text{Reliability coefficient}}$$

By substituting the values noted in Table G-1 this standard error of measurement works out to be 3.31.

The standard error of measurement tells us the width of the confidence band within which a true score lies. The observed score can be thought of as one of an infinite sample of scores that the person might obtain on the test. The mean of that infinite series, when errors are random, is the person's true score. The standard deviation of these scores is the standard error of measurement. Thus, the obtained score, plus and minus 1 standard deviation, contains 68 percent of the cases. Thefore, the true score for a person lies within +1 and -1 standard error of the obtained score about 68 percent of the time. If we needed to be quite sure about someone's true score, say if we were deciding whether to recommend the person for promotion or retention in a course, we might want to use plus or minus 2 standard errors, which would give us 95 percent confidence that we had bracketed the person's true score.

A quick way for teachers to determine the standard error of measurement is given in Table G-2. If the standard deviation and reliability are known, a quick estimate can be obtained without a formula. For a test of high reliability, say .90, and a small standard deviation, say 4, the standard error of measurement is 1.3. Thus, 68 percent of the time a person's true score will be within 13 points of the observed score. But remember that teacher-made tests typically have reliabilities well below .80. The standard errors become large when the standard deviation is over 10 and reliabilities are under .80. Most teacher-made tests have large errors of measurement.

The concept of reliability is important because it enters into estimating the standard error of measurement. To give you an even more dramatic example, suppose you were giving course grades and trying to end up with a distribution of 5 percent A's, 25 percent B's, 40 percent C's, 25 percent D's, and 5 percent F's, as was once common in many university courses. The percentage of mis-classifications you would make for given test reliabilities is given in Table G-3.

Table G-2
Estimated Standard Errors of Measurement for Given Values of Reliability and for Given Standard Deviations

Standard Deviation	Reliability Coefficients					
	.95	.90	.85	.80	.75	.70
30	6.7	9.5	11.6	13.4	15.0	16.4
28	6.3	8.9	10.8	12.5	14.0	15.3
26	5.8	8.2	10.1	11.6	13.0	14.2
24	5.4	7.6	9.3	10.7	12.0	13.1
22	4.9	7.0	8.5	9.8	11.0	12.0
20	4.5	6.3	7.7	8.9	10.0	11.0
18	4.0	5.7	7.0	8.0	9.0	9.9
16	3.6	5.1	6.2	7.2	8.0	8.8
14	3.1	4.4	5.4	6.3	7.0	7.7
12	2.7	3.8	4.6	5.4	6.0	6.6
10	2.2	3.2	3.9	4.5	5.0	5.5
8	1.8	2.5	3.1	3.6	4.0	4.4
6	1.3	1.9	2.3	2.7	3.0	3.3
4	.9	1.3	1.5	1.8	2.0	2.2
2	.4	.6	.8	.9	1.0	1.1

Source: The Psychological Corporation, *Test Service Bulletin No. 50* (June, 1950).

Table G-3
Estimates of Misgrading for Various Test Reliabilities

Test Reliability	Incorrect Classifications
.98	9%
.95	15
.90	23
.80	33
.70	40

Source: Adapted from Ebel (1965).

With typical teacher-made tests that have reliabilities of under .80, over one-third of the students will probably be given a grade that is not the one they really deserve. True, A students will usually not receive D's, nor will many F students receive C's. But many students will receive a grade that is higher or lower than the grade they should have received if measurement had been error-free.

REFERENCES

DIEDRICH, P. D. (1964) Short-cut statistics for teacher-made tests. Princeton, N.J.: Educational Testing Service. Evaluation and Advisory Service Series, No. 5.

EBEL, R. L. (1965) Measuring educatonal achievement, Englewood Cliffs, N.J.: Prentice-Hall.

SABERS, D. L. and KLAUSMEIER, R. D. (1971) Accuracy of short-cut estimates for standard deviation. Journal of Educational Measurement, 8:335-339.

Students	Total Score	Scores on Odd Items	Scores on Even Items
Roddy	18	11	7
Robert	39	17	22
Bethann	19	10	9
Brett	37	20	17
Murry	20	9	11
Lee Ann	21	10	11
Michelle	28	14	14
Sheila	32	14	18
James	30	16	14
Kelly	36	16	20
Mark	33	15	18
Edna	37	21	16
Greta	30	14	16
Ferdinand	22	10	12
Douglas	29	14	15
Landers	34	21	13
Keith	29	14	15
Mike	26	13	13
Irving	28	16	12
Seth	32	13	19
Charles	35	19	16
David	29	13	16
Nathaniel	33	16	17
Natalie	27	13	14
Carmine	24	12	12
Cassandra	30	16	14
Zelda	26	14	12
Juanita	30	13	17
Shirley	25	15	10
Henry	31	16	15
Sum of scores	870	435	435
Mean	29.0	14.5	14.5
Standard deviation	5.6	3.2	3.3
Variance	31.36	10.24	10.89
Reliability	.65		
Standard error of measurement	3.31		

Table G-1
Students' Scores, Computing Formulas, and Descriptive Statistics on a Classroom Botany Test

Formulas:

$$\text{Mean} = \frac{\text{Sum of scores}}{\text{Number of scores}}$$

$$\text{Standard deviation} = \frac{\text{Sum of top 1/6 of students' scores} - \text{Sum of bottom 1/6 of students' scores}}{1/2 \text{ of the number of scores}}$$

$$\text{Variance} = (\text{Standard deviation})^2$$

$$\text{Reliability} = 2\left(1 - \frac{\text{Variance of odd scores} + \text{Variance of even scores}}{\text{Variance of total scores}}\right)$$

$$\text{Standard error of measurement} = \left(\begin{array}{c}\text{Standard deviation}\\\text{of total scores}\end{array}\right)\sqrt{1 - \text{Reliability}}$$

CHAPTER 26 STANDARDIZED TESTS AND THE TEACHER

OBJECTIVES

The student should be able to

o state some common uses and misuses of standardized tests

o interpret and convert scores reported as T scores, standard scores, stanines, grade-level scores, and percentile values

o apply twelve criteria in rating the utility of a standardized test

o distinguish between aptitude and achievement tests

o compare and contrast standardized tests and teacher-made tests on the criteria of reliability, validity, quality of test items, administration, scoring, and interpretation

o locate the review of any standardized test in the Mental Measurements Yearbook

REMINDER

Chapter 26 dealt with the uses, misuses, evaluation, and interpretation of standardized tests by the classroom teacher. You learned about criteria a teacher can use to select and evaluate a standardized test, including descriptions of behavior measured, validity, reliability, teaching feedback, examinee appropriateness, ease of administration, ethical propriety, retest potential, and cost. If they are administered and interpreted correctly, norm-referenced standardized tests provide an objective and general appraisal of a student's abilities and aptitudes. Such tests have the advantage of typically being accompanied by detailed administrative directions and information as to reliability and validity. The misuses of standardized tests by the classroom teacher can take the forms of regarding the scores obtained as perfectly reliable, confusing norms with desirable standards, or evaluating teacher performance. You also learned how to convert standardized test scores into standard scores, T scores, age-level scores, grade-level scores, and percentile ranks to make them more easily interpreted.

DEFINITIONS OF KEY CONCEPTS

The following key concepts were discussed in this chapter. In your own words, write the definition of each concept in the space provided.

1. A norm-referenced standardized test _____

_____

_____

2. A criterion-referenced standardized test _____

_____

_____

3. Aptitude tests _____

_____

_____

4. Standardized achievement tests _____

_____

_____

5. Noncognitive standardized tests _____

_____

_____

6. A percentile rank _____

_____

_____

7. A frequency distribution _____

_____

_____

8. The median _____

_____

_____

9. The arithmetic mean _____

_____

_____

10. A standard score _____

_____

_____

11. A standard deviation _____

_____

_____

12. A T score _____

_____

_____

13. A stanine _____

_____

_____

14. An age or grade norm _____

_____

_____

APPLICATION OF KEY CONCEPTS

The terms listed below refer to important concepts that were discussed in this chapter. Carefully read each statement, and identify the concept or concepts each statement implies. Place the corresponding letter(s) of the concept(s) you select in the space provided.

Concepts

A. noncognitive standardized test
B. frequency distribution
C. criterion-referenced standardized test
D. arithmetic mean
E. stanine
F. standard score
G. aptitude test

H. median
I. standardized achievement test
J. norm-referenced standardized test
K. T score
L. standard deviation
M. percentile rank
N. grade norm

Descriptive statements

_____ 1. This type of converted score fits easily onto an IBM card.

_____ 2. The State Board Examination in Nursing requires candidates to answer a given number of questions correctly in order to be licensed.

_____ 3. The algebra teacher converts her students' raw scores on tests so that she can compare their relative performance; a negative converted score indicates performance below the class average and a positive converted score indicates performance above the class average.

_____ 4. I was so happy when I saw my score--86! That means I did better than 86% of the others taking the test.

_____ 5. Half of the boys on the junior varsity basketball team are below 5' 9" and half are over 5' 9".

_____ 6. Three people in our class got a score of 10, five got a score of 9, eight got a score of 7, eight got a score of 6, seven got a score of 4, one got a score of 2, and four people got a score of zero.

_____ 7. He recently took the State French Reading Comprehension Examination.

_____ 8. Ellen scored quite high on the verbal part of the College Admissions Test.

_____ 9. I was reading the pamphlet that accompanied the test. It gives specific directions about administration and provides a chart to be used in interpreting students' scores. The chart was based on information about the test performances of over ten thousand students who had taken the test.

_____ 10. It would be much more reasonable to interpret these test scores knowing the mean and degree of variability of the scores. I should compute the latter statistic.

_____ 11. The average score on reading comprehension for all the sixth-graders in the district was 82.

_____ 12. The average score of our class on the test was 11 right out of 15 items. We figured it by adding up all the students' scores and dividing by 23, the number of students in our class.

_____ 13. It's often convenient to convert z scores in order to eliminate the minus signs and decimals.

_____ 14. I'd like to give my ninth-grade students Brown and Holtzman's "Survey of Study Habits and Attitudes" so that I can use the results to help them study more effectively.

MULTIPLE-CHOICE SELF-TEST

Select the response that best answers the question or completes the statement. Place the letter of the chosen answer in the space provided.

_____ 1. Which of the following types of school personnel probably makes the most use of knowing that Linda scored very high on standardized spatial and mechanical aptitude tests?
A. The school principal

B. The school counselor
C. The student's teacher
D. An evaluator studying the effects of a new science curriculum

_____ 2. What is the relationship between scores on standardized tests and student practice with various item types and test formats?
A. Practice increases test scores.
B. Practice decreases test scores.
C. Aptitude test scores cannot be improved with practice, but achievement test scores can.
D. There is no consistent relationship between practice and test scores.

_____ 3. On a particular test, a T score of 65 and a z score of +1.5 will turn out to have
A. raw scores that are close in magnitude.
B. raw scores on different sides of the mean.
C. identical raw scores.
D. different grade-equivalent scores.

_____ 4. You know that students are studying for tomorrow's test. The likelihood is that it is a
A. standardized achievement test.
B. standardized aptitude test.
C. teacher-made test.
D. interest battery to be used for guidance purposes.

_____ 5. In relation to your own tests in science, the content validity of a standardized science test is likely to be
A. about the same.
B. higher.
C. lower.
D. sometimes higher, sometimes lower.

_____ 6. The Center for the Study of Evaluation (CSE) has rated many standardized tests. In general, the reliability and validity of the tests are rated as
A. poor.
B. good.
C. excellent.
D. outstanding.

_____ 7. Standardized tests are predominantly
A. criterion-referenced.
B. norm-referenced, using an immediate peer group.
C. norm-referenced, using a distant peer group.

_____ 8. Because of budget limitations, the school district has sent us dittoed, instead of printed, copies of the test. In many instances smudging of the ink has made the items difficult to read. This test would not pass the criterion of
A. teaching feedback.
B. ethical propriety.
C. retest potential.
D. examinee appropriateness.

_____ 9. In general the best source for obtaining an objective and comprehensive evaluation by experts of standardized tests is

        A. the test manual.
        B. the publisher's catalog.
        C. Mental Measurements Yearbook.
        D. taking the test yourself.

_____ 10. What is the median of the following distribution of raw scores: 10, 7, 3, 5, 8, 2, 6?
        A. 5
        B. 6
        C. 3
        D. There is no median

_____ 11. What is the mean of the following distribution of raw scores: 4, 6, 11, 7, 9, 5?
        A. 5
        B. 6
        C. 7
        D. There is no mean

PROJECTS AND ACTIVITIES

1. Go to a school testing office or university library and take out a standardized test and the administrator's booklet and technical report that accompany the test. Read these materials carefully and judge whether you think the test can be administered easily, gives reliable information, is valid for its purposes, can be interpreted by you, and will make sense to the student.

2. In the section on information sources at the end of this study guide are listed a number of test publishers. With some classmates, write to some of these publishers and ask for reports on their standardized tests in your subject matter area. When some of these are received, go over them carefully and see what claims are made and whether or not they can be substantiated. In particular, check whether the norming group used by the test publisher is appropriate for their standardization and your purposes.

SUGGESTIONS FOR TERM PAPERS

1. Student reactions to standardized tests

2. Pros and cons of standardized testing

3. Standardized testing and minority groups

4. Why standardized tests should be abolished

5. A review of the ____ test for measuring achievement in reading/mathematics /science/etc.

CHAPTER 27   TEACHER-MADE TESTS

OBJECTIVES

The student should be able to

o construct a table of specifications for building a test

o compare and contrast essay, short-answer, true-false, multiple-choice, and matching questions

o develop criteria for grading an essay test

o write acceptable multiple-choice items

o perform item analyses to estimate the sensitivity to instruction, difficulty, and discrimination indexes of a test's items

o state the uses of four types of achievement tests

o explain how microcomputers can be of use in writing teacher-made tests

REMINDER

Chapter 27 considered the advantages of teacher-made criterion-referenced tests--for evaluating students against the objectives of your own teaching and their own learning. That is, student achievement should be evaluated in terms of what it is important for students to have learned. You will remember that in constructing criterion-referenced tests, the teacher must consider what kinds of achievement are important, what types of questions will elicit student performance revealing those kinds of achievement, and how student achievement can be evaluated in ways that will help the teacher become more effective.

Chapter 27 also indicated how, after testing, you can peform item analyses to estimate the difficulty, discrimination, and sensitivity to instruction indexes of your test questions. Finally, you learned about four kinds of achievement tests--placement, formative, diagnostic, and summative--and their various uses.

DEFINITIONS OF KEY CONCEPTS

The following key concepts were discussed in this chapter. In your own words, write the definition of each concept in the space provided.

1. Domain-referenced testing _____

_____

_____

2. A table of specifications for an achievement test _____

_____

_____

3. Essay questions _____

_____

_____

4. Supply short-answer questions _____

_____

_____

5. Select short-answer questions _____

_____

_____

6. Acquiescent reponse set _____

_____

_____

7. Multiple-choice questions _____

_____

_____

8. Power tests _____

_____

_____

9. Speeded tests _____

_____

_____

10. Item analysis _____

_____

_____

11. Item sensitivity to instruction _____

_____

_____

12. Item analysis in criterion-referenced testing _____

_____

_____

13. An index of item difficulty _____

_____

_____

14. An index of item discrimination _____

_____

_____

15. Placement tests _____

_____

_____

16. Formative tests _____

_____

_____

17. Diagnostic tests _____

_____

_____

18. Summative tests _____

_____

_____

APPLICATION OF KEY CONCEPTS

The terms listed below refer to important concepts that were discussed in this chapter. Carefully read each descriptive statement, and identify the concept or concepts each statement implies. Place the corresponding letter(s) of the concept(s) you select in the space provided.

Concepts

A. supply short-answer question
B. acquiescent response set
C. select short-answer question
D. index of item difficulty
E. item analysis
F. speeded test
G. placement test
H. item sensitivity to instruction

I. index of item discrimination
J. summative test
K. formative test
L. power test
M. multiple-choice question
N. diagnostic test
O. essay question
P. domain-referenced test

Descriptive statements

_____ 1. If you are stumped by a particular test item, skip it and go on to the next question. You can always go back to those items if time allows. It is very important for you to answer as rapidly as you can. I'll tell you when it's 10:30, which means half the session is over. It is exactly 10:00 o'clock now, so begin.

_____ 2. I gave my students a quiz asking them to write the name of each of the 20 bones indicated with numbers on the skeleton. I inferred that the students who got all the items on the test right know the names of all the bones in the body.

_____ 3. You'll have two hours to complete the test. If you finish before that time, turn your test materials in to me, and you may leave. Carefully think through your answers--you'll have plenty of time to finish.

_____ 4. I passed the spelling and punctuation test, so now I can enroll in Creative Writing.

_____ 5. The "Big Four"--Charles Crocker, Collis Huntington, Leland Stanford, and Mark Hopkins--were responsible for the construction of a ___ that drastically altered the population of the Far West in the late nineteenth century.

_____ 6. Mrs. Richvale gave us a short quiz yesterday on safety rules for use of the equipment. Today she said we still need "a bit more work" in that area before we can use the table saws.

_____ 7. I just passed my Red Cross life-saving exam! Now I'm fully certified to be a lifeguard.

_____ 8. Why is it difficult to identify a mineral by its color?
A. The color surface of many minerals tarnishes, making identification very unreliable.
B. Minerals take on a different color when they are exposed to heat and moisture.
C. Traces of impurities can cause color variation in minerals.
D. The same mineral has a wide range of possible color.

226

_____ 9. Match the word in the right column with the correct word or phrase in the left column.

__1.	Real or imagined pattern of stars	A. nebula
__2.	Stars whose brightness periodic change	B. cepheid
		C. constellation
__3.	Star in a late stage of development	D. quasar
		E. red giant

_____10. Ms. O'Rourke gave me some extra reading on the digestive system to do at home. She said my test showed that I really understood the physiology of all the body's systems except that one.

_____11. Define the economic principle of diminishing returns and describe how it operates in a free enterprise economy. Provide at least two applications of the principle to a hypothetical economic situation.

_____12. Whenever I'm not sure about a statement on a true-false test, I answer "true"; I figure I'd be more apt to recognize a false statement than one that was true.

_____13. I'm definitely going to add this item to my item pool to use next term. The students who got the highest test scores seem to be getting it correct, whereas the lower-scoring students generally answered it incorrectly.

_____14. After looking at the breakdown of student response to each item, I decided to retain only about half of the items, and to generate other new items to use for next year's class.

_____15. This item is a very easy one--all the students in the class but one got it correct.

_____16. I'm pretty pleased with this test item. Most of the students missed it before we covered the material, but after studying the unit most of them got it right.

MULTIPLE-CHOICE SELF-TEST

Select the response that best answers the question or completes the statement. Place the letter of the chosen answer in the space provided.

_____ 1. An advantage of the select type of short-answer test item over the supply type of item is that select items can
A. be constructed more easily.
B. be scored more reliably.
C. be less ambiguous.
D. tap more complex mental processes.

_____ 2. An item on a multiple-choice test has a discrimination index of .48. How would you rate this item?
A. Excellent
B. Good
C. Fair
D. Poor

_____ 3. Sally wants postinstruction items that have difficulty indexes of about .50.

Charlie wants postinstruction items that have difficulty indexes of about .90.
Without knowing much other information, you might conclude that
A.   Sally and Charlie are building criterion-referenced tests.
B.   Sally is building a criterion-referenced test; Charlie is building a norm-referenced test.
C.   Sally and Charlie are building norm-referenced tests.
D.   Sally is building a norm-referenced test; Charlie is building a criterion-referenced test.

_____ 4.   Giving students a choice of essay questions is
A.   recommended, because students like the options.
B.   recommended, because a wide sampling of desired learning outcomes can be chosen.
C.   not recommended, because of the difficulty of preparing essay questions.
D.   not recommended, because it is difficult to get a set of essay questions that demand the same things from learners.

_____ 5.   On a particular test, the nubmer of distractors for a multiple-choice item
A.   should remain the same.
B.   should preferably be varied from item to item.
C.   may be varied according to the number of plausible distractors possible for the gi item.

_____ 6.   This question appeared on a test: "Compute the difficulty index of an item where all 10 scorers got the item right and none of the 10 low scorers got the item right." This kind of question would probably be classified as
A.   application.
B.   synthesis.
C.   analysis.
D.   evaluation.

_____ 7.   In item 6, the difficulty index actually is
A.   1.00.
B.   .75.
C.   .50.
D.   .00.

_____ 8.   When scheduling tests, you should probably try to create a system that tests students
A.   infrequently, with longer tests.
B.   frequently, with shorter tests.
C.   infrequently, with shorter tests.
D.   frequently, with longer tests.

_____ 9.   The research on the reliability of grading essay tests shows that teachers tend
A.   not to agree with other teachers, but to agree with themselves over time.
B.   not to agree with other teachers and not even to agree with themselves over time.
C.   to agree with other teachers and with themselves over time.
D.   to agree with other teachers but not to agree with themselves over time.

_____ 10.   The ordering of test types from least likely to adequately sample a domain to most likely to adequately sample a domain is

A.   essay, short answer, multiple-choice.
B.   essay, multiple-choice, short answer.
C.   short answer, essay, multiple-choice.
D.   short answer, multiple-choice, essay.

_____11.   If you are interested in measuring students' ability to use higher-order cognitive processes, such as analysis and evaluation, which type of tst question format would be best?
A.   Essay
B.   Matching
C.   True-false
D.   Incomplete sentence

_____12.   Which kind of select-type test question is the most flexible?
A.   True-false
B.   Matching
C.   Multiple-choice
D.   All are equally flexible

_____13.   After calculating test items, sensitivity to instruction, which items would you revise or eliminate?
A.   Those equal to 1.00
B.   Those that are .80 or higher
C.   Those that are close to 0.00
D.   Those that students said were difficult
E.   Those that students said were easy

_____14.   Good test items are those that students answer
A.   correctly both before and after instruction.
B.   correctly before instruction and incorrectly after instruction.
C.   incorrectly before instruction, and correctly after instruction.
D.   incorrectly both before and after instruction.

_____15.   What do the authors of your text suggest regarding tstudent choice among essay questions?
A.   Students should be given several alternatives form which to select.
B.   Students should answer all questions.
C.   Students should be required to answer half the questions.
D.   Students should answer half the questions in class and half on a take-home exam.

_____16.   The incorrect alternative responses, or distractors, in a multiple-choice question should be
A.   plausible.
B.   implausible.
C.   shorter than the correct response.
D.   a phrase.

PROJECTS AND ACTIVITIES

1. Construct a behavior-content table of specifications for a course or subject matter area you are likely to teach. Ask a colleague to criticize it. You might also give it to a student of such a course, and see whether the student would judge it to be fair.

2. In your subject matter area, and for the grade level you will teach, try writing 10 multiple-choice test items. Have a colleague do the same. Then criticize each other's items. In writing the items, follow the advice given on pages 000 of the text, and use your best educational judgment in making your critique.

3. See whether you can obtain a teacher-made test in some subject matter area. Check the test for content coverage and analyze the items for their quality. Then do an item analysis and fed those results back to the teacher. You should learn a lot about classrom tests and their revision throught this activity.

SUGGESTIONS FOR TERM PAPERS

1. The development of a behavior-content matrix and associated items for the teaching fof fifth-grade social studies/junior high school science/twelfth-grade/English/etc.

2. The essay test: pros and cons from the student's and teacher's perspectives.

3. A history of classroom testing practices in the United States

4. Anxiety in classroom testing: Why anxiety occurs and how to reduce it

5. How to use a microcomputer for writing better tests

CHAPTER 28   GRADING AND MARKING

OBJECTIVES

The student should be able to

o specify a grading sytem for his or her own course or subject matter area

o write a brief essay on the pros and cons of using tests and grades as a motivational device

o differentiate between normative, absolute, and pseudo-absolute standards

o create a criterion-referenced reporting system

REMINDER

Chapter 28 addressed the reasons for, and problems with, teacher evaluation of students. You read about such controversial issues as: teacher variability in grading, grading as a motivational device, effects of pass/no credit grading, and the relationship between testing and student anxiety. You also learned about techniques for gathering information about students--both from formal testing situations and from careful observation of students in other settings. Your evaluations and use of grades can be helpful in vocational counseling, determining admission to programs, and providing feedback to parents.

DEFINITIONS OF KEY CONCEPTS

The following key concepts were discussed in this chapter. In your own words, write the definition of each concept in the space provided.

1. Convergence technique in student evaluation _____

_____

_____

2. Marks in student evaluation _____

_____

_____

3. Bias in evaluation _____

_____

_____

4. Absolute standards _____

_____

_____

5. Pseudoabsolute standards _____

_____

_____

6. Relative standards _____

_____

_____

7. Report cards _____

_____

_____

8. Normative reporting _____

_____

_____

9. Parent conferences _____

_____

_____

10. Anecdotal reports _____

_____

_____

APPLICATION OF KEY CONCEPTS

The terms listed below refer to important concepts that were discussed in this chapter. Carefully read each descriptive statement, and identify the concept or concepts that each statement implies. Place the corresponding letter(s) of the concept(s) you select in the space provided.

Concepts

A. bias in evaluation
B. relative standards
C. anecdotal report
D. marks
E. report card

F. convergence technique
G. parent conference
H. pseudoabsolute standards
I. absolute standards
J. normative reporting

Descriptive statements

_____ 1. To receive an A grade in lab section, you have to corrrectly perform three experiments from each chapter in the chemistry workbook; to receive a B grade, you must correctly perform two experiments from each chapter in the workbook.

_____ 2. Mrs. Jacoby, you can see from my notes about Suzie's playground behavior that she gets along very well with the other girls, but is shy about playing with any of the boys.

_____ 3. I grade students on the curve to prevent them from working together on take-home exams.

_____ 4. I make sure I have an estimate of a student's performance on at least five homework assignments, three essay tests, and an individual project before midterm evaluation.

_____ 5. Now I have to go back over all the assignments in Carolyn's folder. If I overlooked her spelling errors on this paper, I might have done the same on her other papers. I guess I wasn't too attentive because she is the brightest student in the class and all.

_____ 6. Let's see. Jamie's test scores fall right about midway between the scores of the other students in the class; therefore, he'll get a B- on his report card.

_____ 7. It's very important that you take these forms home. They're for your parents to use to indicate what time is most convenient for them to come in and have a talk with me about the work you're all doing.

_____ 8. I got a B+ on my book report!

_____ 9. My grading system is very efficient. The students whose average composite percentage from all tests and assignments is 85 percent or higher get an "outstanding"; those with percentages between 65 percent and 85 percent get a "satisfactory"; and everybody with percentages below 65 percent receives an "unsatisfactory." But, if more than half the class falls into either the "outstanding" or the "unsatisfactory" category, then I have to adjust the cutoff points.

_____ 10. I got five "satisfactories" and one "improvement needed" at the end of the term.

MULTIPLE-CHOICE SELF-TEST

Select the response that best answers the question or completes the statement. Place the letter of the chosen answer in the space provided.

_____ 1. Using many different sources of information about a student's achievement
A. provides too much divergent information to be used sensibly.
B. increases the errors inherent in marks.
C. improves the validity of marks.

_____ 2. The number of A's or F's given by teachers of different classes in different schools has been found to
A. vary markedly.
B. vary slightly.
C. be fairly constant.
D. be related to socioeconomic status.

_____ 3. Severe grading of student performance
A. provides the motivation needed for greater achievement.
B. does not seem to affect students' behavior in any noticeable fashion.
C. eliminates lower grading standards.
D. creates a threat that some students will avoid by not enrolling in a course.

_____ 4. Bridgham examined secondary school science enrollments as a function of ease of grading. He found that when the ease of grading in chemistry was made equal to that in other disciplines subsequent enrollment in physics classes tended to increase for
A. girls only.
B. boys only.
C. Both girls and boys.
D. neither girls nor boys.

_____ 5. When pass/no credit grading is used rather than conventional grades, the performance of students is
A. somewhat lower.
B. somewhat higher.
C. much higher.
D. not significantly different.

_____ 6. When graduate students were compared on the amount of work they did on their research papers for a course, it was found that they did more work when graded
A. on a pass/no credit basis.
B. competitively.
C. noncompetitively.
D. by means of verbal comments without grades.

_____ 7. You probably should not combine scores from
A. norm-referenced tests.
B. speeded tests.
C. power tests.
D. criterion-referenced tests.

_____ 8. Generally, when evaluating student achievement, you should
A. take into account your estimates of student effort.

B. keep your estimates of student effort separate from your evaluation of achievement.
C. ignore the student's achievement and evaluate whether or not the student has tried to the best of his or her ability.

_____ 9. Absolute standards are used when we have a system that is
A. norm-referenced.
B. expressed in percentile scores.
C. achievement-oriented.
D. criterion-referenced.

_____ 10. Research on bias in grading was conducted by Zillig. The findings might lead you to predict that
A. better students will get more breaks in grading than less able students.
B. better students will get fewer breaks in grading than less able students.
C. less able students will receive lower grades than they deserve.
D. students in the middle of the ability range get the best breaks in grading.

PROJECTS AND ACTIVITIES

1. Conduct a survey among your fellow students in this course to tap attitudes toward grading practices. Find out whether they think they learn as much in pass/no credit courses as in graded courses. Ask them to describe fair and unfair grading practices they have encountered. How would they envision an optimal grading system? How can you apply what you learned from your suvey to the grading practices you will use when you teach?

2. Conduct a survey of some students and their parents, asking what they like and don't like about report cards. See whether either the students or their parents can tell you what information needs they have that are not being met. Try to find out how important report cards are to parents by asking if they reward or punish their children on the basis of those reports. See whether you can include different social class groups in your limited survey, and whether the perceptions of students and parents in the different social class groups differ.

3. Carry out with your colleagues an exercise in role-playing a parent-teacher conference. Try to role-play reports on different types of children, such as the anxious student, the achievement-oriented student, the very low ability student, the belligerent type, etc. Also try to role-play an angry father, one who will punish his child; then try to role-play a parent who accuses the teacher of incompetence, or one who fawns over the teacher, etc. Such an exercise will help you to consider your role during parent-teacher conferences.

SUGGESTIONS FOR TERM PAPERS

1. Toward the abolition of report cards

2. Developing a fair grading system for English/social studies/gym/etc.

3. Teacher bias in grading practices

4. Society's needs for evaluation: A defense of equitable grading programs

5. In defense of pass/no credit grading systems in high school and college courses

TECHNICAL NOTE H

COMBINING AND WEIGHTING NORM-REFERENCED DATA

COMBINING TEST DATA

A way of converting the various scores from many and diverse tests into a standardized scoring system is presented in Table H-1. <u>The standardized scores can be averaged</u> because the conversion puts all the tests into the same <u>metric</u>, or measuring, scale. In these standard scores, each test is made to have the same mean $\overline{(50)}$ and the same standard deviation (10). These standard scores are called $\underline{T}$ scores, and their relationships to other types of standard scores have already been described in Chapter 26 of the text. These standard, or $\underline{T}$, scores also are converted into a normal or bell-shaped frequency distribution, regardless of the shape of the original distribution of the raw scores. The various interchangeable scoring systems, including $\underline{T}$ scores, were displayed in relation to the normal curve distribution of scores in Figure 5-1 (p. 76).

All you need to convert the many different kinds of raw scores to a common metric is the ability to rank-order the students on some dimension of performance. Suppose you had given five tests of arithmetic. On the first test, Marco ranked 13th out of the 24 students who took the test. Using Table H-1, we find that Marco's standard score would be 49. This score could be given to Marco, or it could be used simply for combining purposes. You may actually have to give him 80 percent because he got 16 out of 20 items correct. Or you may have given him a B or simply 16. On his second test, when 31 students were present, he may have scored 20 correct out of 40 problems. You might choose to give him a mark of 20, 50 percent, or C. However, ultimately, for combining his test scores you will want his rank in the class. If on the second test he was 27th out of the 31 students taking the test, his standard score, according to Table H-1, would be 39. Marco's standard scores on these different tests--49 on the first test, 39 on the second test, and, say 45, 62, and 38 on the other three tests--can be averaged together. A single composite standard score is then arrived at; in this case, it is 46.6

The conversion to $\underline{T}$ scores and averaging of the tests should be done for all students. The range of standard scores will go from about 25 to 75 in large classes, with a smaller range appearing in smaller classes. The mean will remain at 50. The distribution of standard scores for the entire class can be used easily to assign summary letter grades, percentages, or any other single mark to reflect a composite drawn from many tests, papers, and projects.

WEIGHTING TESTS

We recommend that very complex systems for weighting tests, papers, or projects be used only in unusual and well-thought-out cases. Each weighting system should be defensible by the teacher and clearly understood by the students.

Sometimes, unless explicit weights are used, all tests and papers, the short quiz and the long final, end up making the same contribution toward a student's grade. If all projects, papers, and tests were simply converted to standard scores with the aid of table H-1, when averaged together they would make equal contributions to a final grade.

A weighted composite of some kind is needed to give the more important and less important sources of information about a student more or less emphasis. The moderately complex example we shall use to illustrate how to weight tests and papers is intended as an illustration rather than a recommendation. You will have to determine your own weighting system by carefully thinking through your values and your evaluation system. Suppose you want to weight tests and student projects differentially, according to their importance as you see them, in your attempt to achieve the goals of your course. Perhaps you have three quizzes and decide they should contribute 10 percent each toward the final grade. You may choose to count a midterm examination 20 percent, a term paper 20 percent, and a final examination 30 percent toward the final grades for your students. Table H-2 shows the steps to be taken for each student, as the marks assigned to tests and papers are converted to standard scores, weighted, and summed to determine a weighted composite, or summary score, for a particular student.

All tests, papers, and projects are graded and converted to a common metric weighted according to some prearranged plan, an a summary standard score is computed for each student. The ranking of these standard scores can be used to assign letter grades or percentage grades.

TableH-2
Computing a Weighted Composite of Six Scores for a Single Student

	Step 1	Step 2	Step 3	Step 4	Step 5
Quiz 1	80%	11/27	53	.10	5.3
Quiz 2	70%	11/30	54	.10	5.4
Midterm	+48	7/30	58	.20	11.6
Quiz 3	38%	24/29	41	.10	4.1
Term paper	B−	10/29	55	.20	11.0
Final exam	+109	31/30	63	.30	18.9

Weighted Composite 56.3
Standard Score

Step 1: Record original mark
Step 2: Record original rank
Step 3: Use Table 34-1 to convert to standard scores
Step 4: Record weight assigned
Step 5: Multiply standard score by weight, and sum to determine weighted composite

TableH-1

Standard Scores for
Groups of Students Who
Have Been Ranked

Rank	5	6	7	8	9	10	11	12	13	14	15	16	17	18	19	20	21	22	23	24	25
1	63	64	65	65	66	66	67	67	68	68	68	69	69	69	70	70	70	70	70	70	71
2	55	57	58	59	60	60	61	62	62	62	63	63	64	64	64	64	65	65	65	65	66
3	50	52	54	55	56	57	57	58	59	59	60	60	60	61	61	62	62	62	62	63	63
4	45	48	50	52	53	54	55	55	56	57	57	58	58	59	59	60	60	60	61	61	61
5	37	43	46	48	50	51	52	53	54	54	55	55	56	56	57	57	58	58	59	59	59
6		36	42	45	47	49	50	51	52	53	53	54	55	55	56	56	56	57	57	57	58
7			35	41	44	46	48	49	50	51	52	52	53	54	54	55	55	55	56	56	56
8				35	40	43	45	47	48	49	50	51	51	52	53	53	54	54	55	55	55
9					34	40	43	45	46	47	48	49	50	51	51	52	52	53	53	54	54
10						34	39	42	44	45	47	48	49	49	50	51	51	52	52	53	53
11							33	38	41	43	45	46	47	48	49	49	50	51	51	52	52
12								33	38	41	43	44	45	46	47	48	49	49	50	51	51
13									32	38	40	42	44	45	46	47	48	48	49	49	50
14										32	37	40	42	43	44	45	46	47	48	48	49
15											32	37	40	41	43	44	45	46	47	47	48
16												31	36	39	41	42	44	45	45	46	47
17													31	36	39	41	42	43	44	45	46
18														31	36	38	40	42	43	44	45
19															31	36	38	40	41	43	44
20																30	35	38	40	41	42
21																	30	35	38	39	41
22																		30	35	37	39
23																			30	35	37
24																				30	34
25																					29

Total Number of (students ranked — column headings 5 through 25)

Rank continues: 26, 27, 28, 29, 30, 31, 32, 33, 34, 35, 36, 37, 38, 39, 40, 41, 42, 43, 44, 45 (no entries)

This table converts rankings to a standard score scale with a mean of 50 and a standard deviation of 10. To use the table, first determine the number of persons ranked. Then enter the table with the rank of the individual. A rank of 2 indicates a person who is second from the top. At the intersection of the row indicating rank and the column indicating number of persons ranked will be found the standard score. For example, the 4th person in a group of 22 would have a score of 60. The 17th person in a group of 30 would have a score of 49. When a tie exists, the individuals in the tie receive the middle rank. If 3 students tie for the 5th rank, they would actually cover the 5th, 6th, and 7th ranks. Each would receive the rank of 6, and the next highest score would receive the rank of 8. If two scores were tied for 10th rank, they would hold the 10th and 11th ranks, and would each receive a rank of 10.5. The corresponding T-score value would be between ranks 10 and 11.

Source: Air Training Command (1952).

Students Ranked

26	27	28	29	30	31	32	33	34	35	36	37	38	39	40	41	42	43	44	45	Rank
71	71	71	71	71	71	71	72	72	72	72	72	72	72	72	72	72	73	73	73	1
66	66	66	66	66	67	67	67	67	67	67	67	68	68	68	68	68	68	68	68	2
63	63	63	64	64	64	64	64	64	65	65	65	65	65	65	65	66	66	66	66	3
61	61	62	62	62	62	62	62	63	63	63	63	63	64	64	64	64	64	64	64	4
59	60	60	60	60	61	61	61	61	61	62	62	62	62	62	62	62	63	63	63	5
58	58	59	59	59	59	59	60	60	60	60	60	61	61	61	61	61	61	62	62	6
57	57	57	58	58	58	58	59	59	59	59	59	60	60	60	60	60	60	60	61	7
56	56	56	57	57	57	57	57	58	58	58	58	59	59	59	59	59	60	60	60	8
54	55	55	55	55	56	56	56	57	57	57	57	58	58	58	58	58	58	59	59	9
53	54	54	55	55	55	55	56	56	56	56	57	57	57	57	57	58	58	58	58	10
52	53	53	54	54	54	54	55	55	55	55	56	56	56	56	56	57	57	57	57	11
51	52	52	53	53	53	54	54	54	54	55	55	55	55	55	56	56	56	56	57	12
50	51	51	52	52	52	53	53	53	54	54	54	54	55	55	55	55	56	56	56	13
50	50	50	51	51	52	52	52	53	53	53	53	54	54	54	54	55	55	55	55	14
49	49	50	50	50	51	51	52	52	52	52	53	53	53	54	54	54	54	54	55	15
48	48	49	49	50	50	50	51	51	51	52	52	52	53	53	53	53	54	54	54	16
47	47	48	48	49	49	50	50	50	51	51	51	52	52	52	52	53	53	53	53	17
46	46	47	47	48	48	49	49	50	50	50	51	51	51	52	52	52	52	53	53	18
44	45	46	46	47	48	48	48	49	49	50	50	50	51	51	51	51	52	52	52	19
43	44	45	45	46	47	47	48	48	49	49	49	50	50	50	51	51	51	52	52	20
42	43	44	45	45	46	46	47	47	48	48	49	49	49	50	50	50	51	51	51	21
41	42	43	43	45	46	46	47	47	48	48	48	48	49	49	50	50	50	51	51	22
39	40	41	42	43	44	45	45	46	46	47	47	48	48	48	49	49	49	50	50	23
37	39	40	41	42	43	44	44	45	46	46	47	47	47	48	48	49	49	49	49	24
34	37	38	40	41	42	43	44	44	45	45	46	46	47	47	48	48	48	49	49	25
29	34	37	38	40	41	42	43	43	44	45	45	46	46	46	47	47	48	48	48	26
	29	34	36	38	39	41	41	42	43	44	44	45	45	46	46	47	47	47	48	27
		29	34	36	38	39	40	41	42	43	43	44	45	45	46	46	46	47	47	28
			29	34	36	38	39	40	41	42	43	43	44	44	45	45	46	46	47	29
				29	33	36	38	39	40	41	42	42	43	44	44	45	45	46	46	30
					29	33	36	37	39	40	41	41	42	43	44	44	44	45	45	31
						29	33	36	37	38	40	40	41	42	43	43	44	44	45	32
							28	33	35	37	38	39	40	41	42	43	44	44	44	33
								28	33	35	37	38	39	40	41	42	43	43	43	34
									28	33	35	37	38	39	40	41	42	42	43	35
										28	33	35	37	37	39	40	41	41	42	36
											28	32	35	36	38	39	40	40	41	37
												28	32	35	37	38	39	40	40	38
													28	32	35	36	37	38	39	39
														28	32	34	36	37	38	40
															28	32	34	36	37	41
																27	32	34	36	42
																	27	32	34	43
																		27	32	44
																			27	45

INFORMATION SOURCES

When the need for information in an area of educational psychology arises, a good starting point for obtaining that information is the subject index and list of references in your textbook, the third edition of Educational Psychology. But sometimes questions arise on topics not addressed in the textbook, or you may need an extensive review of an area for a project. For these situations, there are other information sources that may prove useful to you. We have listed some of the more accessible and comprehensive sources with annotations to help you choose the documents to consult. In addition, we have listed some of the major test distributors from which you can obtain information about standardized tests.

GENERAL GUIDES TO A WIDE RANGE OF LITERATURE

Current Index to Journals in Education (CIJE). New York: CCM Information Sciences, 1969.

Five hundred or more educational journals are indexed, by author, subject, and institution. Brief resumes of juournal articles are given. Issued monthly, with a yearly index.

Education Index. New York: H.W. Wilson, 1932-

The basic index to the periodical literature in education, including book reviews. The index, by author and subject, is issued 10 times a year. Almost all subject matter fields, all grade levels from preschool to adult, teacher education, counseling, and educational psychology are covered.

Psychological Abstracts Washington, D.C.: American Psychological Association, 1927-.

The first place to look for anything having to do with topics in any aspect of psychology, including those in educational psychology. Monthly listings of nonevaluative abstracts of journal articles, books, dissertations, and government docuemtns, including the literature of other countries.

Research in Education (RIE). Washington, D.C.: U.S. Government Printing Office, 1967-.

The monthly abstracting report from ERIC (Educational Resources Information Centers), consisting of 16 clearinghouses located around the U.S.A. Reports of excellent research efforts are indexed by subject, author, and institution.

ERIC systems will also conduct computer searches at low cost if you furnish one or more keyword descriptors. These searches can be made at many sites throughout the country and will turn up hundreds of abstracts for you to look at on the topic you described. Check with the reference service at your school district, college, or university for more information about ERIC computer searches.

REVIEW OF RESEARCH

Review of Research in Education. Itasca, Ill.: F.E. Peacock for the American Educational Research Assocation, 1973-.

Presents expert review of the research literature on selected topics. Major areas are updated annually.

Review of Educational Research. Washington, D.C.: American Educational Research Association, 1931-.

Unsolicited reviews on various topics provide the latest syntheses of information in diverse research areas. Published quarterly.

BASIC REFERENCE BOOKS USED IN EDUCATIONAL PSYCHOLOGY

Anastasi, Anne. Differential Psychology (3rd ed.).
New York: Macmillan, 1958

A comprehensive, well-written textbook on the differences between people. Includes perspectives on racial, social class, sex, and urban-rural differences in intelligence, temperament, personality, interests, and achievement.

Berelson, Bernard, and Steiner, Gary. Human Behavior: An Inventory of Scientific Findings. New York: Harcourt, Brace and World, 1967.

Presents 1,045 numbered propositions, hypotheses, or assertions about human behavior. Nontechnical summaries of the literature of psychology, sociology, anthropology, and education. Fascinating reading.

Buros, Oscar K. (Ed.) The Eighth Mental Measurements Yearbook. Highland Park, N.J.: Gryphon Press, 1978. 2 vols.

Psychologists, teachers, and psychometricians review hundreds of published tests. Whatever information you may need about a test, including exhaustive bibliographies, can usually be found in this or previous yearbooks in the series.

Ebel, R. L. (Ed.) Encyclopedia of Educational Research (4th ed.). New York: Macmillan, 1969

Presents scholarly, alphabetically arranged articles with bibliographies on many different topics to which educational research is addressed.

Gage, N. L. (Ed.) Handbook of Research on Teaching. Chicago: Rand McNally, 1963.

Experts in various fields wrote 24 chapters on such topics as classroom observation; statistical methods; experimental design; teacher personality; and the teaching of social studies, reading, and other subject matter areas. Excellent biliographies. Partially updated by the Second Handbook of Research on Teaching, edited by Travers, listed below.

Good, Carter V. Dictionary of Education (3rd ed.). New York: McGraw-Hill, 1973.

Carefully constructed definitions of terms used in educational psychology and related areas.

International Encyclopedia of the Social Sciences. New York: Macmillan, 1968. 17 vols.

Provides a good start on just about any social science topic.

Travers, R. N. W. (Ed.) Second Handbook of Research on Teaching. Chicago: Rand McNally, 1973

Experts review the literature on teaching in many different areas. Includes chapters on the teaching of all major subject matter areas, as well as theory in research on teaching, early childhood education, instructional technology, etc.

DISTRIBUTORS OF EDUCATIONAL AND PSYCHOLOGICAL TESTS

These test distributors can supply you with information, sample tests, and guides for the administration of the tests. All kinds of tests are sold by these distributors, and you should first obtain their catalogs so that you can decide which ones you want further information about.

American College Testing Program, P.O. Box 168, Iowa City, IA 55240

American Guidance Services, Inc., Publishers Building, Circle Pines, MN 55014

Australian Council for Educational Research, Frederick St., Hawthorn E.2, Victoria, Australia

Bobbs-Merrill Company, Inc., 4300 East 62nd St., Indianapolis, IN 46206.

Bureau of Educational Measurements, Kansas State Teachers College, 1200 Commercial St., Emporia, KS 66801.

California Test Bureau (CTB), Del Monte Research Park, Monterey, CA 93940.

Consulting Psychologists Press (CPP), Inc., 577 College Ave., Palo Alto, CA 94306.

Educational and Industrial Testing Services (EITS), P.O. Box 7234, San Diego, CA 92107.

Educational Records Bureau, 21 Audubon Ave., New York, NY 10032.

Educational Testing Services (ETS), Princeton, NJ 08540.

Grune & Stratton, Inc., 381 Park Ave. South, New York, NY 10016.

Harper & Row, Publishers, 49 East 33rd St., New York, NY 10016.

Harcourt Brace Jovanovich, Inc., 757 Third Ave., New York, NY 10017.

Houghton Mifflin Company, One Beacon St. Boston, MA 02108.

Institute for Personality and Ability Testing (IPAT), 1602 Coronado Dr., Champaign, IL 61820.

National Foundation for Educational Research in England and Wales, The Mere, Upton Park, Slough, Bucks, England.

Newnes Educational Publishing Company Ltd., Tower House, 8-11 Southampton St., Strand, London W.C. 2, England

Ohio Scholarship Tests, Station C, Department of Education, State of Ohio, 751 Northwest Blvd., Columbus, OH 43212.

Personnel Press, Inc., 20 Nassau St., Princeton, NJ 08540.

Psychological Corporation, 304 East 45th St., New York, NY 10017.

Psychological Test Specialists, Box 1441, Missoula, MT 59804.

Psychometric Affiliates, 1743 Monterey, Chicago, IL 60643.

Public Personnel Asociation, 1313 East 60th St., Chicago, IL 60637.

Research Psychologists Press, Goshen, NY 10924.

Richardson, Bellows, Henry & Co., Inc., 324 Balter Bldg., New Orleans, LA 70712.

The Riverside Publishing Company, 8420 Bryn Mawr Avenue, Chicago, IL 60631.

Scholastic Testing Service, Inc., 480 Meyer Rd., Bensenville, IL 60106.

Science Research Associates (SRA), Inc., 259 East Erie St., Chicago, IL 60624.

Sheridan Supply Co., P.O. Box 837, Beverly Hills, CA 90213.

C.H. Stelting Co., 424 North Homan Ave., Chicago, IL 60624.

University of London Press Ltd., Little Paul's House, Warwick Sq., London E.C. 4, England.

Western Psychological Services, 12035 Wilshire Blvd., Los Angeles, CA 90025.

CHAPTER 1   HOW EDUCATIONAL PSYCHOLOGY HELPS WITH THE PROBLEM
OF TEACHING

ANSWER GUIDE TO DEFINITIONS OF KEY CONCEPTS

1. Educational objectives are those statements that tell what students should be able to do and what they will do if given an opportunity (p. 9).

2. Individual differences in students are those characteristics in which students differ--such as age, sex, previous achievement of certain kinds, social class, and ethnic background-- that will affect what they are ready to learn and how they will learn it (p. 9).

3. Correlation is the degree to which various characteristics do or do not go together (p. 10).

4. Teaching methods are the procedures by which students can be helped to move from their initial ways of behaving to those that have been set up as objectives (p. 11).

5. Evaluation is a method of assessing students' learning or achievement of educational objectives (p. 12).

6. "Grading on the curve" is a method that evaluates students according to what percentage of their group they have excelled (p. 12).

ANSWER GUIDE TO APPLICATION OF KEY CONCEPTS

1.	C	4.	E
2.	B	5.	F
3.	A	6.	D

ANSWER GUIDE TO MULTIPLE-CHOICE SELF-TEST

1.	D	4.	A
2.	B	5.	E
3.	C	6.	B

ANSWER GUIDE TO DEFINITIONS OF KEY CONCEPTS

1. The empirical approach is the study of phenomena based on experience (p. 18).

2. Variables are attributes that vary among individuals or events (p. 22).

3. Concepts in educational psychology are variables that refer to aspects of the behavior of people as they become involved in educational activity and parts of the environment that are related to such behavior (p. 22).

4. Principles are the relationships between concepts (p. 25).

5. Laws are firmly established principles (p. 25).

6. Understanding is the ability to account for relationships between variables in ways that obey the laws of logic (p. 25).

7. Prediction is the ability to foretell, given the value of one variable, the subsequent value of another variable with better than chance accuracy (p. 25).

8. Control is the ability to manipulate one variable in such a way as to bring about desired values in another variable (p. 25).

9. A correlational relationship is one that exists if certain values of one variable tend to be found together with certain values of the other variable (p. 28).

10. A causal relationship is one that exists if changes in one variable bring about changes in the other variable (p. 29).

11. Manipulation of a variable is administration of the variable in varying amounts to objects, organisms, persons, or groups of these (p. 29).

12. Independent variables are the variables that are manipulated in an experiment (p. 29).

13. Dependent variables are the variables that are measured after the independent variable has been manipulated in an experiment (p. 29).

14. Random assignment is the selection of a random sample of persons to receive each of the values of the independent variable in an experiment (p. 30).

15. Correlation coefficients are numbers varying from -1.00 through zero to +1.00 that tell the direction and degree of closeness of the relationship between two variables (p. 31).

16. Experimentation is the situation in which the independent variable is manipulated and the values of the dependent variable are measured (p. 32).

17. Statistics are numerical procedures used to estimate whether research findings might be due to chance factors operating or not (p. 33).

ANSWER GUIDE TO APPLICATION OF KEY CONCEPTS

1.		E, L	5.	D	9.
2.	K	6.	C, J	10.	G
3.	F, H	7.	A, C	11.	I
4.	B	8.	A	12.	N

ANSWER GUIDE TO MULTIPLE-CHOICE SELF-TEST

1.	B	7.	A	13.	A
2.	A	8.	B	14.	B
3.	D	9.	B	15.	D
4.	C	10.	C	16.	B
5.	B	11.	D	17.	C
6.	A	12.	C		

CHAPTER 3   THE FORMULATION OF OBJECTIVES AND THEIR JUSTIFICATION

ANSWER GUIDE TO DEFINITIONS OF KEY CONCEPTS

1. Objectives are the desired outcomes of some activity (p. 41).

2. Terminal behaviors in educational objectives are those behaviors to be exhibited by the student as evidence that the objective has been achieved (p. 42).

3. Conditions of performance in educational objectives are the important conditions under which the desired student behavior is expected to occur (p. 42).

4. Levels of performance in educational objectives are the criteria of success to which the learner's achievement of an objective is compared (p. 43).

5. A behavior-content matrix is a framework for formulating educational objectives--one that uses types of student behaviors as columns, and categories of curriculum content as rows (p. 45).

6. Expressive objectives are those that describe an educational encounter, such as an activity to be engaged in; they differ from behavioral objectives in that they purposely do not specify the behavior that the learner is to exhibit after having engaged in a learning activity (p. 51).

ANSWER GUIDE TO APPLICATION OF KEY CONCEPTS

1.	C	4.	D	
2.	A	5.	E	
3.	B			

ANSWER GUIDE TO MULTIPLE-CHOICE SELF TEST

1.	B	6.	D	10.	D
2.	D	7.	C	11.	C
3.	B	8.	A	12.	D
5.	D	9.	A	13.	A

CHAPTER 4   DIFFERENT KINDS OF OBJECTIVES AND THEIR ORGANIZATION

ANSWER GUIDE TO DEFINITIONS OF KEY CONCEPTS

1. Taxonomy of educational objectives is a classification scheme that divides the field of objectives into three domains: cognitive, affective, and psychomotor (p. 57).

2. Cognitive objectives are those dealing primarily with intellectual processes (p. 57).

3. Affective objectives are those dealing primarily with emotional and attitudinal processes (p. 57).

4. Psychomotor objectives are those dealing with skills that primarily require physical movement (p. 57).

5. Knowledge is the ability to remember facts or ideas, in a situation in which certain cues are given to elicit effectively whatever knowledge has been stored (p. 58).

6. Comprehension is the ability to receive what is being communicated and make use of it, without necessarily relating it to other materials or seeing its implications (p. 58).

7. Application is the ability to use abstractions, rules, principles, ideas, and methods in particular and concrete situations (p. 58).

8. Analysis is the ability to break down a communication into its constituent elements or parts (p. 58).

9. Synthesis is the ability to work with pieces, parts, or elements and combine them in some way to form a whole or make a new pattern or structure (p. 59).

10. Evaluation is the ability to make quantitative and qualitative judgments about the extent to which materials and methods satisfy criteria (p. 59).

11. Learning hierarchy is the structure of material to be learned, ranging from simple to complex (p. 60).

12. Signal learning is the habit of making some kind of emotional response to a stimulus or signal (p. 60).

13. Stimulus-response learning is the ability to make relatively precise movements of the muscles in response to specific stimuli or combinations of stimuli (p. 61).

14. Chaining is the ability to connect a series of previously learned stimulus-response connections (p. 61).

15. Verbal association learning is a subvariety of chaining that occurs when stimuli and responses in the chains consist of words or syllables (p. 61).

16. Discrimination learning is the ability to distinguish among a set of stimuli in such a way as to make the appropriate response to each member of the set (p. 61).

17. Concept learning is the ability to respond to various instances of something by giving the appropriate abstract category or name (p. 61).

18. Rule learning is the ability to respond to a class of stimulus situations with a class of related performances (p. 61).

19. Structure of content is the relation between parts of the content to be learned (p. 62).

20. Mode of knowledge is the way in which knowledge is portrayed, for example, concretely, graphically, or symbolically (p. 65).

21. Economy of knowledge is the ability to represent a domain of knowledge with only a small amount of information to be kept in mind and processed (p. 65).

22. Power of knowledge is the value of the knowledge for generating new propostions, ideas, and principles (p. 66).

ANSWER GUIDE TO APPLICATION OF KEY CONCEPTS

1. E	4. B, H	7. A
2. B, H	5. D	8. C
3. G	6. F	

ANSWER GUIDE TO MULTIPLE-CHOICE SELF-TEST

1. A	6. C	11. C
2. C	7. B	12. A
3. B	8. D	13. B
4. B	9. A	
5. B	10. A	

ANSWER GUIDE TO DEFINITIONS OF KEY CONCEPTS

1. Intelligence is the ability to deal with abstractions, learn, and solve problems (p. 73).

2. Binet intelligence tests were those developed by French psychologist Alfred Binet at the turn of the century and used to differentiate between dull and normal children as judged by teachers (p. 72).

3. Raw test scores are those resulting from a summation of points earned on all the questions of a test (p. 75).

4. Test norms indicate the frequency with which various test scores have been obtained by the members of a particular norm group (p. 76).

5. Standardized test scores are those resulting from a conversion of raw scores by statistical procedures to standard scores with a mean of a given value (p. 76).

6. Standard deviation is a measure of variability of the scores in a group (p. 76).

7. Percentile rank is a standardized test score that tells what percentage of the norm group is surpassed by a person with that rank (p. 76).

8. A normal distribution is a fequency distribution that occurs whenever the magnitude of a variable is determined by many independent factors of roughly equal importance (p.76)

9. Reliability refers to the degree of consistency, dependability, or stability in the results of a test (p. 77).

10. Achievement tests are tests used to measure knowledge and ability taught directly in schools (p. 82).

11. Crystallized intelligence is ability resulting from the application of general mental ability to subject matter fields, such as history, mathematics, or geography (p. 83).

12. Fluid intelligence is ability requiring adaptation to new situations (p. 83).

13. The self-fulfilling prophecy phenomenon occurs when what is expected of a person strongly influences what, in fact, he or she becomes; in other words, the expectation of the outcome increases the probability of its occurrence (p. 85).

ANSWER GUIDE TO APPLICATION OF KEY CONCEPTS

1. B	5. J	9. B
2. I	6. F	10. A
3. D	7. E	11. H
4. C	8. K	12. G

ANSWER GUIDE TO MULTIPLE-CHOICE SELF-TEST

1. A	9. A	17. A
2. B	10. D	18. A
3. C	11. A	19. B
4. B	12. D	20. B
5. B	13. C	21. C
6. A	14. B	22. D
7. D	15. A	23. B
8. C	16. C	

CHAPTER 6   HEREDITY, ENVIRONMENT, AND GROUP DIFFERENCES IN INTELLIGENCE

ANSWER GUIDE TO DEFINITIONS OF KEY CONCEPTS

1. Selective placement is placement of children with foster parents whose cultural and educational level resembles that of the biological parents (p. 93).

2. Longitudinal studies are studies in which the same persons are tested in successive years (p. 103).

3. Social class is a variable measured by one or more of the following kinds of indices: father's occupation, family income, place of residence, and parents' educational level (p. 106).

4. "The poverty circle" refers to the fact that parents low in scholastic ability and, consequently, educational level tend to create environments in their homes and neighborhoods that produce children similarly low in scholastic ability and achievement (p. 108).

5. Selective migration refers to the movement of more able persons into the more advantaged social classes, occupations, regions, and communities (p. 110).

6. Environmental influences are the sights and sounds, words and ideas, problems and solutions a child is exposed to that facilitate the skills and knowledge measured by intelligence tests (p. 111).

7. Test bias is the degree to which intelligence tests involve content and processes that are more accessible to children in the advantaged groups (p. 112).

8. Culturally fair intelligence tests are tests designed to eliminate middle-class or other cultural bias (p. 112).

9. Early intervention refers to attempts to improve the intelligence of preschool age children (p. 118).

10. Cultural deprivation is inadequate opportunity to have rich and varied experiences that promote ability to learn (p. 118).

11. The <u>linguistic-deficit approach</u> maintains that the cognitively deficient linguistic systems of the culturally deprived are a key variable in accounting for differences in intellectual performance between middle-class and lower-class children (p. 119).

12. <u>Mediated learning</u> is learning that is assisted by an adult who focuses, elaborates, and corrects in order to help the learner understand and solve a problem (p. 125).

ANSWER GUIDE TO APPLICATION OF KEY CONCEPTS

1.	H	6.	E
2.	B	7.	F, I
3.	A	8.	D
4.	C	9	J
5.	G		

ANSWER GUIDE TO MULTIPLE-CHOICE SELF-TEST

1.	E	9.	A	17.	A
2.	D	10.	A	18.	D
3.	A	11.	A	19.	C
4.	A	12.	C	20.	B
5.	B	13.	A	21.	B
6.	B	14.	D	22.	E
7.	C	15.	C	23.	B
8.	B	16.	A		

CHAPTER 7   THE DEVELOPMENT OF COGNITIVE FUNCTIONS AND LANGUAGE

ANSWER GUIDE TO DEFINITIONS OF KEY CONCEPTS

1. The <u>sensorimotor stage</u> is a developmental stage characterized by the child's growth in ability in simple perceptual and motor activities (p. 132).

2. <u>Object permanence</u> is the cognitive ability, acquired during the sensorimotor stage to know that objects continue to exist even when they cannot be seen (p. 132).

3. The <u>preoperational phase</u>, the first phase of the preoperational stage of development, is characterized by the child's use of language to help learn concepts (p. 134).

4. The <u>intuitive phase</u>, the second phase of the preoperational stage of development, is characterized by the child's ability to reach conclusions that are based on nonverbal impressions and perceptual judgments (p. 135).

5. <u>Conservation</u> is the idea that the amount of something, either liquid or solid, remains the same regardless of changes in its shape or the number of pieces into which it is divided (p. 136).

6. The <u>concrete operational stage</u> is a developmental stage characterized by the child's ability to perform logical operations with concrete objects or information (p. 138).

7. <u>Composition</u> refers to the notion that whenever two elements of a system are combined, another element of the system results (p. 139).

8. <u>Associativity</u> refers to the notion that the sum of elements is independent of the order in which they are added (p. 139).

9. <u>Reversibility</u> refers to the fact that if a series of moves are made to get from place or state A to place or state B, the reverse order can be used to get from B to A (p. 139).

10. The <u>formal operational stage</u> is a developmental stage characterized by the child's ability to think logically with abstractions (p. 140).

11. <u>Hypothetico-deductive thinking</u> is the process of developing hypotheses, offering interpretation, and drawing conclusions (p. 140).

12. <u>Propositional thinking</u> is the process of combining one set of propositions into new, higher-order propositions (p. 140).

13. <u>Assimilation</u> is the process of changing what is perceived to fit existing cognitive structures (p. 143).

14. <u>Accommodation</u> is the process of changing existing cognitive structures to fit what is perceived (p. 143).

15. <u>Cognitive schema</u> is cognitive organization and structure (p. 144).

16. <u>Disequilibrium</u> is the cognitive state experienced when one is confronted with new events that do not fit with one's perceptions (p. 144).

17. The <u>enactive stage</u> is a developmental stage in which nonthinking action and simple motor behavior provide the only ways in which the child can understand the world (p. 146).

18. The <u>iconic stage</u> is a developmental stage characterized by the child's dependency on perceptual information to understand the world (p. 147).

19. The <u>symbolic stage</u> is a developmental stage characterized by the child's ability to use symbol systems (p. 147).

20. <u>Intellectual empathy</u> is the process of adults putting themselves in the child's place so that they can see phenomena and problems in the same way the child does (p. 147).

21. The <u>inductive approach</u> to teaching allows the child to acquire an understanding of concepts and principles through personal discovery (p. 148).

22. A <u>language acquisition device</u> in a theoretical construct used to explain how human beings acquire language given exposure to language; it contains a system of preconceptions about the formal nature of language (p. 151).

23. A <u>rationalist view of language acquisition</u> suggests that children learn by impliictly determining the rules of their language community (p. 151).

24. <u>Holophrastic speech</u> refers to the one-word utterances of young children used to express complex ideas. They are equivalent to the full sentences of adults (p. 152).

25. <u>Linguistic competence</u> is a speaker's knowledge of the finite system of rules that enable the comprehension and production of an infinite number of novel sentences (p. 152).

26. <u>Linguistic performance</u> is the expression or realization of linguistic competence in behavior (p. 152).

27. <u>Inflections</u> are the endings of word stems that express grammatical relationships (p. 153).

28. <u>Metalinguistic awareness</u> is the ability to think, at a conscious level, and comment about the sounds in words, the ordering of words in spoken or written sentences, and the selection of the most appropriate linguistic form to convey a given meaning (p. 158).

29. <u>Sociolinguistic competence</u> is the knowlege of the social rules governing the use of language in the classroom environment (p. 160).

ANSWER GUIDE TO APPLICATION OF KEY CONCEPTS

1. L	9. D, E	17. W
2. Q, S	10. N, T	18. M, S
3. N, W	11. K	19. F, H, I
4. F, O	12. P	20. F
5. N, R, W	13. J	21. E
6. C, H	14. U	22. B
7. V	15. G	23. I
8. A, N	16. B, X	

ANSWER GUIDE TO MULTIPLE-CHOICE SELF-TEST

1. C	8. B	14. C
2. A	9. A	15. B
3. B	10. C	16. C
4. B	11. B	17. C
5. C	12. B	18. C
6. B	13. D	19. B
7. D		

CHAPTER 8   THE DEVELOPMENT OF PERSONALITY

ANSWER GUIDE TO DEFINITIONS OF KEY CONCEPTS

1. Personality refers to the integration of all of a person's traits, abilities, and motives, as well as temperament, attitudes, opinions, beliefs, emotional responses, cognitive styles, characteristics, and morals (p. 165).

2. Crises in psychosocial development are events in an individual's environment at a given stage of development that result in progress or regression in personality growth, and influence whether the individual's personality becomes more integrated or more diffuse (p. 166).

3. Crisis of trust vs. mistrust occurs in infancy and is determined by the quality of love, attention, touch, and feeding relationships the child receives (p. 167).

4. Crisis of autonomy vs. shame occurs during early childhood and is characterized by the degree of development of self-control (p. 167).

5. Crisis of initiative vs. guilt occurs in middle childhood and is characterized by the degree of development of a realistic sense of purpose and the formation of a conscience (p. 167).

6. Crisis of accomplishment vs. inferiority occurs between the years of kindergarten and puberty and is characterized by the child's degree of need to do and make some things well, or even perfectly (p. 167).

7. Crisis of identity vs. confusion occurs during adolescence and is characterized by degrees of feelings of diffusion, estrangement, and unattachment resulting from psycholigical and physiological sexual changes and the struggle to establish an identity (p. 168).

8. Crisis of intimacy vs. isolation occurs after identity is functionally established and is characterized by the individual's ability or inability to establish intimate relationships (p. 169).

9. Crisis of generativity vs. stagnation occurs in adulthood and is characterized by the individuals, degree of interest in being creative and productive, and guiding the next generation (p. 169).

10. Crisis of integrity vs. despair occurs in old age and is characterized by the degree of the individual's sense of being satisfied with himself or herself and what he or she has accomplished (p. 170).

11. Moral development is an individual's formation of ideas concerning what is right and what is wrong (p. 170).

12. Preconventional level of moral development is a stage characterized by the child's ability to respond to cultural labels of good and bad, and attend mainly to the physical or pleasure-pain effects of action or the physical power of those in authority (p. 172).

13. Conventional level of moral development is a stage characterized by an individual's valuing loyalty to, and support of, the social order (p. 172).

14. **Postconventional level of moral development** is a stage characterized by an individual's effort to define moral principles that are valid apart from the authority of other persons holding them or one's identification with particular groups (p. 172).

15. **Morality** is a principle governing behavior that defines what is intrinsically just in terms of how the rights and well-being of others are affected (p. 174).

16. **Convention** is a principle governing behavior that defines what is right in terms of societal consensus regarding proper behavior (p. 174).

17. **Traits** are the relatively stable and enduring aspects of a person's behavior across a variety of situations (p. 175).

18. **Creativity** refers to originality, flexibility in thinking, and fluency in the production of ideas (p. 181).

19. **"Govering skill" in problem solving** is a skill that helps a person to organize and manage the problem-solving activities necessary for productive or creative solutions (p. 185).

20. **Self-concept** is the totality of one's perception of oneself, including one's attitude towards oneself and the language used to describe oneself (p. 186).

21. **Anxiety**, as a trait, refers to a person's general disposition to feel threatened by a wide range of nonharmful conditions; as a state, it refers to the same feeling of threat, but only in particular environmental situations (p. 190).

ANSWER GUIDE TO APPLICATION OF KEY CONCEPTS

1.	K	7.	I	13.	N
2.	F	8.	C	14.	G
3.	A, B, E, L	9.	Q	15.	E
4.	P	10.	H	16.	L
5.	J	11.	O	17.	B
6.	M	12.	D		

ANSWER GUIDE TO MULTIPLE-CHOICE SELF-TEST

1.	B	8.	C	15.	H
2.	A	9.	C	16.	G
3.	B	10.	A	17.	E
4.	A	11.	C	18.	C
5.	A	12.	D	19.	A
6.	D	13.	B		
7.	B	14.	F		

CHAPTER 9   THE DEVELOPMENT OF SEX DIFFERENCES

ANSWER GUIDE TO DEFINITIONS OF KEY CONCEPTS

1. <u>Sex bias in intelligence tests</u> refers to the degree to which intelligence tests involve content and processes that are more accessible to a child because of his or her sex (p. 199).

2. <u>Cross-sex parental linkage</u> is the genetic transmission of a parental characteristic to a child of the opposite sex (p. 201).

3. <u>Spatial ability</u> is skill in orienting or visualizing the location of oneself or real objects in space (p. 201).

4. <u>Field dependence</u> is the degree to which the context of a problem affects the solving of the problem (p. 201).

5. <u>"Category width" in conceptual learning tasks</u> is the degree to which something differing from a standard is judged to be the same as the standard (p. 202).

6. <u>Androgyny</u> refers to sex-role adaptability, that is, possession of both feminine and masculine psychological characteristics to a high degree regardless of one's physiological sex (p. 207).

7. <u>Sex-role stereotypes</u> are roles commonly accepted as being more or less appropriate for an individual depending on his or her sex (p. 211).

8. <u>Title IX of the Education Amendments</u> is a federal regulation prohibiting sex discrimination in any education program or activity receiving federal funds (p. 213).

ANSWER GUIDE TO APPLICATION OF KEY CONCEPTS

1.	F	5.	A
2.	C	6.	G
3.	B	7.	E
4.	H	8.	D

ANSWER GUIDE TO MULTIPLE-CHOICE SELF-TEST

1.	B	7.	B	13.	C
2.	C	8.	C	14.	B
3.	B	9.	B	15.	A
4.	C	10.	C	16.	C
5.	B	11.	A	17.	B
6.	A	12.	B	18.	A

257

ANSWER GUIDE TO DEFINITIONS OF KEY CONCEPTS

1. Exceptional students are those whose education must be specially designed to meet their particular mental, sensory, physical, social, and communication characteristics and abilities (p. 220).

2. P.L. 94-142, the Education for All Handicapped Children Act, is a federal law assuring that all handicapped children have a free and appropriate public education available to them (p. 220).

3. The least restrictive environment refers to the placement of exceptional children with their nonexceptional peers in regular classrooms to the maximum extent possible (p. 220).

4. Mainstreaming refers to the inclusion of exceptional students in the least restrictive enviroment to assure that their special needs are met and their abilities developed as fully as possible (p. 221).

5. An individualized education program, or IEP, is the written statement indicating explicitly how a particular exceptional student will be helped to reach agreed-upon objectives, including the special educational and administrative services needed by the student (p. 222).

6. Specific learning disabilities is a category of exceptionality referring to students whose abilities are judged to be much higher than their actual performance (p. 227).

7. Behavior disorders is a category of exceptionality referring to inability to learn that cannot be explained by other factors, inability to have satisfactory relationships, inappropriate behavior or feelings under normal circumstances, general mood of depression, or the tendency to develop physical symptoms associated with problems (p. 231).

8. Mental retardation is a category of exceptionality referring to students who are below average in both IQ and adaptive behavior (p. 233).

9. Severely or profoundly mentally retarded students are those requiring custodial supervision and training in self-care skills (p. 233).

10. Trainable mentally retarded students are those requiring training in self-care, language usage, independent living, perceptual-motor abilities, social interaction, and vocational skills (p. 233).

11. Educable mentally retarded students are those who show inadequate adaptive behavior in school settings (p. 233).

12. Speech disorders is a category of exceptionality referring to speech that deviates so far from the speech of others that it calls attention to itself, interferes with communication, or causes the speaker or listener to be distressed (p. 234).

13. Language disorders is a category of exceptionality referring to students' basic misunderstanding of the symbols used to convey ideas (p. 234).

14. Hearing impairment is a category of exceptionality, ranging from hard-of-hearing to deaf, that causes the student to lack proficiency in speech, language use, and reading (p. 235).

15. Visual impairment is a category of exceptionality, ranging from limited vision to blindness, that causes the student to have difficulty in orientation and mobility, communication skills, and access to information (p. 237).

16. Physical and health impairment is a category of exceptionality referring to disorders of (a) the skeleton, joints, and muscles, and (b) those health conditions that affect students' educational performance (p. 240).

17. Giftedness and talent is a category of exceptionality referring to students who demonstrate high performance in intellectual ability, specific academic aptitude, creative thinking, leadership, visual and performing arts, or psychomotor ability (p. 240).

18. Acceleration is an approach to helping gifted students by exposing them to learning experiences designed for older students (p. 241).

19. Enrichment is an approach to helping gifted students by providing experiences and training that enhance regular classroom instruction (p. 242).

20. An aptitude-treatment interaction is the situation that occurs when students high in a characteristic ("aptitude") learn better when taught by one method ("treatment"), whereas students low in that characteristic learn better when taught by another method (p. 242).

ANSWER GUIDE TO APPLICATION OF KEY CONCEPTS

1. E	7. O, N	13. C
2. M	8. P	14. N
3. A	9. D	15. K
4. J, N	10. Q	16. L
5. F	11. G	17. H
6. B	12. I	

ANSWER GUIDE TO MULTIPLE CHOICE SELF-TEST

1. C	9. E
2. B	10. C
3. C	11. C
4. B	12. A
5. D	13. D
6. A	14. A
7. E	15. C
8. C	16. A

ANSWER GUIDE TO DEFINITIONS OF KEY CONCEPTS

1. Learning is the process whereby an organism changes its behavior as a result of experience (p. 252).

2. Maturation is behavioral change resulting from changes that occur during the normal process of an organism's physiological growth and development (p. 253).

3. Respondent learning is acquiring the capacity to have a response, particularly a visceral or an emotional response, elicited by a known stimulus (p. 254).

4. An unconditioned stimulus is a stimulus that elicits a seemingly instinctive or unlearned response (p. 255).

5. An unconditioned response is a response that is seemingly instinctive or unlearned, and that is elicitied by an unconditioned stimulus (p. 255).

6. A conditioned stimulus is a stimulus that was previously neutral but that when associated with an unconditioned stimulus, can, over time, become able to elicit a response very similar to the one given to the unconditioned stimulus (p. 256).

7. A conditioned response is a response that is elicited by a conditioned stimulus (p. 256).

8. Contiguity learning is a change in behavior brought about by the pairing or association of a stimulus and a response (p. 258).

9. Operant conditioning is the kind of learning that takes place as the result of reinforcement (p. 260).

10. The consequences of a behavior are the events that immediately follow the emission of a behavior (p. 260).

11. A reinforcer is any event or stimulus that increases the strength of a behavior (p. 260).

12. Operant level is the frequency of behavior prior to the occurrence of conditioning (p. 261).

13. Contingent reinforcement is a reward that is received only upon the emission of a certain behavior (p. 261).

14. Observational learning is a change in behavior brought about by imitating the behavior of a significant other (p. 261).

15. Inhibition is the process of restraining a response or making a response less frequent (p. 264).

16. Disinhibition is the process of freeing from restraint, thus allowing a response to occur (p. 264).

17. Cognitive learning is the change in behavior brought about by a process that entails insight, thinking, reasoning, or deductive and inductive logic (p. 266).

ANSWER GUIDE TO APPLICATION OF KEY CONCEPTS

1. A	6. B	11. N	
2. G	7. C	12. H, M	
3. D	8. J	13. A, E, L	
4. I	9. F	14. M	
5. E	10. K	15. E	

ANSWER GUIDE TO MULTIPLE-CHOICE SELF-TEST

1. A	10. D	18. C
2. B	11. A	19. R
3. B	12. B	20. R
4. A	13. A	21. C
5. A	14. B	22. O
6. A	15. C	23. R
7. A	16. D	24. C
8. C	17. C	25. O
9. A		

CHAPTER 12   OPERANT CONDITIONING: A PRACTICAL THEORY

ANSWER GUIDE TO DEFINITIONS OF KEY CONCEPTS

1. Positive reinforcers are those that increase the probability of a certain response because they provide a positively valued stimulus (p. 272).

2. Negative reinforcers are those that increase the probability of a certain response because they discontinue an aversive or negatively valued event (p. 272).

3. Primary reinforcers are stimuli that satisfy physiological needs (p. 274).

4. Secondary reinforcers are stimuli that can be made reinforcing through association with primary reinforcers (p. 275).

5. Continuous reinforcement is reinforcement of every response of a given type (p. 276).

6. Intermittent reinforcement is reinforcement of only a fraction of reponses of a given type (p. 276).

7. A ratio schedule of reinforcement reinforces one out of every N responses of a given type (p. 276)

8. An interval schedule of reinforcement reinforces one out of every N responses of a given type (p. 276).

9. A fixed-ratio schedule of reinforcement reinforces after a fixed number of nonreinforced reponses (p. 276).

10. A token reinforcement system is a management system in which objects redeemable for desired things or events are used as reinforcers (p. 277).

11. A variable-ratio schedule of reinforcement reinforces responses on a certain average ratio, but the number of responses intervening between reinforcements varies from one reinforcement to the next (p. 278).

12. A fixed-interval schedule of reinforcement reinforces the first response given after some fixed time interval measured from the last reinforcement (p. 279).

13. A variable-interval schedule of reinforcement reinforces a response made after a varying time period since the previous reinforcement (p. 280).

14. Contingency management provides for reinforcement under certain circumstances and withholds reinforcement if those circumstances are not appropriate (p. 281).

15. The Premack principle states that behaviors with higher probabilities of occurrence can be used as reinforcers for behaviors with lower probabilities of occurrence (p. 282).

16. Successive approximations are rough approximations of the desired behavior that are reinforced initially when shaping behavior; later, reinforcement is withheld until the approximations more and more closely resemble the desired behavior (p. 283).

17. Stimulus control is the reinforcement of a response after the occurrence of a given stimulus, and nonreinforcement of the response if it is not preceded by the given stimulus (p. 285).

18. Stimulus discrimination is the ability to respond differently to stimuli that may appear to be quite similar (p. 286).

19. Stimulus generalization is the ability to make the same response to similar but not identical stimuli (p. 287).

20. Extinction is the decrease in rate of occurrence of a response as a result of nonreinforcement (p. 288).

21. Differential reinforcement of other behavior is a technique to reduce or eliminate behavior by reinforcement of all kinds of behavior other than the behavior to be eliminated (p. 290).

22. Differential reinforcement of low response rates is a technique to reduce or eliminate behavior by reinforcement of that reduction (p. 290).

23. Punishment I is the presentation of a negative stimulus after a response (p. 291).

24. Punishment II is the discontinuation of a positive reinforcement after a response (p. 292).

25. <u>Time out</u> is a procedure used to reduce or eliminate a response by deprivation of the opportunity to obtain reinforcement when certain undesirable behavior occurs (p. 292).

26. <u>Response cost</u> is the contingent removal of previously attained reinforcement (p. 292).

27. <u>Behavioral humanism</u> is the merging of behavioral and humanistic views, resulting in the use of operant techniques to develop self-regulatory mechanisms in people whose freedom of choice has been limited by self-impairing behavior (p. 296).

28. <u>Intrinsic reinforcement</u> is the occurrence of rewards that arise in a way that is naturally a part of the learning activity itself (p. 296).

ANSWER GUIDE TO APPLICATION OF KEY CONCEPTS

1.	G	7.	D	13.	B, F, I, N
2.	B	8.	J	14.	B, I
3.	H	9.	C, N	15.	E
4.	A, B	10.	H	16.	B, P
5.	B, O	11.	L	17.	B, F, N
6.	Q	12.	M	18.	K

ANSWER GUIDE TO MULTIPLE-CHOICE SELF-TEST

1.	D	12.	A	23.	D
2.	B	13.	B	24.	C
3.	D	14.	C	25.	D
4.	C	15.	B	26.	A
5.	A	16.	C	27.	B
6.	A	17.	A	28.	D
7.	B	18.	C	29.	C
8.	A	19.	B	30.	E
9.	C	20.	E	31.	D
10.	B	21.	A	32.	C
		22.	A		

CHAPTER 13   THE COGNITIVE PROCESSING OF INFORMATION

ANSWER GUIDE TO DEFINITIONS OF KEY CONCEPTS

1. <u>Short-term sensory store</u> (STSS) is the part of the memory system that briefly stores an exact replica of raw sensory information (p. 301).

2. <u>Short-term memory</u> (STM) is the conscious memory of all the information a person is aware of at one time, with storage limited to about seven chunks of information (p. 301).

3. <u>Working memory</u> (WM) is the part of the memory system that is used for conscious mental operations (p. 301).

4. <u>Long-term memory</u> (LTM) is the part of the memory system that has unlimited capacity for the permanent storage of information (p. 301).

5. <u>Orienting responses</u> are investigative responses made to changes in a stimulus or to unique stimulus characteristics (p. 300).

6. <u>Psychophysical stimulus properties</u> are physical stimulus characteristics, such as variation of intensity, size, color, and pitch, that can elicit an orienting response (p. 303).

7. <u>Emotional stimulus properties</u> are stimulus characteristics that quicken the pulse and raise the level of activity through the arousal of emotional responses (p. 303).

8. <u>Discrepant stimulus properties</u> are stimulus characteristics that depend for their effect on deviation from the expected (p. 304).

9. <u>Manding stimuli</u> are verbal statements that have a highly probable consequence associated with them (p. 304).

10. <u>Propositions</u> are the smallest unit of language that can stand alone as a separate assertion (p. 312).

11. <u>Propositional networks</u> are the intersections of nodes consisting of a proposition, its relations, and its arguments (p. 312).

12. <u>Mediation</u> is the process of creating meaningful links between terms or ideas that are not clearly related (p. 313).

13. An <u>advance organizer</u> is a brief, general introduction of information to be presented (p. 314).

14. <u>Schemata</u> are abstract structures that represent the knowledge stored in memory (p. 317).15.<u>Mathemagenic behaviors</u> are those that give birth to learning (p. 319).

16. <u>Recitation</u> is a technique for learning material by reciting it out loud (p. 321).

17. <u>Overlearning</u> is a process that occurs when a person has recalled something perfectly, and then goes on to engage in continued study of the material (323).

18. <u>Mnemonic devices</u> are techniques to help in remembering (p. 324).

19. <u>Imagery</u> is the mnemonic device of linking pictorial images to verbal symbols to enhance the codability and retrievability of the symbols (p. 326).

20. <u>The method of loci</u> is the mnemonic device of placing to-be-remembered material at imaginary ordered locations in memory (p. 326).

21. <u>The keyword method</u> is the mnemonic device of selecting a familiar association for new information to be remembered and visualizing the new and the familiar images together (p. 328).

ANSWER GUIDE TO APPLICATION OF KEY CONCEPTS

1.	G	9.	A, E
2.	J	10.	B
3.	O, L	11.	N
4.	I, K	12.	L
5.	I	13.	K
6.	D	14.	M, L
7.	E, G	15.	A, H, M
8.	F	16.	C

ANSWER GUIDE TO MULTIPLE-CHOICE SELF-TEST

1.	D	7.	D	13.	C
2.	A	8.	B	14.	D
3.	B	9.	A	15.	D
4.	B	10.	C	16.	A
5.	C	11.	C	17.	A
6.	C	12.	A	18.	B

CHAPTER 14   SOCIAL LEARNING THEORY

ANSWER GUIDE TO DEFINITIONS OF KEY CONCEPTS

1. Observational learning is the change in one's potential or actual knowledge, skills, and attitudes as a result of observation of the behavior of others (p. 334).

2. The attentional phase is the first component in learning from models, that is, attending to the behavior of others, especially those models perceived to have high status, competence, and expertise (p. 335).

3. The retention phase is the second component in learning from models, that is, symbolically representing the model's performance in long-term memory (p. 337).

4. The reproduction phase is the third component in learning from models, that is, using symbolic representation to guide actual performance of the newly acquired behavior (p. 337).

5. The motivational phase is the fourth component in learning from models, that is, performing the behavior learned from the model; it is dependent on the reinforcing or punishing consequences for the behavior (p. 340).

6. Vicarious reinforcement leads to the increase in occurrence of the learner's behavior as a result of observing the consequences of the behavior for the model (p. 341).

ANSWER GUIDE TO APPLICATION OF KEY CONCEPTS

1. B, C   4.   E, C
2. D   5.   F
3. A

ANSWER GUIDE TO MULTIPLE-CHOICE SELF-TEST

1. B   7.   B
2. E   8.   D
3. C   9.   C
4. C   10.   A
5. A   11.   B
6. C

CHAPTER 15   IMPROVING THE TRANSFER OF LEARNING

ANSWER GUIDE TO DEFINITIONS OF KEY CONCEPTS

1. Transfer of learning is the process that enables the making of previously learned responses in new situations (p. 352).

2. Theory of identical elements is the theory that transfer of learning takes place to the extent that the stimuli and responses called for across situations are similar (p. 353).

3. Doctrine of formal discipline is the view that the value of studying certain subjects is that they provide principles useful in other subjects (p. 353).

4. Identity of substance refers to the one-to-one correspondence between the elements of what is studied and what is to be done in real life (p. 354).

5. Identity of procedure refers to the learning of general habits, attitudes, principles, and procedures that facilitate learning in a wide variety of situations (p. 354).

6. The transfer value of principles refers to the generalizability of principles, which makes it easier to solve problems and learn things that seem quite different (p. 355).

7. Negative transfer is the process of applying a principle that is helpful for one set of problems to a new problem with inefficient or inaccurate results (p. 356).

8. Metacognition is knowledge about one's own cognitive system (p. 358).

9. Cognitive-skill training is training with the goal of teaching transfer of what has been learned (p. 362).

10. Stimulus predifferentiation is making students aware of the similarities and differences among stimuli so that they can determine what kind of response is called for (p. 366).

ANSWER GUIDE TO APPLICATION OF KEY CONCEPTS

1.	D	5.	F
2.	B	6.	E
3.	A	7.	C
4.	D	8.	G

ANSWER GUIDE TO MULTIPLE-CHOICE SELF-TEST

1.	A	8.	A
2.	B	9.	C
3.	A	10.	C
4.	D	11.	B
5.	C	12.	D
6.	C	13.	C
7.	A	14.	A

CHAPTER 16   THE INFLUENCE OF MOTIVATION ON LEARNING

ANSWER GUIDE TO DEFINITIONS OF KEY CONCEPTS

1. Motivation is what energizes a person and directs his or her activity (p. 372).

2. Traits are the stable, long-lasting dispositions of an individual (p. 373).

3. States are the temporary, short-term dispositions of an individual (p. 373).

4. Interest is what determines a person's selection of stimuli to attend to (p. 374).

5. Need is the lack of something that a given activity or outcome can provide (p. 374).

6. A value is an orientation toward a whole class of goals that are considered important in one's life (p. 375).

7. An attitude is a feeling for or against something (p. 376).

8. Aspiration is one's hope or longing for a certain kind of achievement (p. 376).

9. Incentive is something one perceives as having the capability of satisfying an aroused motive (p. 376).

10. Overachievement is achievement greater than that predicted on the basis of an individual's intelligence or scholastic aptitude (p. 379).

11. Underachievement is achievement less than that predicted on the basis of an individual's intelligence or scholastic aptitude (p. 379).

12. <u>Psychogenic needs</u> are needs with a nonphysiological base (p. 381).

13. <u>Self-actualization</u> is a level of functioning at which basic needs have been met and the individual is motivated by needs to be open, to love, to act ethically and morally, to express autonomy and creativity, to be curious and spontaneous (p. 384).

ANSWER GUIDE TO APPLICATION OF KEY CONCEPTS

1.	I	5.	G	9.	J
2.	B	6.	D	10.	A
3.	F	7.	K	11.	A, H
4.	E	8.	C		

ANSWER GUIDE TO MULTIPLE-CHOICE SELF-TEST

1.	D	5.	B	9.	E
2.	D	6.	C	10.	D
3.	B	7.	A	11.	B
4.	C	8.	C	12.	A

CHAPTER 17   PERSONALITY FACTORS IN MOTIVATION

ANSWER GUIDE TO DEFINITIONS OF KEY CONCEPTS

1. The <u>Thematic Apperception Test</u> is a test that can measure motive strength by eliciting stories in response to a series of ambiguous pictures (p. 388).

2. <u>Autonomous achievement motivation</u> is motivation in which persons compare their performance against their previous performance (p. 393).

3. <u>Social achievement motivation</u> is motivation in which persons compare their performance against that of others (p. 394).

4. <u>Achievement motivation</u> is the desire to be good at doing something because one is motivated to succeed, or to avoid failure, or both (p. 395).

5. <u>Internal locus of control</u> is the attribution of success and failure to one's own personal effort or ability (p. 399).

6. <u>External locus of control</u> is the attribution of success and failure to luck or the difficulty of the task (p. 399).

7. <u>Learned helplessness</u> is a motivational pattern in which students do not see effort as related to achievement (p. 399).

8. An "origin" is a person who feels in control of his or her own fate (p. 409).

9. A "pawn" is a person who feels his or her fate is in the hands of others (p. 409).

10. Affiliation motives refer to the degree to which an individual wants and needs friendly relationships with other persons (p. 405).

11. Power motives refer to an individual's desire to influence other persons (p. 406).

12. Need for approval is a motive pattern typified by an excessive need to be recognized by others, and associated with a conforming and submissive attitude (p. 407).

ANSWER GUIDE TO APPLICATION OF KEY CONCEPTS

1.	B	6.	F
2.	H	7.	K
3.	C, I, L	8.	C, I
4.	G, E	9.	A
5.	D	10.	J

ANSWER GUIDE TO MULTIPLE-CHOICE SELF-TEST

1.	C	8.	B	15.	D
2.	C	9.	C	16.	A
3.	A	10.	A	17.	B
4.	B	11.	A	18.	C
5.	B	12.	C	19.	B
6.	B	13.	A	20.	D
7.	C	14.	C		

CHAPTER 18   ENVIRONMENTAL FACTORS IN MOTIVATION

ANSWER GUIDE TO DEFINITIONS OF KEY CONCEPTS

1. Intrinsic motivation is that which is maintained without apparent reinforcement or reward, or by rewards that occur naturally in the activity itself (p. 412).

2. Extrinsic motivation is that which is maintained with observable rewards (p. 412).

3. An incentive is the promise or expectation of reinforcement (p. 415).

4. Discontinued reinforcement is the withholding of expected rewards -- withholding that causes change in the energy and directionality of the student's behavior (p. 417).

5. Frustrated behavior is behavior--characterized by emotionality, withdrawal, regression, overactivity, or aggression--that is caused by preventing an individual from initiating or completing responses leading to reinforcement (p. 418).

6. <u>Token economies</u> are systems that provide reinforcement, in the form of tokens redeemable for goods, services, or special privileges, that is contingent upon academic achievement or other desirable behavior (p. 418).

7. <u>Motivational contracts</u> are formal or informal contracts between teachers and students specifying what particular student behaviors are required to receive what particular reinforcements (p. 421).

8. <u>Social rewards</u> are rewards, such as approval, promotion, graduation, raise in pay, etc., that are motivating because they are recognized by others (p. 431).

9. <u>Epistemic curiosity</u> is aroused behavior that is aimed at acquiring knowledge (p. 432).

10. "<u>Ethos</u>" refers to the fundamental values or spirit of a particular group (p. 437).

11. <u>Reward power</u> is an individual's ability to influence another person's behavior by dispensing rewards (p. 439).

12. <u>Coercive power</u> is an individual's ability to influence another person's behavior by dispensing punishments (p. 440).

13. <u>Legitimate power</u> is power derived from the assignment of reward or coercive power to an individual through either law or custom (p. 440).

14. <u>Referent power</u> is an individual's ability to influence another person because that person identifies with the influential individual (p. 440).

15. <u>Expert power</u> is an individual's ability to influence another person because of the expertise or special competence he or she possesses (p. 440).

ANSWER GUIDE TO APPLICATION OF KEY CONCEPTS

1. L	7. C	13. A
2. M, N, P	8. I	14. F
3. G	9. O	15. B, N, O
4. B, D	10. H	16. P
5. E, F, G	11. J	17. M
6. B	12. K	

ANSWER GUIDE TO MULTIPLE-CHOICE SELF-TEST

1. D	7. C	13. A
2. C	8. C	14. B
3. B	9. D	15. C
4. B	10. B	16. C
5. C	11. D	17. B
6. B	12. B	

ANSWER GUIDE TO DEFINITIONS OF KEY CONCEPTS

1. Teaching methods are recurrent patterns of teacher behavior that are applicable to various subject matters, characteristic of more than one teacher, and relevant to learning (p. 445).

2. Teaching techniques are teacher behaviors that are useful in the teaching of specific subject matter (p. 445).

3. The lecture method of teaching involves relatively long, uninterrupted, formal discourses (p. 452).

4. Explanations are shorter teacher discourses, lasting approximately 30 seconds to 5 minutes (p. 452).

5. The equalization effect is the result that occurs when students compensate for the inadequacies of the teaching methods by which they are taught--a result that tends to reduce differences in the effects of the various teaching methods on student achievement (p. 456).

6. Motivational cues are cues a teacher uses to motivate learning by telling students which ideas are important, which topics are to be covered in examinations, or which ideas or techniques are difficult (p. 459).

7. Clarity of aims refers to teachers making explicit the purposes of the lesson that is being taught (p. 460).

8. Advance organizers are statements made by a teacher telling students in advance about the way in which a lecture or short talk is organized, the abstract and general concepts to be used, and the inferences and generalizations to be concerned with in order to improve students' comprehension and ability to recall and apply the material they've heard (p. 460).

9. Student oportunity to learn is the extent to which the material that students are to learn, or the material that is required to answer test questions, was covered in the teacher's lecture or lesson (p. 462).

10. Transitional statements are statements used by a lecturer to highlight the relationship among the units of a lecture (p. 463).

11. Discontinuity in a lecture refers to the teacher's digressions or irrelevancies that negatively affect student achievement and student attitude toward the teacher's performance and content of the lesson (p. 463).

12. Component relationships in a lecture deals with helping students understand the larger idea and how smaller ideas are subsumed under it (p. 464).

13. Classification hierarchy is the organization of facts, concepts, and principles presented in a lecture under a common, unifying heading (p. 464).

14. Sequential relationships in a lecture refers to the chronological and cause-and-effect organization of ideas presented (p. 465).

15. Material-to-purpose (relevance) relationships in a lecture refers to the identification of a central idea and the exclusion of ideas lacking consistency with the total group of ideas presented (p. 465).

16. Chaining is a technique of organizing ideas in a lecture into a sequence of events in logical, cause-and-effect, or chrononological order (p. 466).

17. Connective relationships in a lecture indicate the component parts of a series (p. 466).

18. A model for organizing an explanation entails (1) understanding the question that necessitates the explanation, (2) identifying the elements involved, (3) identifying the relationships between the elements, and (4) showing how these relationships are instances of a more generalized relationship (pp. 469).

19. The rule-example-rule technique is the pattern of giving an explanation in a sequence as follows: presentation of the main idea, examples or instances of the main idea, and a restatement of the main idea (p. 471).

20. Explaining links are prepositions and conjunctions that indicate that the cause, result, means, or purpose of an idea or event is being presented (p. 472).

21. Interlecture structuring is the lecturer's indication to students of the nature of the next lecture (p. 481).

ANSWER GUIDE TO APPLICATION OF KEY CONCEPTS

1.	C	8.	A
2.	B	9.	I
3.	G	10.	J
4.	D	11.	E
5.	F	12.	H
6.	M	13.	L
7.	I, K		

ANSWER GUIDE TO MULTIPLE-CHOICE SELF-TEST

1.	C	10.	A
2.	D	11.	D
3.	D	12.	C
4.	B	13.	C
5.	C	14.	C
6.	A	15.	A
7.	C	16.	D
8.	B	17.	B
9.	B		

ANSWER GUIDE TO DEFINITIONS OF KEY CONCEPTS

1. Small-group teaching is a teaching method that entails face-to-face, multi-channelled communication between student and student and between student and teacher for the purpose of exchanging, evaluating, and responding to information and ideas (p. 486).

2. High-consensus fields are subjects of study whose major concepts, principles, and methods are so well established that no competent person can raise serious doubts about them (p. 488).

3. Low-consensus fields are subjects of study whose major concepts, principles, and methods are so poorly established that any competent person can raise serious doubts about them (p. 488).

4. "Intellectual agility" is the ability to follow the course of a discussion without losing track of the argument or losing patience with its complexity (p. 490).

5. The discovery method is a teaching method that requires students to find their own concepts, principles, and solutions, rather than receiving them from a teacher or textbook (p. 490).

6. Extemporaneous speech is impromptu speaking, such as takes place during the course of a discussion or lecture (p. 491).

7. Communication networks are the patterns of verbal interactions in a discussion group that prescribe the permissible channels for the flow of messages among members of the group (p. 496).

8. Logical fallacies are errors in logic that divert an argument from its main concerns or lead it into inappropriate areas (p. 502).

9. The cognitive map approach is a group discussion structure that consists of chronological steps, beginning with a definition of terms and concepts and continuing through actual discussion of the topic, application of the issues, and evaluation of the discussion and the participants (pp. 503).

10. Intellectual pitfalls are those teacher behaviors during a discussion that bias, encourage yielding, withhold crucial information, or continue the discussion of a dead topic (p. 505).

11. Biasing the discussion means giving the students cues that tend to subvert their intellectual or rational processes so that they yield to authority or group pressure (p. 506).

12. Social-emotional pitfalls are those arising from the attitudes of students toward themselves, other students, or the teacher that reduce the value of the discussion by hurting participants' feelings or encouraging nonparticipation (p. 508).

273

13. The next-in-line phenomenon occurs when the student who is to speak next in a discussion concentrates hard on what he or she is going to say, paying little attention to the previous speaker (p. 511).

14. Group cohesiveness is the degree to which group members want to stay in the group, like each other, and care about one another (p. 513).

15. Role-playing is a teaching technique allowing students to understand viewpoints and feelings of others, and to practice alternative solutions to problems, by assuming various roles in imaginary settings (p. 514).

16. Cooperative learning is a teaching technique whereby the teacher gives assignments and projects to small groups of students; the students then divide the labor among themselves, help one another, and praise or criticize one another's efforts and contributions (p. 516).

ANSWER GUIDE TO APPLICATION OF KEY CONCEPTS

1.	D	8.	I
2.	F	9.	C
3.	E	10.	N
4.	L	11.	B, K
5.	A	12.	H
6.	G, M	13.	H
7.	B		

ANSWER GUIDE TO MULTIPLE-CHOICE SELF-TEST

1.	B	6.	B	11.	D
2.	D	7.	C	12.	D
3.	B	8.	D	13.	B
4.	A	9.	A	14.	C
5	B	10.	C	15.	D

CHAPTER 21 INDIVIDUAL INSTRUCTION

ANSWER GUIDE TO DEFINITIONS OF KEY CONCEPTS

1. Individualized instruction is a method of teaching that requires students to progress at their own rate, working on tasks appropriate to their particular abilities and using techniques and styles of learning appropriate to their temperament (p. 523).

2. Ability grouping is the placing of students in a classroom, grade, or school with other students of about the same ability (p. 523).

3. Homogeneous grouping is the placement of students in groups that differ less widely in abilities than does the classroom group as a whole (p. 524).

4. Independent study is a teaching method that requires a one-to-one relationship between student and teacher to plan each student's pursuit of a different course of study or research project (p. 524).

5. Self-directed study is a teaching method that preserves formal course structure, yet reduces the number of formal classes attended by the student in order to increase intellectual curiosity (p. 525).

6. SQ3R is an acronym referring to a survey-question-read-recite-review sequence in studying material to be learned (p. 526).

7. A multiple correlation coefficient is a number expressing the degree and direction of the relationship between one variable and a combination of variables (p. 527).

8. A partial correlation coefficient is a number expressing the degree and direction of the relationship between one variable and another, with the possible effects of other variables not of primary interest held constant (p. 527).

9. A contract is an agreement between teacher and student that specifies what is to be learned, how learning will be demonstrated, what steps will be taken and what resources used, the intermediate steps toward contract agreement, and the overall time schedule (p. 528).

10. The Keller plan is a system of individualized instruction that is individually paced, mastery oriented, and guided; it uses both tutoring and traditional instructional techniques (p. 529).

11. Mastery learning is an approach to individual instruction that provides students with whatever time and assistance they need to meet established criteria for success in an area of curriculum (p. 533).

12. Diagnostic tests are tests to determine the level of mastery a student has attained in an area of curriculum; they are used to make prescriptions regarding what needs to be done next in order to reach specified levels of mastery (p. 534).

13. Tutoring is a method of individualized instruction requiring the tutor to diagnose the learning progress of a tutee and prescribe remediation, while constantly encouraging and supporting the tutee (p. 539).

14. Programmed instruction is an individualized system of instruction in which each student is presented with content, is required to respond overtly to that content, and is immediately informed as to whether or not the response is correct (p. 544).

15. A frame in programmed instruction is a relatively brief presentation of about a sentence or a paragraph of instructional material and a question to be answered by the student (p. 545).

16. Computer-assisted instruction is a computerized system of programmed instruction that allows for the presentation of content to students, in addition to storing, retrieving, and statistically processing the responses of individual students or groups of students (p. 547).

ANSWER GUIDE TO APPLICATION OF KEY CONCEPTS

1.	L	8.	G, K
2.	A	9.	J
3.	B	10.	D
4.	C	11.	G
5.	M	12.	H
6.	F	13.	I
7.	E, G		

ANSWER GUIDE TO MULTIPLE-CHOICE SELF-TEST

1.	A	7.	B	13.	C
2.	D	8.	A	14.	A
3.	B	9.	B	15.	B
4.	A	10.	A	16.	D
5.	A	11.	C	17.	A
6.	A	12.	D	18.	C

CHAPTER 22   OPEN AND HUMANISTIC APPROACHES TO TEACHING

ANSWER GUIDE TO DEFINITIONS OF KEY CONCEPTS

1. Humanistic approaches to teaching are those that give equal status to the role of the teacher and that of the student, and are aimed at the student determining what is to be learned so that he or she may become more self-directed and independent (p. 558).

2. Self-actualization is the inherent ability in everyone to be perceptive, spontaneous, expressive, genuine, merry, and unafraid (p. 560).

3. Confluent education is educational procedures that bring the cognitive and affective domains together by incorporating feelings into the curriculum (p. 566).

4. Facilitator of learning is a role requiring a teacher to act as a guide to learning, as a model of problem solving, as a catalyst and aid for learning processes, and as a friend to whom students can go for help (p. 568).

5. Integrated-day plans are British early education programs that emphasize an individualized approach in an open-education environment (p. 570).

6. Project AWARE is an affective education program at the elementary level aimed at understanding feelings, accepting individual differences, and developing social living skills (p. 574).

7. Affective education is education aimed at improving students' emotional well-being and social skills (p. 574).

ANSWER GUIDE TO APPLICATION OF KEY CONCEPTS

1. B
2. E
3. A, E
4. C
5. D

ANSWER GUIDE TO MULTIPLE-CHOICE SELF-TEST

1. D   6. C
2. A   7. A
3. C   8. B
4. D   9. A
5. C

CHAPTER 23   CLASSROOM: PLANNING AND MANAGEMENT

ANSWER GUIDE TO DEFINITIONS OF KEY CONCEPTS

1. Classroom teaching is a synthesis of various combinations of lecturing and explaining, the discussion method, various methods for teaching students individually, and humanistic approaches in varying proportions (p. 584).

2. Recitation is a relatively short instructional segment in which the teacher calls on individual students to answer questions, read in turn, or give answers to homework (p. 584).

3. Structuring is a classroom teaching behavior that sets the context for classroom behavior by starting or ending an interaction and indicating its nature (p. 587).

4. Soliciting is a classroom teaching behavior of seeking a response (p. 587).

5. Responding is a classroom teaching behavior of fulfilling the expectation set by the soliciting move (p. 587).

6. Reacting is a classroom teaching behavior of modifying or evaluating a previous move (p. 587).

7. The preinteractive phase of teaching is the planning phase that occurs before a course or school term begins, and also before each meeting of the class (p. 593).

8. The "integrated ends-means model" is a planning model in which the teacher takes the viewpoint that ends do not necessarily need to be specified before the means are selected (p. 596).

9. <u>Withitness</u> refers to the teacher's ability to know what is going on all around the room (p. 602).

10. <u>Overlappingness</u> refers to the teacher's ability to handle two or more behavior problems at the same time (p. 602).

11. <u>Momentum</u> refers to the teacher's ability to keep the classroom free from slowdowns (p. 602).

12. <u>Smoothness</u> refers to the teacher's ability to keep the class free from distractions during changes in activities (p. 602).

13. <u>Group alerting</u> refers to the teacher's ability to manage recitations in ways that keep students involved and attentive, as well as involving nonparticipating students (p. 602).

14. <u>Bias in teacher-student interaction</u> is the tendency, whether conscious or unconscious, of teachers to interact more frequently or favorably with some categories of students (boys vs. girls, more able vs. less able, those who sit in the front vs. those who sit in the back, etc.) than with other categories of students (p. 609).

15. <u>Variation in classroom teaching</u> is diversification in the length of teaching segments, the style and method of teaching, or the teaching materials and facilities (p. 614).

16. <u>Style in classroom teaching</u> refers to the manner in which teachers express themselves, as reflected in their gestures, movement about the room, volume of voice, and degree of enthusiasm (p. 614).

17. <u>Method in classroom teaching</u> refers to the more formal and self-conscious aspects of teaching, such as the way the teacher interacts with students, the kinds of questions asked, and the social arrangement of the classroom (p. 614).

18. <u>Flexibility in classroom teaching</u> refers to the frequency with which the teacher changes from one behavior to another (p. 615).

ANSWER GUIDE TO APPLICATION OF KEY CONCEPTS

1. C	6. A	11. M
2. D	7. L	12. I
3. K	8. E	13. F
4. O	9. N	14. G
5. B	10. J	15. H

ANSWER GUIDE TO MULTIPLE-CHOICE SELF-TEST

1. E	7. C	13. D
2. C	8. A	14. A
3. C	9. D	15. A
4. B	10. D	16. C
5. C	11. B	17. A
6. B	12. C	

ANSWER GUIDE TO DEFINITIONS OF KEY CONCEPTS

1. Classroom seatwork is a component of classroom teaching that consists of the pupils' working by themselves or with others on assigned or self-selected tasks in textbooks and workbooks (p. 623).

2. Classroom recitation is a teaching method consisting of a repeated sequence of events in which, initially, the teacher provides structuring and solicits input by asking a question, a student responds, and the teacher reacts (p. 623).

3. Academic learning time is the amount of time, in hours per 150-day school year, that students are learning academic subject matter, as a function of the time teachers allocate for subject matter, student engagement, and difficulty level of material (p. 624).

4. Monitoring is the teacher behavior of circulating around the classroom during seatwork to check on students and comment on how they are doing (p. 626).

5. Signal giving is a structuring behavior indicating that one part of the lesson has ended and another is to begin (p. 629).

6. Discontinuities are disorderly transitions within a lesson or a topic from one point to another (p. 630).

7. Lower-order questions are those that require students to recall knowledge that they have heard or read (p. 635).

8. Higher-order questions are those that require students to use such more complex cognitive processes as application, analysis, synthesis, and evaluation (p. 635).

9. Wait time I is the length of time after the teacher asks a question before the student responds (p. 636).

10. Wait time II is the length of time after a student answers a question until the teacher speaks (pp. 636, 641).

11. "Call-outs" are answers to questions given by students who do not wait for the teacher's permission to respond (p. 638).

12. Redirecting is asking a student the same question previously asked of another student (p. 638).

13. Probing is continuing to question the same student until more of his/or her knowledge or understanding about an issue has been brought out (p. 639).

14. Acceptance of student ideas is a teacher reaction that consists of using the contributions of a student in the subsequent discussion (p. 643).

ANSWER GUIDE TO APPLICATION OF KEY CONCEPTS

1.	E	8.	M
2.	B	9.	L
3.	G	10.	C
4.	D	11.	I
5.	J	12.	B, K
6.	A,I	13.	H
7.	F		

ANSWER GUIDE TO MULTIPLE-CHOICE SELF-TEST

1.	D	8.	B
2.	A	9.	B
3.	D	10.	C
4.	A	11.	B
5.	B	12.	B
6.	C	13.	C
7.	A	14.	C

CHAPTER 25   BASIC CONCEPTS IN MEASUREMENT AND EVALUATION

ANSWER GUIDE TO DEFINITIONS OF KEY CONCEPTS

1. A test is a systematic procedure for measuring a sample of a person's behavior in order to evaluate that behavior against standards or norms (p. 654).

2. A behavior sample is a selection of only a small number of the many possible behaviors of a given kind that an individual can display (p. 655).

3. Evaluation is the process by which we attach value to something (p. 656).

4. A test standard is the established criterion of acceptable competence in a given subject matter area (p. 656).

5. Norm-referenced tests are tests that use the performance of other persons on the same measuring instrument as a basis for interpreting a person's relative test performance (p. 657).

6. Criterion-referenced tests are tests that measure a person's ability with respect to some criterion or specified level of achievement (p. 658).

7. Test reliability refers to the degree of precision, consistency, or stability of a test score over different testings and time spans (p. 662).

8. Test-retest reliability is the degree to which the rank ordering of student scores on one test occasion is the same as the rank ordering of scores they would receive if they were tested again on a different occasion (p. 662).

9. Internal-consistency reliability is the correlation between the rank ordering of scores received by students on one test and on a hypothetical second test given at the same time (p. 664).

10. The standard error of measurement is a statistic indicating the estimated amount of error, or deviation from the true score, associated with an observed score (p. 664).

11. A confidence band is the width of an interval around an observed score, used to estimate the limits within which a true score lies (p. 665).

12. Validity refers to how well test procedures and interpretations measure what the test purports to measure (p. 666).

13. Content validity of a test refers to the degree to which the test measures knowledge in an instructional domain by the inclusion of an adequate sample of test items that tap the various kinds of knowledge and skill in the domain (p. 667).

14. Construct validity of a test refers to the degree to which a test measures the attribute or psychological dimension it is intended to measure (p. 668).

15. Criterion validity refers to the degree to which a test predicts how well individuals will do in a given course, program, or job (p. 692).

16. Formative evaluation is the examination of a given program for the purpose of revising it so that it works as intended (p. 671).

17. Summative evaluation is the examination of a given program for the purpose of judging how well it yields the outcomes intended (p. 671).

ANSWER GUIDE TO APPPLICATION OF KEY CONCEPTS

1.	H	7.	L
2.	J	8.	C
3.	G	9.	F
4.	A	10.	E
5.	D	11.	K
6.	B	12.	I

ANSWER GUIDE TO MULTIPLE-CHOICE SELF-TEST

1.	B	6.	C
2.	A	7.	B
3.	C	8.	B
4.	A	9.	D
5.	A		

ANSWER GUIDE TO DEFINITIONS OF KEY CONCEPTS

1. A norm-referenced standardized test is a test that has been given to a large and representative sample of some population so that an individual's score on the test can be compared with the scores of the people in the sample (p. 678).

2. A criterion-referenced standardized test is a test that has been constructed by experts and for which detailed instructions are provided about how it should be administered in order to give information about how well a student has performed in relation to some specific criterion (p. 679).

3. Aptitude tests are standardized tests measuring specific kinds of intellectual abilities, or other characteristics, that are used to predict the outcomes of future learning experiences (p. 680).

4. Standardized achievement tests are tests measuring specific kinds of achievement of the objectives of instruction in a given course, or other curriculum unit, and that are used to evaluate the outcomes of learning experiences (p. 680).

5. Noncognitive standardized tests are tests that measure such nonintellectual variables as attitudes, interests, motives, temperament, and values (p. 684).

6. A percentile rank is a statistic, converted from a raw score, that tells what percentage of students in a comparison group is excelled by that particular raw score (p. 694).

7. A frequency distribution is a tabular summarization of data in which the test-score values are arranged, in order of size and the frequency with which each score value occurs is indicated (p. 695).

8. The median is the score that is higher than half and lower than half of the scores in a frequency distribution (p. 695).

9. The arithmetic mean is the score obtained by summing the scores in a frequency distribution and dividing the total by the number of scores (p. 695).

10. A standard score is a converted score that indicates a raw score's deviation from the mean measured in standard deviation units (p. 695).

11. A standard deviation is a statistic that reflects the variability, or spread, of scores in a frequency distribution (p. 697).

12. A T Score is a statistic obtained by multiplying the standard score by 10 and adding 50 (p. 697).

13. A stanine is a converted score that has a mean of 5 and a standard deviation of approximately 2 (p. 697).

14. An <u>age</u> or <u>grade norm</u> is the raw score obtained, on the average, by students of a given age or grade (p. 698).

ANSWER GUIDE TO APPLICATION OF KEY CONCEPTS

1.	E	6.	B	11.	N
2.	C	7.	I	12.	D
3.	F	8.	G	13.	K
4.	M	9.	J	14.	A
5.	H	10.	L		

ANSWER GUIDE TO MULTIPLE-CHOICE SELF TEST

1.	B	7.	C
2.	A	8.	D
3.	C	9.	C
4.	C	10.	B
5.	C	11.	C
6.	A		

CHAPTER 27   TEACHER-MADE TESTS

ANSWER GUIDE TO DEFINITIONS OF KEY CONCEPTS

1. <u>Domain-referenced testing</u> is the testing of knowledge in a given area of study or domain with a representative sample of test items, to evaluate student achievement of knowledge in the whole domain (p. 703).

2. <u>A table of specifications for an achievement test</u> is a behavior-content matrix crossing the two dimensions of curriculum content and types of student cognitive performance (p. 703).

3. <u>Essay questions</u> are questions used to evaluate a student's ability to organize and produce a fairly complex written, verbal response to a problem (p. 703).

4. <u>Supply short-answer questions</u> are questions used that require the student to supply a brief, perhaps one-word or one-phrase, response to a question or an incomplete statement (p. 709).

5. <u>Select short-answer questions</u> are questions that require the student to select the correct response to a question from alternatives that are provided (p. 709).

6. An <u>acquiescent response set</u> is a consistent tendency to respond "true" to a true-false question when in doubt about the correct response (p. 711).

7. Multiple-choice questions are select short-answer questions consisting of an item stem, in the form of a question or incomplete statement, and a list of alternative responses (p. 713).

8. Power tests are tests that allow students ample time to attempt all test items (p. 716).

9. Speeded tests are tests in which individual differences in achievement depend on speed of performance (p. 716).

10. Item analysis is a posttest examination of items for purposes of test revision in terms of their statistical properties as determined by student responses (p. 719).

11. Item sensitivity to instruction is a number computed by (a) subtracting the number of students answering correctly before instruction from (b) the number of students answering correctly after instruction, and dividing by the total number of students (p. 720).

12. Item analysis in criterion-referenced testing is the process of analyzing the responses of instructed and uninstructed students until a set of good items is created (p. 719).

13. An index of item difficulty is a number computed by adding (a) the proportion of student scoring high on the test who got the item correct to (b) the proportion of students scoring low on the test who got the item correct, and dividing by 2 (p. 721).

14. An index of item discrimination is a number computed by subtracting (a) the proportion of students scoring low on the test who got the item correct from (b) the proportion of students scoring high on the test who got the item correct (p. 722).

15. Placement tests are a type of achievement test used to determine whether or not students have entry-level skills (p. 723).

16. Formative tests are a type of achievement test used to provide feedback regarding mastery of content to both teachers and students (p. 723).

17. Diagnostic tests are a type of achievement test used to indicate specific learning problems for a particular student (p. 724).

18. Summative tests are a type of achievement test given at the end of instruction to certify student mastery of content (p. 724).

ANSWER GUIDE TO APPLICATION OF KEY CONCEPTS

1.	F	9.	C
2.	P, K	10.	N
3.	L	11.	O
4.	G	12.	B
5.	A	13.	I
6.	K	14.	E
7.	J	15.	D
8.	M	16.	H.

ANSWER GUIDE TO MULTIPLE-CHOICE SELF-TEST

1.	B	9.	B
2.	A	10.	A
3.	D	11.	A
4.	D	12.	C
5.	C	13.	C
6.	A	14.	C
7.	C	15.	B
8.	B	16.	A

CHAPTER 28   GRADING AND MARKING

ANSWER GUIDE TO DEFINITIONS OF KEY CONCEPTS

1. Convergence technique in student evaluation is the teacher's use of several sources of evidence, such as performance on multiple-choice tests, essay tests and student projects, and participation in large-group, small-group, and individual activities, in evaluating student achievement (p. 738).

2. Marks in student evaluation are summary symbols, such as A, P, or 73%, that are intended to represent achievement in some area of education (p. 738).

3. Bias in evaluation refers to teacher-misperceived reality regarding errors made on student work because of the teacher's belief that brighter students are less likely to make errors (p. 740).

4. Absolute standards are the established criteria for acceptable performance against which students' performances can be judged (p. 741).

5. Pseudoabsolute standards are standards used for evaluating a student's performance on the basis of percentage correct scores that are not based on present criteria or performance (p. 742).

6. Relative standards are standards used for evaluating a student's performance on the basis of how well he or she is doing relative to other students in a class, grade, age, or ability level (p. 742).

7. Report cards are vehicles for communicating the teacher's judgments and assignment of marks and grades regarding student achievement to students and their parents (p. 743).

8. Normative reporting is a reporting system using a predetermined category system, such as letter grades, to evaluate student achievement relative to other students in the class (p. 744).

9. Parent conferences are a type of reporting medium allowing for two-way communication between the home and the school (p. 748).

10. <u>Anecdotal reports</u> are a type of reporting medium requiring the teacher to collect information about students in the form of observational notes about samples of student behavior in different situations--notes that can be shared with both parents and students (p. 750).

ANSWER GUIDE TO APPLICATION OF KEY CONCEPTS

1.	I	6.	B, J
2.	C	7.	G
3.	B	8.	D
4.	F	9.	H
5.	A	10.	E

ANSWER GUIDE TO MULTIPLE-CHOICE SELF-TEST

1.	C	6.	B
2.	A	7.	D
3.	D	8.	B
4.	A	9.	D
5.	A	10.	A